ROYAL BOROUGH OF GREENWICH

Follow us on twitter @greenwichlibs

gural year of 1914 when the continued legacy of European imperialism was yielding to the rising global American power and the transition framing the eventual formation of postcolonial nation-states that seem to be crumbling right in front of our eyes today. More critical and informed studies like McMillan's are much needed if the cascade of the daily news is 'c-ing ahead in an increasingly tumultuou al moment."

—Hamid Dabash
Studies and Com
USA, a

n
y,
d

"To begin understanding why the Middle East is falling apart today, read M. E. McMillan's beautifully written and admirably succinct book *From the First World War to the Arab Spring: What's Really Going On in the Middle East?* She unravels with verve the clash of empires that preceded the violent dismantling of the Ottoman Empire during World War I. But most importantly, she analyzes with clarity the contradictory principles and conflicting interests that were embedded in the new Middle East. Not only were borders drawn haphazardly at war's end, but also the Great Powers insisted that Middle Eastern peoples take on new identities. Enlightenment concepts such as nationalism, constitutionalism, and separation of church and state were imposed at the point of a gun. Today, that order is in shambles, despite—or perhaps because of—multiple interventions. McMillan is a wonderful guide. I will be assigning it to my students."

—Joshua Landis, Director of the Center for Middle Eastern Studies and Associate Professor at the College of International Relations, University of Oklahoma, USA

"A lively and engaging book that sheds great clarity on a century of Middle Eastern conflict."

—Eugene Rogan, Associate Professor of the Modern History of the Middle East and Director of the Middle East Centre, St Antony's College, University of Oxford, UK, and author of *The Arabs: A History* and *The Fall of the Ottomans: The Great War in the Middle East*

Middle East Today

Series editors:
Fawaz A. Gerges
Professor of International Relations
Emirates Chair of the Modern Middle East
Department of International Relations
London School of Economics

Nader Hashemi
Director, Center for Middle East Studies
Associate Professor of Middle East and Islamic Politics
Josef Korbel School of International Studies
University of Denver

The Iranian Revolution of 1979, the Iran-Iraq War, the Gulf War, and the US invasion and occupation of Iraq have dramatically altered the geopolitical landscape of the contemporary Middle East. The Arab Spring uprisings have complicated this picture. This series puts forward a critical body of first-rate scholarship that reflects the current political and social realities of the region, focusing on original research about contentious politics and social movements; political institutions; the role played by nongovernmental organizations such as Hamas, Hezbollah, and the Muslim Brotherhood; and the Israeli-Palestinian conflict. Other themes of interest include Iran and Turkey as emerging preeminent powers in the region, the former an "Islamic Republic" and the latter an emerging democracy currently governed by a party with Islamic roots; the Gulf monarchies, their petrol economies and regional ambitions; potential problems of nuclear proliferation in the region; and the challenges confronting the United States, Europe, and the United Nations in the greater Middle East. The focus of the series is on general topics such as social turmoil, war and revolution, international relations, occupation, radicalism, democracy, human rights, and Islam as a political force in the context of the modern Middle East.

Ali Shari'ati and the Shaping of Political Islam in Iran
Kingshuk Chatterjee

Religion and the State in Turkish Universities: The Headscarf Ban
Fatma Nevra Seggie

Turkish Foreign Policy: Islam, Nationalism, and Globalization
Hasan Kösebalaban

Nonviolent Resistance in the Second Intifada: Activism and Advocacy
Edited by Maia Carter Hallward and Julie M. Norman

The Constitutional System of Turkey: 1876 to the Present
Ergun Özbudun

Islam, the State, and Political Authority: Medieval Issues and Modern Concerns
Edited by Asma Afsaruddin

From the First World War to the Arab Spring

What's Really Going On in the Middle East?

M. E. McMillan

palgrave
macmillan

First published 2016 by
PALGRAVE MACMILLAN

The author has asserted their right to be identified as the author of this work in accordance with the Copyright, Designs and Patents Act 1988.

Palgrave Macmillan in the UK is an imprint of Macmillan Publishers Limited, registered in England, company number 785998, of Houndmills, Basingstoke, Hampshire, RG21 6XS.

Palgrave Macmillan in the US is a division of Nature America, Inc., One New York Plaza, Suite 4500, New York, NY 10004-1562.

Palgrave Macmillan is the global academic imprint of the above companies and has companies and representatives throughout the world.

Hardback ISBN: 978–1–137–52201–6
Paperback ISBN: 978–1–137–52204–7
E-PUB ISBN: 978–1–137–52203–0
E-PDF ISBN: 978–1–137–52202–3
DOI: 10.1057/9781137522023

Distribution in the UK, Europe and the rest of the world is by Palgrave Macmillan®, a division of Macmillan Publishers Limited, registered in England, company number 785998, of Houndmills, Basingstoke, Hampshire RG21 6XS.

Library of Congress Cataloging-in-Publication Data

McMillan, M. E., author.
From the First World War to the Arab Spring : what's really going on in the Middle East? / M.E. McMillan.
pages cm.—(Middle East today)
Includes bibliographical references and index.
ISBN 978–1–137–52201–6 (hardback)—
ISBN 978–1–137–52204–7 (paperback)
1. Middle East—History—20th century. 2. Middle East—History—21st century. 3. Middle East—Politics and government—20th century. 4. Middle East—Politics and government—21st century. 5. Political culture—Middle East. I. Title.
DS62.8.M46 2015
956.04—dc23   2015018133

A catalogue record for the book is available from the British Library.

For my late grandfather William (Bill) Milford

And for my great friend Rosie Cleary

Contents

Acknowledgments

I would like to thank everyone who helped me to see this through. Special thanks to my parents; to Yaron and Dayse (without whom I could never have understood certain aspects of the Middle East), Anna Maria, Leah, Natalia, and, as ever, massive thanks to Lee.

I have been very lucky with the people who have taught me over the years: to Professor Jeremy Johns, thank you for teaching me stuff I can still remember 20 years on (who knew the *amsar* would figure in a book like this?!) and for changing the way I look at the world. To Professor Alan Jones, thank you for being the greatest mentor ever. And to the still-very-much-missed Dr. Elizabeth A. M. Warburton, thank you for giving me the chance and for so much else.

A big thank you to the fantastic team at Palgrave Macmillan for all the help and support: Veronica Goldstein, Sara Doskow, Erin Ivy, and especially Alisa Pulver for going above and beyond the call of duty on this project, and Dr. Farideh Koohi-Kamali for making it happen in the first place. I would also like to thank the anonymous reviewer for his very helpful comments and for giving this project the green light. Thanks, too, to the Newgen team including copy editor Pradeep Kumar for doing such a wonderful job with the text.

Along with Palgrave Macmillan, I would also like to thank the trustees of the E. J. W. Gibb Memorial Trust and acknowledge the material derived from Professor Alan Jones's English translation of the Quran, published by the E. J. W. Gibb Memorial Trust and reproduced here with the kind permission of the trustees.

Finally, thanks to my great friend Rosie Cleary for her words of wisdom; and to my late grandfather William (Bill) Milford for seeing me on my way. This one is for you.

All errors are my own.

Note on Conventions

Every effort has been made to make Arabic names as easy as possible to read. Names have not been transliterated according to academic convention but simplified for the general reader. This might horrify purists, but it will hopefully make it easier for anyone approaching this subject for the first time.

For the same reason, place names have been simplified throughout. The nation-states of the Middle East are relatively recent creations, and as this text also deals with the period before they were created, in order not to burden it with various names for the same place, phrases like "modern-day Jordan" are used rather than the historic names.

Abbreviated references are given in the notes. These include the author's name, book title, and page number. Full references including year and name and location of publisher are given in the Bibliography.

Introduction

Lost in the Labyrinth: What's Really Going On in the Middle East?

If you have been following recent events in the Middle East and you are confused by the tangled web of wars and proxy wars, sectarian splits, revolutions, and counter-revolutions that are convulsing the region, do not worry. You are not alone. Policy makers, prime ministers, and presidents alike have been wrong-footed by the dizzying speed of change as the old order in the Arab world collapses and a new one fights its way into existence. The post–Arab Spring Middle East is rife with contradictions, inconsistencies, and the kind of complications that make your head spin. Finding your way through this labyrinth is no easy task.

Take Syria, for example. What began with a group of teenage schoolboys scribbling graffiti in Deraa calling for the overthrow of the dictator in Damascus has escalated into a catastrophic civil war with consequences far beyond Syria. Syria started off fighting one war—the people versus the unelected president—and is now fighting more than half a dozen. Damascus, the city that once ruled the Arab world, has become the stage for just about every power struggle in the region. Democracy versus dictatorship. Sunni versus Shi'i (which really means Saudi Arabia versus Iran). Militants versus moderates. The sacred versus the secular. Arab versus Arab (which really means Saudi Arabia versus Qatar). Even East versus West, as old and supposedly forgotten Cold War rivalries resurface with a new, twenty-first-century twist.

Then, to complicate things further, militants started fighting each other. And their fighting did not stop with them. The rise of the Islamic State of Iraq and the Levant (ISIL—rebranded as the Islamic State in the summer of 2014) pulled yet another group into the vortex of violence: the

Kurds. Without a state of their own, the Kurds are caught in the crossfire of other people's wars. When ISIL attacked Kurdish villages on Syria's northern border and in Iraq, the Kurds fought back and a whole new front opened up. ISIL, for their part, extended their reach beyond the battle-fields of the Middle East. Lone wolf attacks and assassinations of soft targets in Western cities—attacks that are deliberately designed to draw a Western military response—opened up yet another front in this seem-ingly endless war.

All of these competing camps fight it out daily in the streets and squares of Syria, while the Syrians are left to fend for themselves, aban-doned and betrayed by an international community that has utterly failed to stop the slaughter.

And even if Syrians do manage to escape the carnage, they are still not safe. The refugee camps are not always places of refuge. All sorts of horror stories have emerged about wealthy men from the Gulf "buying" teen-age brides from the camps. In desperation to help their destitute families, these girls are prepared to marry men they have never met: men who often turn out to be three or four times their age and who cast them off as soon as they become pregnant. But with essentials like food in such short supply (the World Food Program fears its supplies are about to run out), desperation has become a daily reality for hundreds of thousands of Syrian families whose lives have been devastated by the war.

The chaos and contradictions of the new Middle East are not limited to Syria. At the gateway to the Persian Gulf sits the tiny island kingdom of Bahrain. Bahrain means "two seas," and the country's strategic posi-tion on the Strait of Hormuz has long made it the envy of empires—be it the Portuguese or the Ottoman Empire in the medieval era or the British and American in the modern era. Bahrain's geopolitical position has for centuries given it a priority in international affairs far beyond its size and strength. Over one-fifth of the world's crude oil passes through the Strait of Hormuz. Little wonder, then, that the US Navy's Fifth Fleet is based in the kingdom to protect that supply route. The oil-dependent global econ-omy cannot survive without that oil and the leading industrial nations will do whatever needs to be done to safeguard it.

In February 2011, the kingdom was rocked by the Arab Spring. The people of Bahrain had had enough of the Khalifa family that had been in power without plebiscite since 1783. People took to the streets in peaceful protest calling for a democratic change.

They did not get it.

On March 14, 2011, over a thousand Saudi soldiers along with five hundred from the United Arab Emirates arrived in Bahrain to save the Bahraini king from his own people. The Saudi ruling family, which had so much to say about the rights of Syrians to determine their future, had nothing at all to say about the rights of Bahrainis to determine theirs. The crackdown that followed was as swift as it was bloody. Protestors were mowed down as they slept in their tented city at Pearl Roundabout in the nation's capital, Manama. Even hospitals were not immune from the crackdown. Doctors treating the wounded were arrested and given hefty prison sentences.

All of which left the Western allies of Bahrain in a difficult position. As democracies, the countries of the West publicly welcomed the Arab Spring. They said they wanted to see democracy in the region. As proof of their good intentions, they initiated military action against one of the region's worst dictators. At the time of the Saudi-UAE intervention in Bahrain, the United States, the United Kingdom, and France were frantically tabling a motion in the UN Security Council to protect the people of Libya from Gaddafi's dictatorship. That motion, UN Security Council Resolution 1973, was passed just days after the crackdown started in Bahrain. Almost overnight, NATO jets were in action in Libya attacking regime positions.

In light of the support Western countries gave to the people of Libya in their fight for freedom, the people of Bahrain might well have expected a similar backing. But they would be proved wrong.

The Western response to the use of violence by the Bahraini regime against the Bahraini people was muted. There were no UN resolutions. There were no sanctions. There were no travel bans. Thanks to the intervention of Western lobbyists and PR firms in the pay of the Bahraini ruling family, the story dropped out of international news agendas. Bahrain's King Hamad was not to be an international pariah like Syria's Bashar al-Asad or Libya's Colonel Gaddafi. In fact, less than six months after the crackdown, British Prime Minister David Cameron welcomed the king at Downing Street. Among other things, they discussed the situation in Syria. They did not discuss the situation in Bahrain.

If what happened in Bahrain showed some of the inconsistencies of Western foreign policy in the post–Arab Spring Middle East, then what happened in Egypt in the summer of 2013 shone a spotlight on them.

In February 2011, Egyptians took to the streets in their millions calling for the overthrow of Hosni Mubarak and the military regime he headed. Egyptians wanted change and, unlike the Bahrainis, they got it. In June 2012, Muhammad Morsi of the Muslim Brotherhood became the first democratically elected president in Egypt's seven-thousand-year history.

Barely a year later, Egyptians took to the streets again. This time calling for the overthrow of Morsi. Rival demonstrations called for him to stay. The military, backed by money from the Gulf, played on these divisions and seized their chance to reclaim power. They deposed Morsi, installed an interim regime with no democratic mandate, and began a crackdown that was so brutal; it made the crackdown in Bahrain look mild in comparison.

Once again, the West had little to say. When questioned about events in Egypt, British Foreign Minister William Hague resorted to all manner of verbal gymnastics to avoid saying the "c" word. Because if what happened in Egypt were to be acknowledged as a coup, US aid would be cut. EU assistance would be stopped. And much-needed IMF funds for cash-strapped Egypt would be off the table. Egypt would then be obliged to look beyond the West for financial help. Perhaps to Moscow. And Moscow was already reclaiming too much influence in the Middle East for the West's liking.

There was also the issue of Israel. Egypt was the first Arab country to strike a peace deal with Israel—a deal largely underwritten by American money and military aid. The Israeli security establishment doubted whether President Morsi and the Muslim Brotherhood would honor the treaty.

There were also behind-the-scenes murmurings that Israel's political establishment had no desire to see a close ally of Hamas in power in the Arab world's biggest country. But with the army-backed regime in Cairo promising to maintain the status quo and with Morsi in prison awaiting trial on trumped-up charges, there was no chance of anything changing. Stability was assured. Israel's southern border appeared to be safe.

The chaos in Syria, the crackdown in Bahrain, and the coup in Egypt are just three examples of a region in flux. Across the Middle East and North Africa, there are further examples.

Yemen, scene of another coup, has become another failed state and a battlefield for another proxy war. Libya is so rife with armed militias that in 2013 even the prime minister was not safe from kidnap. By early 2015, the country had two rival governments. Lebanon, by contrast, did not even have one: the country's politicians could not agree on a president. Even worse, the country has been sucked into Syria's wars and will probably not survive the crisis in its current form. Iraq is also in crisis. In 2013, the country saw a spike in violence that is nothing short of horrific. By the summer of 2014, the country had all but collapsed. Divided among the Kurds in the north, ISIL in the center, and the Shi'is in the south, Iraq is no longer functioning as a coherent political unit. To fight ISIL, Baghdad has had to turn to Iran for help.

And in the background, far down news agendas until a new eruption of violence explodes onto our screens and briefly reclaims the world's attention, the region's longest running conflict between Israelis and

Palestinians chugs along, as far from resolution as it was back in 1948 when the two peoples went to war for the first time.

If all of this leaves you wondering what's really going on in the Middle East, how this mess happened, and what is likely to happen next, the place to start looking for answers is not in the great imperial Arab cities of Baghdad, Cairo, or Damascus. It is not even in the sacred cities of Mecca, Medina, or Jerusalem. The place to start looking is not in the Middle East at all.

It is in the Balkan city of Sarajevo where on a sunny summer day, over a century ago, a man driving a car took a wrong turn and changed the course of history.

Part I

The Tangled Web: Why the Great Powers of Europe Became Involved in the Middle East

1

Sarajevo: Sunday, June 28, 1914

The man's name was Franz Urban.

He was a chauffeur and his passengers on that sunny summer day a century ago were two of the most important people in Europe: the heir to the Austro-Hungarian Empire, Archduke Franz Ferdinand, and the archduke's wife, Sophie.

The Austro-Hungarian Empire was one of the largest in Europe. It was also one of the oldest. It was the latest reinvention of the Habsburg Empire whose territories in the sixteenth century had extended far beyond Europe to include huge chunks of central and southern America. By the twentieth century, the Habsburg dynasty had survived wars, revolution, and bankruptcy to emerge as rulers of a central European empire stretching from Austria in the west to Ukraine in the east, Poland in the north to Bosnia in the south. The great cities of Vienna, Budapest, and Prague all fell within the Habsburg realm.

Multiethnic, multifaith, and multicultural, the Austro-Hungarian Empire was an intellectual powerhouse. It was here that Sigmund Freud founded a new science of psychoanalysis and, in doing so, forever changed how we see ourselves and how we understand sex and sexuality. It was here that Gustav Klimt founded a new school of art, the Secessionist, and painted the gold-hued modern icon *Portrait of Adele Bloch-Bauer 1* that would break sales records in 2007 when Ronald S. Lauder, son of cosmetics giant Estée, bought it for his New York museum for a staggering sum of $135,000,000, and the story of which became a major motion picture in 2015, *Woman in Gold*, starring Helen Mirren and Ryan Reynolds.

And it was here that Theodor Herzl founded a new political ideology that would have profound consequences for the future of the Middle

East: the belief that the Jewish people were a people like any other and should have a national home of their own, an idea that came to be known as Zionism.

Ruling such a diverse and dynamic empire meant power on a truly grand scale, but for Archduke Franz Ferdinand, the chance to exercise that power came at considerable personal cost. In an era of empires and elites, the sons of one royal house were expected to marry the daughters of another. Royal marriages were not just personal. They were political: a good way to cement relations between foreign powers. A king could hardly go to war with a country whose head of state was married to his sister and whose children called him uncle. Or so the elites of Europe thought.

This line of thinking led Europe's royal families to become so interconnected that the Romanian king was genetically German; the Greek monarchs were really Danish; and one of the most famous Russian royals, Catherine the Great, was not Russian at all. She was a German named Sophie. But it was Britain's Queen Victoria who set new benchmarks in imperial intermarriage. Her children (particularly her daughters) married so strategically that by 1914 the thrones of no fewer than three of Europe's empires—the British, the German, and the Russian—were all occupied by Victoria's direct descendants or in-laws. Kaiser Wilhelm II and Tsar Nicholas II were King George V's full cousins.

In this closed circle of blue blood and imperial alliances, Franz Ferdinand committed the cardinal sin. He put his heart before his head and married beneath him. His wife Sophie did not come from a famous family with impressive imperial credentials. She was not even royal. She was a minor member of the Czech aristocracy whose family had seen better days financially. And Emperor Franz Josef never let her, or her husband, forget it.[1]

Emperor Franz Josef had lived his adult life on the throne. Now 83 years old, he had come to power in 1848 while still a teenager. In the near seven decades of his reign, he had outlived several heirs. Franz Ferdinand, his nephew, was his fourth. The emperor's treatment of his heir suggests that if he could have appointed anyone else to fill the role he would gladly have done so. So low was the emperor's opinion of the archduke's wife that he made his nephew swear an oath that neither Sophie nor her children would ever inherit the empire. To underline the point, the emperor made sure royal protocol was strictly enforced at any event Sophie attended. This led to bizarre scenes at state receptions where Sophie was treated as a low provincial aristocrat rather than the wife of the future emperor. She would be seated at the bottom of the table away from her husband and, in royal processions, was obliged to walk at the end of the line alone.[2]

The royal couple bore these private slights and public humiliations and enjoyed their life together. June 28, 1914, was their wedding anniversary, and photographs taken early in the day show a genuinely happy couple. They sit smiling in the back of their open-top car. Sophie holds a bunch of flowers and looks on while her husband shakes hands with a local dignitary.

Franz Ferdinand and his wife were in Bosnia on official business. The archduke had come to oversee the Fifteenth and Sixteenth Army Corps on maneuvers in the border province. Security was a pressing concern for the empire because the Balkan region was in a state of upheaval. But exactly how much the Habsburgs knew about what was really going on beyond their borders and how prepared they were to deal with it remains an open question. The empire's intelligence chief, Colonel Alfred Redl, had been arrested the year before, caught red-handed passing secrets to the Russians. Partly to keep his personal life private (he was gay) and partly to fund his lavish lifestyle (he had very expensive taste), the colonel had duped his political masters for a decade. After being interrogated, Colonel Redl was given a gun and left alone to do the honorable thing. The scandal was hushed up but the damage was done. At a time when the Habsburg Empire's southern borders were simmering with discontent, Vienna was relying on faulty intelligence.[3]

The province that the archduke was visiting, Bosnia, was bordered by Serbia and Montenegro. Both were newly independent after centuries as provinces of the Ottoman Empire. Other Balkan countries were also recent additions to the map of Europe: Bulgaria, Romania, Albania, and Greece had all recently broken away from Istanbul's control, often with the help of one of the Great Powers. Britain and Russia, in particular, were ruthlessly Machiavellian about using the Balkans to score points against their imperial rival in Istanbul.

For the new Balkan states, however, independence brought new problems. They had freedom but no peace. In 1912, and again in 1913, several of these countries went to war with each other over unfulfilled territorial ambitions. State creation is not an exact science, and the lines on the new map of Europe were not drawn cleanly and people frequently found themselves on the wrong side of a new border. There were, for example, large numbers of Serbs in Bosnia who wanted to be citizens of the Serbian state rather than subjects of the ageing Austrian emperor.

All of this presented a challenge to the Austro-Hungarian Empire. It was not just that Vienna needed to protect the empire's southern border from invasion or another Balkan war. The real threat to the empire was ideological. The newly formed Balkan states were based on the idea of *nation*. A nation-state saw people with a common language and (usually) a common religion draw on their shared historical experience and come together to create a shared future destiny. Italy's city-states did it in 1870, Germany's principalities in 1871. Both were thriving.

At the beginning of the twentieth century, nationalism was one of the most influential political ideologies. With its focus on ethnic unity, it was the polar opposite of the transnationalism of the Austro-Hungarian Empire where no fewer than 12 languages were spoken and at least four religions were freely practiced. To this day, Budapest still has the largest synagogue in Europe.

The problem for a transnational empire like Austro-Hungary was that some of the nationalities in it were more equal than others. The empire's name gave its priorities away: the Austrians and Hungarians were politically more important than everyone else. The Austrians, in turn, were more important than the Hungarians. Franz Ferdinand planned to address this imbalance when he became emperor and aimed to make the empire more equal.[4] In the meantime, nationalism gained strength among the empire's minorities who saw it as a way to achieve their goal of independence.

These minorities were encouraged by the success of their Balkan brothers. Like the minorities in the Austro-Hungarian Empire, the people of the Balkans had once belonged to a vast transnational empire—the Ottoman—that spanned three continents and was a veritable Babel of languages and peoples. But like the empire in Vienna, the one in Istanbul also had a dominant culture. And Istanbul's Turkish and Islamic culture was not shared by the Serbs, Bulgarians, and Greeks who lived in the empire's European provinces. So when the Serbs, Bulgarians, and Greeks broke away from Istanbul, the minorities in the Habsburg Empire started to entertain hopes of breaking free of Vienna.

Discontent had been bubbling beneath the surface in the provinces of the Austrian Empire for years. And on June 28, 1914, the empire's heir and his wife walked blithely into the maelstrom of that long-simmering discontent. The date, emotionally significant for them personally, was even more significant for local Serbs. It was National Day in Serbia, marking one of the defining moments of Serb history: the Battle of Kosovo Polje (the Field of Blackbirds) against the Ottomans in 1389 when the Serbs, led by King Lazar, were defeated. Lazar was killed. The Kingdom of Serbia was reduced to a vassal state of the Ottoman Empire. The saving grace for Serb honor was that they did not go down without a fight. One of their fighters assassinated the Ottoman sultan, Murad I, on the battlefield.[5]

On this day heavy with so much history, the imperial couple began their official visit. Soon after they arrived in the city, a young man in the midst of a crowd of cheering well-wishers lobbed a bomb at their car.

The bomb bounced off and crashed into the oncoming car carrying the archduke's staff. There were injuries but no fatalities. The injured men were taken to hospital. The attacker was caught. The archduke and duchess continued their journey to the City Hall for an official reception. Arriving at the City Hall, the archduke was overheard asking one of the local dignitaries, "So you welcome your guests here with bombs?" But other than that, he and his wife appeared remarkably unruffled by the attempt on their lives.[6]

The attack was carried out by six young Serbs from a radical group called Young Bosnia whose aim was to free Bosnia from Vienna's control and unite it with the rest of Serbia. Trained and armed across the border in Belgrade, the young men were sent into Bosnia with orders to hit at the heart of Austrian imperial power. Franz Ferdinand's visit to Sarajevo provided an ideal, high-profile opportunity to do it.

But the Young Bosnians were not professional soldiers. And as far as would-be assassins went, they were not really up to the job. One of them, Gavrilo Princip, was actually ill with tuberculosis. By the time the archduke arrived at the City Hall, it looked as if their mission had failed miserably.

When the imperial couple finished their visit to City Hall, they decided to deviate from their official agenda and visit the hospital where the injured officers were being treated. This meant a change in their planned route. Their driver, Franz Urban, did not know the new route. When he came to the intersection between Franzjosefstrasse and Appel Quay, he took the wrong turn. The street was so narrow that he could not turn the car around. He had to brake, go into reverse, and go back down the street at a snail's pace.

A young man idling at the street corner suddenly spotted the open-topped car crawling the street. He was Gavrilo Princip. The royal couple were just a few feet away from Princip. The 19-year-old wasted no time. He pulled out his gun and fired twice. Both shots hit their target. Franz Ferdinand and Sophie were dead by the time they reached hospital.[7]

*   *   *

Within weeks, Europe was at war.

The imperial system of alliances, so carefully constructed over so many years to maintain the balance of power in Europe and to prevent war, now kicked in and brought about the very war they were designed to prevent.

After the assassination in Sarajevo, Austro-Hungary issued an ultimatum to Serbia, the terms of which were almost impossible to fulfill. Even so, Serbia tried. But one of the stumbling blocks to any resolution was the rapidly developing international nature of the crisis.

Germany was joined by geography and linked by language with Austro-Hungary, and Berlin now urged Vienna to stand their ground. (Vienna, it has to be said, needed little encouragement.) Russia was Slavic like Serbia and followed the same Orthodox faith, and St. Petersburg now urged Belgrade to stand theirs.

To complicate matters further, Russia was allied by treaty with Britain and France, which meant anyone taking on St. Petersburg would have to fight on more than one front.

It was to avoid that very scenario that Germany decided to invoke the "Schlieffen Plan." Named after the general who devised it, this plan would see Germany invading France from the north, via Belgium and Holland, in a lightning strike that would knock France out of the war and leave Germany free to fight Russia.

The problem for Germany was that Britain and France had been legal guarantors of Belgium's neutrality since 1839. The British government sent an ultimatum to Berlin reminding them as much. The Germans ignored it. On August 4, the day the ultimatum was due to expire, Germany went ahead and invaded Belgium.

Cousinly kinship between the royal houses of Europe counted for nothing now. On August 4, 1914, five of Europe's great empires were at war. On one side were Germany and Austro-Hungary. On the other were Britain, France, and Russia. The Ottoman Empire would soon join the German side. And because these empires, with the exception of Austro-Hungary, all had extensive overseas territories, this war would not be confined to the continent where it started.

The Middle East would be particularly affected. European powers, mainly Britain and France, had taken over much of the region during the nineteenth century. The First World War would provide them with the opportunity to seize control of even more of it.

But what brought these Great Powers into the Arab world in the first place had nothing at all to do with the high politics of war and peace. It was much more mundane than that.

It was money.

2

The British Empire and the Arab World: Ambition, Austerity, and a Class Apart

1

The sovereign of Egypt had grand ambitions.

His name was Ismail (r. 1863–79) and he was the grandson of Muhammad Ali, the man widely regarded as the founder of modern Egypt. Muhammad Ali was one of those giants of history who start with nothing and end with everything. An illiterate soldier from Macedonia, he arrived in Egypt as part of the Ottoman sultan's army against Napoleon's disastrous invasion of 1798. He never left.

His success was based on his military skills, and in 1805 those skills saw him promoted to *pasha*, or ruler. From then, until his death in 1848, he ruled Egypt as his personal fief, his obedience to Istanbul little more than lip service. At times, he fought alongside the sultan's forces—and at times he fought against them. Which side he took depended on where his personal interests lay. In 1841, the Ottoman Sultan Abdulmajid recognized this reality and took a new approach to secure his erstwhile ally's loyalty. He made him royal. Egypt would remain a province of the Ottoman Empire, but Muhammad Ali had the power to appoint his own successors.[1]

On his death, Muhammad Ali was succeeded first by his son Ibrahim (r. 1848), then by a grandson Abbas (r. 1848–54), then by another son Said (1854–63). Said is remembered as the man who commissioned the Suez Canal. But it was Muhammad Ali's grandson Ismail (r. 1863–79) who inherited the full force of the patriarch's driving ambition and who set about remaking Egypt in a modern mold.

Inspired by a visit to France in 1867 for the World Exhibition, Ismail decided to build a New Paris on the Nile. Not for him were the crowded quarters and the twisting, winding alleyways of Cairo's old city. Under Ismail, the medieval was cast aside and Cairo was redrawn to accommodate wide Haussmann-esque boulevards. Entire suburbs were transformed. An opera house was built. Public parks, gardens, and open spaces dotted the city. And the changes were not just cosmetic. The latest technology was imported from Europe along with the latest architecture and culture. Telegraphs, street lighting, railways, irrigation projects, European-style schools including schools for girls and technical colleges, all became part of the landscape of the new Egypt.

And the crowning glory of this modernized Egypt was the Suez Canal. Its construction revolutionized Egypt's place in the world. Egypt was no longer a country off the beaten track that travelers, traders, and troops had to make a special effort to reach. It was now fully incorporated into international trade routes. Thanks to the canal, trade between Europe and the East was able to bypass the long and expensive route round the African Cape. With shipping costs drastically reduced, Egypt became nothing less than the pivot between East and West.

No expense was spared for the canal's grand opening in November 1869. It was a French engineer, Ferdinand de Lesseps, who designed the canal, so the honor of opening it was given to French Empress Eugénie. Legend has it that Ismail had a palace specially built in Cairo's island suburb of Zamalek for her. Verdi was commissioned to write a new opera, *Aida*, for the occasion. (It was not ready in time so they made do with *Rigoletto*.) Egypt's reinvention as a modern nation was complete. Ismail went as far as to declare his country was now part of Europe.

There was just one problem. Egypt did not have the money to pay for any of it. And within six years of the canal opening, Egypt was bankrupt.

In fairness to Ismail, the mess was not all of his making. His uncle Said had launched the Suez project and he awarded the contract for building the canal to his close friend, Ferdinand de Lesseps, and he did so on terms wholly unfavorable to Egypt. Cairo was burdened with all the costs of constructing the canal in return for only a minority share of the potential profits, which meant that even though the canal quickly became a huge financial success, the beneficiaries were the European shareholders of the canal's holding company not the Egyptian exchequer.[2]

Adding to the pile of financial losses, Egypt financed the canal's construction with loans from European banks, which were leveraged at such high rates of interest; it was debatable if Egypt could ever repay them, regardless of how profitable the canal turned out to be.

And, as if all of these were not enough, there were issues about Ismail's rebranding of Egypt as a European country. As part of his strategy, he imported the trappings of European progress but not Europe's economic or political model. The city of Paris, which had impressed him so much during his visit in 1867, was supported by a solid manufacturing industry, a productive farming sector, a thriving banking community, and trade from a worldwide empire. Egypt had none of these. Even its most successful export was not as economically productive as it could have been. Egypt's farming sector was overly reliant on one crop, cotton, and overly reliant on one customer, the mills in Lancashire, England.[3]

Then there was the issue of Ismail's financial relations with Istanbul. In return for doubling the yearly tribute to the Ottoman sultan, from 1866 Ismail was allowed to call himself "*khedive*," the Persian for sovereign. He was also granted the right to introduce the principle of primogeniture. The right of the first-born son to inherit power was not widely practiced in Muslim monarchies. Ever since the dynastic principle was introduced into the Muslim world in the seventh century, the ruling family as a unit took precedence over any individual line of it. Caliphs and sultans often tried to pass power to their direct descendants, but the wider family always won in the end. With this grant from the sultan, Ismail succeeded where so many before him had failed. But he had to pay for the privilege and it was one more thing he could not afford.[4]

In 1875, the entire house of cards collapsed. Egypt's foreign debt was now roughly the same size as the country's entire economy. There was simply no way to balance the books. Bankruptcy prompted a fire sale of assets. The khedive's most desirable financial asset was his 40 percent stake (just over 175,000 shares) in the Suez Canal's holding company, the Compagnie Universelle du Canal Maritime de Suez. The company's majority shareholders were French, and to maintain French influence, a number of French banks expressed interest in buying the khedive out. De Lesseps himself was said to have made an offer.

But this was to be Britain's moment. The world's greatest maritime power with a global empire on which the sun never set needed access to the Suez Canal more than anyone else. British Prime Minister Benjamin Disraeli was acutely aware of just how important the canal was to British imperial interests. He acted swiftly. With an informality that would be unthinkable nowadays, Disraeli rushed round to the house of his friend Baron Lionel de Rothschild and borrowed the four million pounds Britain needed to buy the khedive's shares.

And with that, the deal was done.[5]

2

Buying the khedive's shares was a triumph for Disraeli. By acting so quickly, he made sure Britain had a role in determining the future of the canal. Half of Britain's shipping to India went through Suez. In the short time since the canal opened, it had become too important to Britain's strategic interests to allow London's arch imperial rival, France, to gain control of the company that ran it. Had the French succeeded in doing so, it would have given Paris the power to strangle British shipping. After the sale, Britain and France set their imperial rivalry aside to put up a united front in defense of their own interests against Egypt. It was a policy both parties held right up to the Suez War in 1956.

In 1879, London and Paris began strengthening their position in Egypt by taking control of the country's finances. In theory, the debt management agency, the Caisse de la Dette (or the European Debt Commission), which was set up to sort out Egypt's financial crisis, was neutral of outside political interference. In theory, it was a body made up of independent financial experts whose job was to make sure Egypt did not default on its debts to European banks. In reality, it was the Trojan horse for a full-scale European takeover of Egypt.

In the same year the debt agency started its work, Paris and London put pressure on the Ottoman Sultan Abdulhamid II (himself in the same kind of financial trouble as Khedive Ismail and for much the same reasons) to allow them to depose Ismail in favor of his young son Tawfiq. Needless to say, the sultan who needed a European bailout just as much as the Egyptians did was not about to argue.[6]

To Egyptians, it was clear that the ease with which Britain and France achieved their goals owed less to the power of their ideas than the power of their money. Egyptians knew Egypt could not compete against European domination on those terms, so they turned to the power of their military. The hero of the hour was an army officer named Ahmad Urabi who came from a peasant family. A son of the land himself, Urabi understood the grievances of ordinary people. His rising popularity soon alarmed the British and French. Their worries were validated when Urabi was arrested in 1880, thrown in jail, and the Egyptian army refused to detain him. Instead, he was appointed to the cabinet. Once there, he proceeded to push the khedive out.

That was the final straw for the British. They feared a popular leader who enjoyed the support of the military and the masses would challenge Anglo-French control of the canal. In what was to become a long-standing feature of British policy in this part of the world, London claimed to have no selfish interests in Egypt, to be acting solely against a military dictator, and to have absolutely no intention of occupying the country. Then, with the full backing of the French, they did exactly the opposite and sent the troops in.

What began with a massive naval bombardment on Alexandria on July 11, 1882, ended with the defeat of Urabi's forces in the battle at Tell al-Kabir near Cairo just two months later on September 13. Urabi was sent packing.[7] Later, he would be honored as the founding father of Egyptian nationalism. One of the main streets in downtown Cairo bears his name to this day. But for now, he was off into exile while the British made themselves at home in Egypt. For the next 70 years.

3

For London, victory in Egypt secured a key strategic objective.

Since the opening of the Suez Canal, Egypt had been the missing link on the route from Britain to India. So central was India to British imperial strategy that securing the route was nothing short of an obsession. It was not enough to control the subcontinent itself. Every part of the way there had to be subdued in one way or another; if for no other reason than to prevent an imperial rival hoisting their flag over it. As a result, Britain viewed every country from the English Channel to the Hindu Kush mountain range as future friend or foe.

Prior to 1882, Britain had access to a number of coaling stations in the Mediterranean: Gibraltar, Malta, and Cyprus. London also had treaties with many of the families who ruled the coastal enclaves along the Persian Gulf. Under the terms of these agreements, British ships traveling to and from India were allowed to dock and refuel in their ports in return for British payment and "protection"—a diplomatic way of offering the undiplomatic choice "you are either with us or against us."

From as far back as 1798, the British had worked with the sultan of Muscat in Oman. In 1820, they concluded a treaty with the ruling families of the Trucial States on the eastern side of the Gulf (now known as the United Arab Emirates). In 1839, the British occupied Aden in modern-day Yemen, which was the most important port on the sea route between Egypt and India.

By the middle of the century, it was the turn of the Bu Said family in Oman to join the British sphere of influence. By 1861, the Khalifa family on the island of Bahrain had decided to do the same. These treaties were alliances of mutual convenience. The British used them to secure a key stage of the route to India at minimal cost. The Arab rulers for their part used them to secure power against local rivals. And they did it well: these ruling families remain in power to this day.[8]

With Egypt now a link in this imperial chain of ports and overseas bases, London could relax. British sea power was secure. Now all London had to do was find someone to rule the land of the Sphinx.

They found their man in Evelyn Baring, otherwise known as Lord Cromer.

Baring was a bastion of the British establishment. A military man, Baring was the grandson of an admiral, the son of a member of parliament, and he himself had served as a soldier on three continents before going to work in the Indian service. His paternal family, the Barings, owned the bank of that name.

Aside from securing the Suez Canal, Britain intervened in Egypt to make sure the country repaid its loans to European banks. From London's point of view, who better than a Baring to look after the interests of Britain and her banks?[9]

In 1883, now in his forties, Cromer arrived in Cairo to take up the post of Consul General with powers that would have made a pharaoh blush. Cromer's aim was not to rule Egypt—Britain, to the end, maintained the fiction that Egypt was not a colony—but "to rule the rulers of Egypt." And Cromer had the force of character to impose this system of indirect dictatorship. No shrinking violet, his colleagues in India referred to him as "Over-Baring." To Egyptians, he was simply "The Lord."

For the next 24 years, Cromer ruled Egypt in all but name. With a relatively small number of British troops, he managed to embed British authority across the country. With an equally small number of British bureaucrats, he managed to perform feats of financial wizardry and balance the Egyptian books. Surplus cash was available for investment in public works, especially agriculture and irrigation, and cotton production soared at a time when its price was booming in the international market. It was during Cromer's era that the first Aswan Dam was built (1906). He was also responsible for abolishing the hated *corvée*, the system of forced labor, which allowed wealthy landowners to force ordinary men into unpaid work for unlimited periods of time.[10]

It was measures like these that justified British rule in their own eyes. More than anything else, Cromer and his fellow members of the imperial elite believed Britain brought fiscal stability and the rule of law to Egypt.[11] Corruption was so endemic in the country that wealthy absentee landowners could confiscate the cotton crop of their tenants, plough a road through their holdings, or cut off their water supply, and the farmers could do nothing to stop them.

The British, by contrast, wanted all Egyptians to be subject to the same law. The fact that peasants could not afford access to it was something the British authorities did not seem to consider.

The truth was that the British did not need to justify their occupation of Egypt to themselves. The late nineteenth century was the high watermark of international imperialism, and Egypt was a welcome addition to the British Empire. And Egypt was not just any country. The land of the Sphinx held a special fascination for Victorian England. Victorian society was a curious, contradictory mix of Puritanism and pleasure, and Egypt with its Biblical associations, Classical connections, and exoticism seemed to have something for everyone. It was here that Moses received the Ten Commandments and led the Jews from captivity to freedom in the Promised Land. It was here that Antony romanced Cleopatra in a doomed seduction immortalized by England's national playwright Shakespeare. And it was here that the intrepid explorer, sexual adventurer, and translator of the *Kama Sutra*, Sir Richard Burton, risked his life and liberty to embark on his secret pilgrimage to Mecca in 1853; a feat that so captured the imagination of Victorian society, the book of the journey became a bestseller when it was published in 1855 and continues to sell today.

For the British administrators sent to work in Egypt, the country became a home away from home. Zamalek, the island suburb in the middle of the Nile, was a virtual British enclave where they recreated the world they knew and lived as a class apart. Often their only real contact with anyone Egyptian was with their servants and chauffeurs.

British women yielded nothing to their environment and continued to behave and dress as if they were in a sitting room in Surrey or a ballroom in Belgravia rather than living on the edge of an African desert. Afternoons were whiled away having tea at Shepheard's British Hotel or drinking gin pahits at the country club.

The British sense of splendid isolation extended to education and sport. The British established their own schools where their children were taught in their own language by their own people and where they studied the same subjects they would have studied back in Britain.

They also brought their pastimes to Egypt: most notably, football. To this day, the football club in Zamalek still has not broken fully free of its foreign associations. By contrast, its main Cairo rival, al-Ahly (meaning national) set up in 1907 by Egyptians for Egyptians, has none of Zamalek's imperial baggage.[12]

The British presence in Egypt was reinforced throughout the year by a steady stream of tourists from the home country. Cairo was a mustsee destination for the more adventurous of the Grand Tourists and for travelers en route to the Holy Land. It was also a stopping-off point for the many British administrators traveling to and from India.

But what of the people whose country this was? What did the Egyptians make of the British occupation of their land?

4

As a proud people with a civilization stretching seven millennia, the Egyptians viewed the British occupation as nothing short of a national humiliation. Muslim since 641, part of the Ottoman Empire since 1517, Egypt now had to come to terms with the rule of a non-Muslim power.

The physical occupation and subsequent loss of sovereignty were just one part of the problem. Even more of an affront to Egyptian national pride was the patronizing nature of British power. Repeatedly, the British claimed they were not occupying Egypt. Repeatedly, they claimed they were only there to sort out the country's finances. Repeatedly, they claimed they would leave as soon as they could find a stable government to replace them.

Yet British actions repeatedly contradicted their words. They did nothing to encourage the development of a local political class that could replace them. Quite the reverse: they turned the khedives into little more than figureheads. First, they deposed Ismail (r. 1863–79) and set up a legislative assembly to rubberstamp their decisions. Next, they stripped Ismail's son Tawfiq (r. 1879–92) of any real power. Then, they deposed Tawfiq's successor son Abbas II (r. 1892–1914) at the start of the First World War and declared Egypt a protectorate of the British Empire.

From the outset, Cromer ran Egypt in the interests of the rulers not of the ruled. Even his successful restructuring of the country's debts was for the benefit of Britain's banks, not for the Egyptians themselves. And having made Egypt safe for European capital, Cromer, scion of a banking dynasty that he was, encouraged these same banks to invest there to help small-scale farmers. But this too was done for the benefit of the banks. They needed new markets for their capital and he provided them.[13]

Cromer's capital investment programs, particularly in irrigation and agriculture, were also done with both eyes fixed firmly on Europe. With more land reclaimed and more water available, the country became even more reliant on cotton production than it had been back in the days of Muhammad Ali. This lack of diversification was dangerous in the long term, but, as with the debt program, it was done to meet the needs of the international economy rather than to improve the living standards of the ordinary Egyptian farmer. Under British rule, Egypt was deliberately integrated into the world economy on terms unfavorable to Egypt. The impact was divisive and felt throughout society. The rich elite who traded with Europe became much richer and the poor became much, much poorer. All of this meant wealthy landowners could still exploit the *fellaheen* farmers who worked their land whatever way they wanted, corvée or no corvée.

This structural imbalance in the nation's finances was repeated in the country's education system. Cromer and the men who followed him, such as Consul Generals Sir Eldon Gorst (r. 1907–11) and Lord Kitchener (r. 1911 until the First World War), made little or no investment in the public education system. Rich Egyptians could afford to send their children to private schools—most of which were British-run with classes taught in English—while poor Egyptians had to make do with the underresourced state sector. In such circumstances, social mobility was nonexistent. And in such circumstances, it was unlikely that a class of Egyptians would ever emerge who were rebellious, educated, and articulate. The imperial logic was that the rich Egyptians who benefited from the status quo would not rock the boat and the poor would not know how to.[14]

Divisions in Egypt were further reinforced by the law. The British may well have believed they were making all Egyptians equal before it, but they placed all non-Egyptians above it. To do this, they took advantage of a legal loophole dating back to 1569. Known as the Capitulations, these legal measures allowed foreign citizens living in the Ottoman Empire to claim legal redress under the laws of their own country. The Great Powers exploited the loophole to give their own citizens virtual immunity from prosecution. In Egypt, it was particularly useful for British businesses setting up after 1882 as they were not subject to local law. It was also useful to protect British soldiers from potential prosecution. For Egyptians, this legal gap between occupier and occupied was thrown into sharp relief by what happened in a village in the Nile Delta one summer day in 1906.

In June of that year, a group of British officers went out pigeon-shooting in the village of Dinshaway. They were supposed to seek permission from the locals before doing so and, to avoid any potential accidents, let the villagers know in advance when they were coming. On this occasion, they did neither. In the course of the shoot, a local woman was shot by a British soldier.

Then all hell broke loose. A fight ensued. Shots were fired. There were casualties and fatality on both sides. But only Egyptians were prosecuted. Over two hundred were arrested. After what was little more than a show trial, four residents of Dinshaway were convicted and publicly hanged two weeks later. Local people were forced to go and watch the executions.

Sentences of hard labor were given to two other men, and many more local men were publicly flogged.

For Egyptians, the Dinshaway Incident became a notorious example of the contradictions of the British presence in their country: the British claimed to be in Egypt to uphold the rule of law, but they did so only when it suited their own interests. And there was nothing the Egyptians could do to stop it.

5

One of the most popular children's books in Victorian Britain was Lewis Carroll's *Alice's Adventures in Wonderland* (1865). And the British presence in Egypt had something of a surreal, wonderland quality to it. When the British peered through the looking glass at the country around them, they saw what they wanted to see, not what was there. Empire distorted the view, threw a veil over their real intentions, and created a form of diplomatic doublespeak that exists to this day when it comes to dealing with the realities of the Middle East.

Empire allowed a man like Cromer to assume the right to speak for women in Egypt when he railed against the veil as a symbol of all that was wrong with Islam. Yet back home, he was so opposed to British women being given the vote he founded an organization to lobby against it: the Men's League for Opposing Women's Suffrage.

Empire allowed Cromer to make bold sweeping statements such as: "The Egyptians should be permitted to govern themselves after the fashion in which Europeans think they ought to be governed."[15] As if Egyptians should be given the right to choose their own government when—and only when—they could be relied upon to choose one that matched the ambitions and interests of Europe's Great Powers.

Empire allowed contradictions like these to flourish. On rare occasions, Cromer admitted as much. "The English as imperialists," he said, "are always striving to attain two ideals which are apt to be mutually destructive—the ideal of good government, which connotes the continuing of his supremacy, and the ideal of self-government, which connotes the whole or partial abdication of his supreme position."[16]

It was a contradiction the British never resolved. Their great imperial rivals, the French, would try a different tack in the parts of the Arab world they occupied. But there was one key area of common ground between London and Paris. Like the British, it was not matters of war and peace that brought the French into the Arab world, it was money.

3

The French Empire and the Arab World: From the Crusades to the Civilizing Mission

1

In 1830, the French invaded Algeria. They stayed for the next 132 years. This long occupation that was to culminate in a devastating war with catastrophic consequences for both countries began because of an incident that bordered on the ridiculous.

In the 1820s France owed Algeria money. Algeria supplied France with grain, particularly for the French army, and the French had not paid their bills. In April 1827, a meeting was held between the Algerian ruler, the *dey*, and the French ambassador to discuss the debts. It turned into a showdown.

The dey pressed for payment of the bills. The ambassador fudged. The arguments became heated. Then, as the ambassador later recorded in his official report to Paris, the dey lost his temper and struck him with his fly whisk, an assault the dey vehemently denied.

Given that a fly whisk is not intended for use on anything larger than a fly, it is hard to imagine what damage the dey could have done had he indeed wielded it against the ambassador. But the ambassador was adamant and demanded an apology for the affront to French honor.

The dey refused to apologize for something he had not done. Besides, the French *still* had not paid their debts. Should the ambassador not concentrate on that?

The ambassador, playing the role of wounded party to perfection, ratcheted up the pressure, and before long the diplomatic equivalent of a duel was underway.

Back in Paris, Charles X was only too glad of the distraction. France was again in revolutionary mood. French troops had recently returned from action in the Greek War of Independence. A deployment that had not gone well. A foreign policy success elsewhere was needed to regain lost prestige, and Algeria offered it.[1]

Part of the Ottoman Empire since 1529, Algeria enjoyed a large measure of independence from Istanbul. As long as taxes were paid and the sultan's name was mentioned in Friday prayers, the ruler of Algeria was left to his own devices. From the mid-1600s, the region had been ruled by a military caste, one of whose members took the title "dey." In 1830, the ruling dey, Hussein, was about to find himself facing the full force of French firepower. In the summer of that year, the French navy bombarded the Algerian coast. The Algerian armies were no match for the French forces and the fighting was soon over.

It was a diplomatic and political triumph for the French. Their ambassador had successfully elevated the fly whisk farce into a major international incident and their government had successfully manipulated it into the legal justification for a full-scale assault on Algeria. It said a lot about the asymmetrical nature of imperial finances that, in 1882, Britain would invade Egypt because Egypt owed Britain money, whereas France invaded Algeria even though France owed Algeria money. The sheer scale of imperial power made such inconsistencies irrelevant to the capitals of Europe.

French debts were well and truly forgotten. In this age of empires, the French now had a foothold in Africa and the way south to the heart of the continent lay open before them. All they had to do was secure the rest of Algeria.

This proved to be a much more difficult task than anyone in Paris had anticipated. Resistance came in the form of a 25-year-old named Abd al-Qadir, whose father was leader of the Qadariyya order of Sufi ascetics.[2] Sufis take their name from the Arabic word for wool (*suf*) describing the woolen cloaks they wear to symbolize austerity and their disconnection from worldly affairs. Outside Islam, they are known for the spectacular, near-acrobatic displays of their whirling dervishes. The Sufi laser-like focus on the sacred did not, however, make them retreat from the world in the way Christian monks did. Throughout Islamic history, members of Sufi orders have taken up arms to fight for their faith, and they now did so in Algeria against the French.

Abd al-Qadir mobilized his forces and used Sufi hostels or *khanqa*s as their logistical base. These were buildings run by the Sufis where travelers could stay for the night and perform their prayers in the adjacent mosque. These hostels became the hubs in Abd al-Qadir's network of resistance and enabled his fighters to move across the region, pass on information, and receive arms, all while posing as pilgrims or traders. Abd al-Qadir also enjoyed massive support from tribes across Algeria, as well as the patronage of the ruler of Morocco.

For nine years, from 1832 and 1841, he held this motley band of brothers together and waged his war so successfully that the French were at a loss about how to deal with him.

Ultimately, Abd al-Qadir became a victim of his own success. Since conventional methods were not working against him, the French resorted to unconventional ones. In 1841, a new French general was deployed to Algeria with a new agenda. General Thomas-Robert Bugeaud was determined to subdue the territory whatever it took. In an era long before the Geneva Conventions governed the rules of war, war had no rules. So the French responded to any attack on their authority with overwhelming force. The novelist Maupassant, no fan of French imperial adventures, sums up the army's casual attitude to the people of Algeria with devastating clarity in his novel *Bel-Ami*. He has Georges Duroy (the lead character and the *Bel-Ami* of the title) kill three Arabs during his military service in Algeria and get away with it because the French military did not much care what happened to an Arab.[3]

Right across the region, collective punishment became the norm. Crops were ruined. Villages destroyed. Communities displaced and sometimes killed. All with the aim of dividing to conquer.[4]

And it worked. In 1847, Abd al-Qadir surrendered. He had no choice. His supporters were suffering too much. In victory, the French showed a generosity they had not shown in war. There was no show trial or public execution for the Algerian rebel leader. He was sent into exile, first to Paris where he was received by the great and the good as an equal, and then to Damascus, the city he chose for his retirement.

With Abd al-Qadir gone, the French were free to concentrate on ruling Algeria. Years later, the British were content to rule Egypt from the splendid isolation of their island enclave on the Nile. As long as Egypt paid its debts, grew its cotton, and kept the canal open, the British were content to remain a class apart. Not so the French in Algeria.

The French, unlike the British, were on a mission. They were going to "civilize" Algeria. They were going to turn it into part of France.

2

The efforts to colonize Algeria began in earnest with the arrival of General Bugeaud in 1841. It was not the first time the French had tried to put down roots in Arab land. Nearly eight hundred years earlier, the Crusades had been launched from French soil. It was in the French town of Clermont on November 26, 1095, that Pope Urban II issued a call to arms for Christians to reclaim the Holy City of Jerusalem from the Muslim "infidel." In return, these crusading warriors were promised nothing short of salvation.

Over 150,000 men responded, many of them from France. But this army of Christian soldiers was anything but holy. They were a rag-tag bunch of thrill-seekers looking for excitement, criminals looking for escape, mercenaries looking for plunder, second sons from noble families looking for a fief, traders looking for goods and markets, and penitents looking for redemption. Within two years they were on their way, and within another two, they had succeeded. For the first time since the seventh century, Jerusalem was Christian again.[5]

The loss of Jerusalem, the third Holiest City in Islam, to the Christians in 1099 and the Crusaders' decision to celebrate by massacring the city's population stunned Muslims. The Arab Muslim world was a relatively self-contained one, used to dealing with the outside world on its own terms. This was the first time a European army had penetrated the House of Islam and the experience was so searing that even now, nearly a thousand years later, you can still hear Western intervention in the Middle East referred to as "Crusader aggression."

For the next two centuries, Crusaders carved out principalities along the Mediterranean coastline. Cities like Antioch and Acre, Jaffa and Jerusalem, Tripoli and Tyre had Latin kings rather than Muslim sultans. Many of these Latin kings were French and the mini-states they ruled were the forerunner of nineteenth-century colonies: outposts of European influence backed up by European military might and European popular opinion. A tour of duty in the East became almost a rite of passage for Christian kings. England's Richard the Lion Heart, Germany's Frederick Barbarossa, France's Louis IX: all made their way eastwards to lead Crusades.

Ultimately, it was all to no avail. Saladin, the great hero of the Arabs (who was actually a Kurd), recaptured Jerusalem in 1187. Then Louis IX's Sixth Crusade in 1249–50 ended in defeat for the Europeans in Egypt. And toward the end of thirteenth century, in 1291, the Mamluk military rulers of Egypt took the fight directly to the Crusaders and defeated the last of their strongholds on the coast of modern Lebanon.

But if the Crusades left a lasting impression on the Arab world, they also made an impact in Europe. The great historian of the Middle East, Philip Hitti, notes in his epic *History of the Arabs* that "the Christians came to the Holy Land with the notion that they were far superior to its people, whom they considered idolaters, worshipping Muhammad as God."[6] Although the Europeans who stayed in the Holy Land often lost that sense of superiority, the people who set the Crusades in motion never did. In the highest echelons of the political and religious establishment of Europe, there remained a firm belief that the Crusades were a just cause because they sought to bring enlightenment to a people living in spiritual darkness. According to this view, the fact that Muslims—those people living in spiritual darkness who could not tell the difference between Muhammad and God—had the audacity to *win* left a legacy in Europe of unfinished business with the East.

Centuries later, Napoleon laid claim to that very legacy and that same sense of superiority and crusading zeal to justify his invasion of Egypt in July 1798. Without the slightest hint of irony, Napoleon told Egyptians that he, like them, was a Muslim, and he had come to Egypt because the country's Mamluk rulers were not as good Muslims as the French. He even planned to write his own Quran. What he really meant was he had invaded Egypt to save the Egyptians from themselves.

What made Napoleon's declaration even stranger than his professed belief in Islam was the fact that the French Revolution of 1789 had swept aside *all* religions in favor of reason and rationalism. So the French were not really bringing the enlightenment of their faith to Egypt. They were bringing their ideas. As part of his invasion force, Napoleon brought dozens of scientists who spent their sojourn in Egypt conducting experiments to showcase the power of French ideas and prove the greatness of French civilization. He even tried to bring local learned men on board and appointed the renowned Egyptian scholar al-Jabarti to his grand council. At the time, al-Jabarti was chair of astronomy at al-Azhar University, and his intellectual curiosity led him to go see the public demonstrations carried out by the French scientists. He was both baffled and impressed.[7]

Power politics were also at play in this imperial scheme. By invading Egypt, Napoleon hoped to land a blow on France's great imperial rival, Britain. Napoleon's foreign minister, Talleyrand, a man so politically slippery he would have left Machiavelli in the shade, correctly identified Egypt as the weak link in Britain's route to India.[8] If France controlled Cairo, the British would be in trouble.

For Napoleon, the dream was even bigger. With Egypt in his grasp and India in his sights, he could be the new Alexander the Great.

But the French did not account for Admiral Horatio Nelson. Under his command, the British navy routed the French fleet at the Battle of Aboukir Bay (also known as the Battle of the Nile) on August 1, 1798. Further French defeats followed when Napoleon set off in the footsteps of the Crusaders and headed for the Christian Holy Land, only for his troops to be heavily defeated in the coastal city of Acre by the Ottomans in the summer of 1799. To make matters worse, the British again routed the French in Alexandria on March 21, 1801, a defeat that left them no option but to flee for home.

Napoleon himself had long since fled. After the disaster at Acre, he left his forces to it and set sail in the early hours of August 22, 1799, without a word to anyone. His successor as head of the army, General Jean-Baptiste Kléber, had no idea what was going on until it was too late. Needless to say, he was not too pleased and called his former boss all the names of the day.[9]

Yet even in failure, Napoleon was welcomed home as a conquering hero. In November that year, he was made First Consul. He was not yet 30 years old and all France was his. Defeat had done nothing to diminish his reputation because there was something about the East that brought out the crusading spirit among Europe's elites. This attitude fostered a sense of entitlement, almost of ownership, so that when France occupied Algeria a few decades after Napoleon's misadventure on the Nile, the idea of colonizing the country was not as alien as it might first appear. As far as the French political elite were concerned, General Bugeaud was pushing at an open door.

3

The colonization of Algeria was an old-fashioned land-grab. In 1840, before he was deployed to Algeria, General Bugeaud told the National Assembly in Paris what he intended to do when he arrived in Africa. "Wherever there is fresh water and fertile land, we have to put settlers without concerning ourselves as to whom these lands belong."[10]

He was true to his word. In the 1840s, the general and his forces wasted no time clearing people off their land to make room for the soon-to-arrive French. Once the link between the locals and the land was broken, the farming industry fell apart and famine spread.[11] People were forced to migrate to the cities to look for work and feed their families. Their sense of dislocation was enormous. Their sense of resentment was even greater.

It was not just the land of ordinary farmers that the French seized. Tribal lands were also confiscated. Even religious lands were not safe. Under Islamic law, land and property can be set aside as an endowment (*waqf*) to support charitable causes. The revenues from these lands are used to support ventures such as mosques, religious schools, hospitals, and so on. By providing social services to people who could not otherwise afford them, religious lands functioned as a form of a welfare system.

In 1843, the French changed the law. Religious lands were now no different from any other form of land. Anyone could buy them. Even foreigners. The change had devastating consequences for Algerians. Not only did it show the French had no respect for their Islamic way of life. It destroyed the system many Algerians relied on to educate their children and look after them when they were ill.[12]

The French were only getting started. After their victory against Abd al-Qadir in 1847, they set about bringing the rest of Algeria under their control. Throughout the 1850s, they extended their rule south into the Sahara. This period of conquest and consolidation coincided with the Second Empire (1852–70) of Louis-Napoleon in France. Nephew of the first Napoleon, Louis was elected president of the Second Republic in December 1848. Like his uncle, his ambition knew no limits, and in December 1851, he staged a coup that laid the groundwork for him to become Emperor Napoleon III a year later.

His Second Empire was an exciting era of excess where nothing seemed off limits and anything seemed possible. Paris itself was torn apart in an urban planning project of truly epic proportions. Whole districts were destroyed to make way for Baron Haussmann's city of wide boulevards and elegant design that we know today. (The redesign was not just done for aesthetic reasons. It was also to facilitate the quick movement of troops around the city so that there would be no repeat of the Commune and the barricades of 1848.) The building industry boomed and speculation in land reached fever pitch. Fortunes were made and lost in a day. The wealth sloshing around the city from the new class of property millionaires and financiers fed an industry of arts, entertainment, and leisure. Paris as a city of pleasure was born.

And when all the land that could be bought and sold in Paris had been bought and sold, France's new class of speculators needed new markets to exploit. Thanks to the land-clearing efforts of General Bugeaud, they found them in Algeria. This was France's Gold Rush. Speculating in Algeria (and later in other French colonies across North Africa) became such common practice for French financiers that it seeped into the popular culture of the time. From the works of Balzac to Maupassant to Zola, many of the classic novels of this period feature a character made or ruined by a land deal in North Africa.

That land needed settlers. Algeria became a new frontier for France where ambitious young men could go, like the Crusaders of old, to carve out a new life and make something of themselves. By 1870, there were nearly a quarter of a million Europeans living in Algeria. The result was that Algeria split in two. One Algeria was for the French settlers, the *colons*, who had access to the most productive land and who enjoyed the full support of the French state. The other was for the Algerians themselves who were increasingly pushed to the margins of their own society and who had no such legal protection.

These divisions were reinforced by language and law. The French spoke their own language and made it compulsory for any Algerians wishing to work in the public administration to do so too. Educated Algerians now started to lead a double life. During the working day, they spoke French, dressed in European clothes, and accommodated themselves to the French way of doing things. At home in the evenings, they dropped the mask and lived another life, speaking Arabic, wearing their own clothes, and behaving the way they always had.

Then suddenly, in 1870, disaster struck the Second Empire. The Franco-Prussian war that summer revealed the fragile reality behind the glittering facade of Louis-Napoleon's empire. The French were routed. The Germans were better equipped, better trained, better prepared than the French, and in one battle alone, they inflicted 20,000 fatalities on French forces. For France, the war was a national humiliation. The resource-rich province of Alsace-Lorraine was lost. The Second Empire collapsed. Louis-Napoleon went into exile in England.

For the Algerians, the end of empire was an opportunity to rebel. A tribal leader named al-Muqrani stepped forward to lead his fellow Algerians against the French. Large parts of Algeria rose up with him.[13] But it was no use. France under the Third Republic was every bit as imperial as it had been under Napoleon III, and the Algerians were still no match for the French forces. Colonization continued.

A few years later, in 1874, the French reinforced their authority over the locals and their land through the *code de l'indigénat*. Under this law, Algerian Muslims were subject to all manner of restrictions that did not apply to the French settlers. The law's purpose was to curtail opposition to French rule. As any activity from reading a newspaper critical of French rule to a full-scale assault on French forces was considered opposition, the law's remit was wide indeed. For Algerians to gain more rights, they had to give up who they were. They had to renounce Islam (an offence punishable by death under Islamic law) and renounce Algeria. They had to become French. Few did.[14]

With Algerians out of the equation, the real power struggle in the country was among the French themselves: the settlers and the army. Each party had very different views for the future of Algeria. The settlers wanted Algeria to be part of France. The army wanted it to be a separate entity run by them through the *bureaux arabes*.

Ultimately, the settlers won. And their settler state was so successful that it attracted large numbers of Spanish immigrants as well as those from France. By the end of the nineteenth century, nearly two million hectares of agricultural land were in their hands. They enjoyed so much support in political, business, and financial circles in Paris that the army was obliged to give in and accept Algeria as a *département* of metropolitan France with representation in the Chamber of Deputies.[15]

But there was one issue that neither the settlers nor their supporters ever considered. What would happen if, one day, the Algerians launched a rebellion the French military could not put down? By digging themselves so deeply into land that was not theirs, the French were ensuring that if such a revolt ever occurred, they could not simply cut and run, as the British could—and would—do in Egypt. The French would be obliged to risk everything and fight to the finish. Whatever the cost.

4

As the nineteenth century progressed, France's influence in the Arab world extended far beyond Algeria.

In one area, modern-day Lebanon, French influence owed less to the military might of bayonets and gunboats than to an unlikely combination of schools and silkworms.

Mountainous and far from any center of power, Lebanon had long been a haven for minorities fleeing persecution. As a result, modern-day Lebanon, especially the area around Mount Lebanon, has a large Christian population. And during the nineteenth century, Christian minorities in the Muslim Ottoman Empire looked increasingly to Europe for political protection. With European power on the rise and the Ottoman Empire in dire need of European financial help, sultans had little choice but to step aside and allow European capitals to all but adopt a minority religious group.

Standing up for their co-religionists in the Ottoman Empire was a policy European leaders could sell easily at home. In reality, however, the policy was little more than cover for European powers to meddle in Ottoman affairs. In Lebanon, Christians were mostly Maronite and affiliated to the Catholic Church. As such, they looked to France as the most powerful Catholic country to defend their interests. And France, regardless of the Revolution's separation of Church and State, was only too happy to oblige.

As a result, the shock troops of the French advance into Lebanon were not troops, as was the case in Algeria, but Jesuit priests. In 1853, they set up a printing press in Beirut to produce copies of the Bible in Arabic. They also set about establishing schools that operated outside the official

Ottoman system.[16] Often these schools were established in response to the requests of local families. There were many areas where no schools existed or, if they did, they concentrated on Quran studies and only taught boys.

These Christian missionary schools became very successful, attracting competition from Protestant missionaries whose schools would prove equally successful, but they helped create a two-tier education system with knock-on social effects. In the privately run foreign missionary schools, children were taught in French or English by French or English teachers who often knew little or nothing about the Arab world. And just as workers in the French-run administration in Algeria learnt to act one way at work and another at home, students in these schools had to do the same, but from an earlier age. Europeans, whether they arrived in the Arab world as an invasion force or on a spiritual mission, brought profound cultural changes to the region and disrupted its long-established social fabric.

The Europeans were also revolutionizing local economies. In Egypt, agricultural output was overly concentrated on cotton production for the European market. In Lebanon, agriculture was also heavily weighted in one direction: silkworms for the French textile industry. Whole areas were given over to the production of this one crop. The French textile industry had powerful connections in Paris, and the relationship between Lebanese silk farmers and French clothing manufacturers strengthened French involvement in the region. As a result, the authorities in Paris increasingly came to view this corner of the Ottoman Empire as part of France's sphere of influence.[17]

Consequently, the French were quick to act when sectarian tensions led to a massacre of Christians in Lebanon in 1860. As many as 11,000 men, women, and children were killed, and well over a hundred Christian villages destroyed. The communal conflict between Christians and Druzes stretched back decades and was littered with tit-for-tat killings, but it had worsened in the recent past because the Ottomans played on it in an effort to divide and conquer. France and Britain hurriedly sent gunboats to the Lebanese coast and threatened to invade if the Ottoman authorities did not resolve the crisis.[18]

To make sure a massacre on this scale did not happen again, the French and British called for Mount Lebanon to become autonomous. Because Istanbul had debts to both countries from the Crimean War, the sultan gave way to their demands, and in 1861 the mountain became virtually independent of Ottoman rule. It had its own Christian governor, paid no taxes to Istanbul, and turned toward Europe. Its fortunes flourished.

There was no need for the French to force their way into this part of the Arab world. Here, they were warmly welcomed.

Elsewhere in the Arab world where the population was not Christian, the French were not welcomed quite so warmly.

5

Tunisia was one such place.

In the 1860s, Tunisia suffered much the same fate as its North African neighbor Egypt. Like Egypt, Tunisia was nominally part of the Ottoman Empire. Like Egypt, Tunisia was ruled by a local dynasty. And like Egypt, that dynasty—the Husayni family—borrowed from European banks and spent money it did not have. Years of bad harvests and plagues did the rest and forced the country into bankruptcy in 1867. A debt commission made up of British, French, and Italian representatives was set up in 1869 to sort out Tunisia's finances.

All of that changed in 1878 at the Congress of Berlin. Convened by German Chancellor Prince Otto von Bismarck to sort out problems in the Balkans, the congress of Europe's elites agreed to give France complete control of Tunisia as compensation for France's loss of the coal-rich province of Alsace-Lorraine during the Franco-Prussian War of 1870–1.

What happened in Berlin set a dangerous precedent, which would bear full fruit after the First World War and the effects of which are still with us today in the battlefields of Syria, the carnage in the streets of Iraq, and the instability in Lebanon. At the Congress of Berlin, European leaders showed that harmony in their own continent came through the sacrifices made by the people of another. For Europe to live at peace, France and Germany had to get along. If giving France control of a country on another continent assuaged French pride and made Franco-German cooperation easier, it was a price worth paying. Except that it was not a price being paid by anyone in Europe.

In Tunisia, the French pursued a less-obviously-aggressive policy than they did in Algeria. There was no attempt to turn Tunisia into a settler state or a military colony. Even so, Tunisians were still separated by language and law from the French. They were still second-class citizens in their own country. They were still sidelined economically in favor of French investors and immigrants. And they were no happier about it than the Algerians were about what was happening in their country. But faced with the economic, military, and technical superiority of a European power, they were equally powerless to do anything to stop it.

With Algeria and Tunisia under their control, the French planned to consolidate their control of North Africa by turning their attention to Morocco. Morocco's position on the north-western Atlantic coast of Africa had long helped preserve its independence from the Ottoman Empire. At its political helm was a family, the Alawis, who claimed descent from the Prophet Muhammad. They had ruled the province for centuries, from the 1600s, and their grip on power seemed secure until Sultan Hasan (r. 1873–95) made the same mistake as his counterparts along the coast and borrowed excessively from European banks to fund modernization. In fairness to him, and to them, the structure of the global economy at the time left them with little alternative. If they wished to modernize, they had to borrow to buy the latest technology. And the only people they could borrow such large sums from were the European banks.

In 1899, the French moved in.

They faced opposition not just from the Moroccans but from the Spanish. Since 1580, the Mediterranean port of Ceuta had been Spain's even though it was on Moroccan territory. The nearby city of Melilla also belonged to Spain. As a result, Spain felt Morocco fell within Spain's sphere of influence. The dispute was eventually settled thanks to France's increasingly friendly relations with her great imperial rival, Britain.

In April 1904, Britain and France signed the *Entente Cordiale*. This treaty formalized their relations by continuing the process begun at the Congress of Berlin of carving up various parts of the world to suit European imperial interests. In this case, France recognized Britain's complete control of Egypt and Britain recognized France's complete control of Morocco. As was the case with Tunisia at the Congress of Berlin, the Entente took no account of the wishes of Egyptians or Moroccans.

Morocco's fate was settled at a conference of European powers at Algeciras in southern Spain in January 1906. France, backed by Britain, was allowed to take the bulk of Morocco while the Spanish kept their ports in the north.

In Morocco itself, the French ruled with much the same mix of conquest and colonization as they did elsewhere in North Africa. The sultan became little more than a figurehead, while the power behind the throne was the Resident-General, a French military man, Marshal Lyautey. Under his command, lands belonging to the sultan and the tribes were seized and made available for French settlers. And the French authorities continued their relentless quest to convert the Muslim middle classes to their way of life through the power of the French language and the allure of French culture.

The conference at Algeciras was evidence of the Entente Cordiale in action and showed what the British and the French could achieve in pursuit of their interests when they presented a united front. Less than a decade later, that Entente would take them into war on the same side. Fighting alongside them in that war were the Russians. And they, too, had interests and ambitions in the Arab world. Since the Ottoman conquest of Christian Constantinople on May 29, 1453, the Russian rulers had considered themselves the new Caesars and Russia as the New Rome. The Russians were just waiting for the right moment to seize their destiny.

4

The Russian Empire and the Arab World: Religion, Royalty, and the New Rome

1

In the summer of 1907, Britain and Russia signed a cooperation treaty.

The driving force behind it was much the same as the driving force behind the Entente Cordiale between Britain and France three years earlier: the need for each empire to recognize—and stay out of—the other's sphere of influence.

In the corridors of power in London, Russia's recent intervention in northern Persia and Afghanistan had set alarm bells ringing. These regions were perilously close to India. And Britain, obsessive as ever about securing all routes to the subcontinent, wanted to keep Russia out. For London, a treaty was cheaper than a war. In Russia, defeat abroad (the war with Japan in 1904–5) and political instability at home (the revolution of 1905) led to a reassessment of the country's strategic objectives. Pragmatism won out. For St. Petersburg, too, a treaty was cheaper than a war.

Yet there was more than politics to the Anglo-Russian relationship. These two empires were family. Edward VII of England was related to Russia's Tsar Nicholas II and his wife, the tsarina, by marriage and blood. To understand just how interrelated the royal houses of England and Russia were, a quick detour through Denmark is needed.

It was thanks to Edward VII's Danish wife that he was the tsar's uncle. Edward VII (r. 1901–10) was married to the beautiful Danish princess, Alexandra, whose equally beautiful younger sister, Dagmar, was married to Russia's Alexander III (r. 1881–94). Their son and heir was Tsar Nicholas II (r. 1894–1917).

But it was thanks to Edward VII's own family that he was the tsarina's uncle. Tsar Nicholas II's wife was Alix of Hesse, the daughter of a German duke. However, when Nicholas married her, he married into more than German royalty. He married into the British imperial family. Because Alix was none other than Queen Victoria's granddaughter, as Alix's mother was Victoria's daughter, Princess Alice.

And if Edward's nephew-by-marriage marrying his niece-by-blood is not confusing enough, the long-term effects of these interdynastic marriages ripple to this day. The small Danish royal house continued to punch well above their weight, matrimonially speaking. Alexandra and Dagmar's brother, Prince William, later to become King George I of Greece, married a Russian princess named Olga, and their grandson, Philip, would later marry Britain's future Queen Elizabeth II.

As for Alix herself, she was no ordinary member of Britain's first family. She was Queen Victoria's favorite grandchild. Alix's mother died when Alix was very young and the queen took a close interest in her granddaughter's upbringing. As a young adult, when Alix met and fell madly in love with the future tsar, her grandmother was less than thrilled. Victoria was worried—rightly, as it turned out—that Russia's throne was less secure than it looked and she had no desire for her darling granddaughter to become a victim of the country's political problems.

The queen's arguments fell on deaf ears. Nicholas and Alix were completely lost in love, and if Alix hesitated to commit, it was not because of granny Victoria's dire warnings about Russia's politics. It was Russia's religion that made her dally. Marrying Nicholas meant taking on the Orthodox faith, and Alix, as a German, was a devout Lutheran. Love won out in the end, and Alix abandoned her Protestant principles and embraced Russian Orthodoxy. And with all the zeal of the convert, she became more Russian than the Russians and more royal than their royals.

2

In Russia, royalty mattered because the tsars were so much more than heads of state. In Russia, royalty and religion were inseparable. Which meant that in Russia, the tsar was much more than a defender of the faith, he was almost divine.[1]

Since 1453, when the Ottoman Sultan Mehmed the Conqueror achieved the dream of generations of Muslims and claimed Constantinople for

Islam, Russian royalty took it upon themselves to become the last line of defense for Orthodox Christianity against the seemingly unstoppable Muslim advance. Russia became Holy Russia. Moscow became Byzantium reborn. And the grand dukes of Muscovy became the new Caesars: the tsars.[2]

Ivan III (r. 1462–1505) consolidated Russia's role as the New Rome with one of the most symbolic marriages of the era. In 1472, he married Sofia, the niece of Constantine, the last of the Byzantine emperors. The adoption of the double-headed eagle, the symbol of Byzantium, as the symbol of Russia underlined Moscow's new mission.

In the four centuries from Ivan III to Nicholas II, Russia never lost sight of its role as a sort of Holy Roman Empire for the Orthodox. As a result, it never ceased to cast a covetous eye across the Black Sea at Constantine's city Constantinople, now Islam's Istanbul. The mighty Catherine the Great (r. 1762–96) went so far as to hatch a plan with her long-time lover and advisor Prince Potemkin to bring the city under Russian rule. She was so committed to the plan that she named her second-born grandson Constantine in preparation for him becoming the city's ruler. The plan, in the end, came to nothing.[3]

Its failure did not stop Russia repeatedly going to war against the Ottomans. And it was during Catherine's reign that the Russians scored one of their biggest and most significant successes against Turkish troops, the effects of which are still felt today. For six years, from 1768 to 1774, the two sides fought each other. For the Russians, the breakthrough came in 1771 when they occupied Crimea on the northern shore of the Black Sea. The strategic importance of the province for Russia cannot be underestimated. It gave faraway St. Petersburg direct access to the Black Sea. All that now stood between Russia and the warm-water ports and the trading routes of the Mediterranean was Istanbul.

Which meant Russia had no intention of giving Crimea up. And still does not. One of the most divisive issues facing modern Ukraine has been whether to turn east toward Russia or west toward the European Union. In February 2014, protestors in Ukraine's capital Kiev chose west, but for Crimea, in the east, the answer was different. Crimea's links with Russia are deep. During the Communist era, Crimea provided a naval base at Sevastopol for the Soviet fleet and, after the end of the Soviet Union, the Russian Federation's Black Sea Fleet continued to be based in the port. Links between Crimea and Russia remained so strong that the political crisis in Ukraine in the spring of 2014 led to Russia reclaiming Crimea, a decision which the majority of Crimeans and Russians (although not the rest of Ukraine or the West) enthusiastically endorsed.

That geopolitical connection between Crimea and Russia dates back to Catherine the Great's victory against the Turks in 1774. And in the treaty that ended the war, the Treaty of Küçük Kaynarca (1774), the Ottomans lost not only Crimea to Russia but all of their provinces north of the Black Sea. Until then, the Black Sea had been the sultan's sea. It was completely surrounded by Ottoman lands. After 1774, this was no longer the case. Emboldened by success, Russia set about encircling the Black Sea either directly with conquered territory or indirectly through friendly satellites. In 1783, Russia annexed Crimea outright and large numbers of Russians were settled there in a bid to alter the peninsula's population in favor of Russia, a policy later adopted by Stalin.

Russia's aim was nothing less than to push the sultan out of Europe and reclaim Istanbul. Not only would that strike a blow for Russia's faith, it would guarantee the safe delivery of her food. Russia's grain shipments were vulnerable because they came through the Bosphorus and the Black Sea. The tsars could not afford to have those routes cut off. Throughout the nineteenth century, Russia steadily encroached on more and more territory around the Black Sea. Even defeat in the Crimean War against the combined forces of the British, French, and Ottomans (1853–6) did not stop Moscow's ambitions.

In the battle for the Black Sea, Moscow had a secret weapon. A clause in the 1774 Treaty of Küçük Kaynarca helped Russia achieve an influence in the Ottoman Empire and, by extension, in the Arab world that few could have foreseen at the time but which fundamentally altered relations between East and West. Following Russia's victory, St. Petersburg wanted to reassure Muslims who lived in Crimea and who wished to go on living there that Russia would respect their freedom of worship. The Russian authorities, therefore, allowed Sultan Abdulhamid I (r. 1774–89) and his successors to call themselves "Caliph of all the Muslims."[4] The title "caliph" dated back to 632 when it was adopted by the Prophet Muhammad's first successor, Abu Bakr. Since then, it was used for centuries by Muslim rulers from Damascus to Baghdad and from Cordoba to Cairo. But it was not currently in use. The Ottoman ruler was a sultan, from the Arabic word for power. Abdulhamid's ability to use the title caliph was largely ceremonial and changed little in practical terms for Muslims.

Paradoxically, it was to have a major impact on the lives of the many Orthodox Christians in the sultan's own empire. The Ottoman Empire in the 1700s and 1800s was as much a European empire as a Middle Eastern one. In 1683, Turkish troops penetrated so far into Europe that they reached the gates of Vienna. By the time of the 1774 treaty, the Ottomans still controlled much of south-western Europe: modern-day Greece,

Bulgaria, Romania, and the Balkans. And the majority of people in these regions were Orthodox Christians.

Now that the sultan-caliph had been given a nominal role in the lives of Muslims outside his territorial jurisdiction, the Russian tsarina claimed the same role in the lives of Orthodox Christians outside *her* territorial jurisdiction. The diplomatic-speak of the treaty was deliberately vague, open to any number of interpretations, but Russia's power was on the rise and Catherine the Great knew how to exploit the treaty to get what she wanted.

From then on, Russia became the patron of Orthodox Christians in the Ottoman Empire, both in Europe and the Arab world. Given that Orthodox Christians were the majority Christian community in many parts of the Ottoman Empire, Russia's position as their protector gave the tsars a huge platform to interfere in Istanbul's affairs.

As the nineteenth century progressed and Russia's power grew and Istanbul's declined, that platform grew bigger. As for the Orthodox Christians themselves, they welcomed Russia's protection and patronage. In the European parts of the Ottoman Empire, the Greeks, Serbs, Bulgars, and Romanians used it to further their dreams of independent statehood. Russia encouraged them, seeing any new Slav or Orthodox state as a gain for them and a loss for the Ottomans.

In the Arab part of the Ottoman Empire, Russia's influence was warmly welcomed by the Orthodox community. Russian royalty built churches for the faithful in the birthplace of the faith, Jerusalem. Tsars maintained close links with the famous Orthodox monastery St. Catherine's in the Sinai, said to be built on the very place where Moses received the Ten Commandments. And in Orthodox homes across Syria, the tsar's picture could be seen hanging on the wall alongside religious icons.[5]

That connection with Russia endures to this day. Moscow continues to place Syria within its sphere of influence and that influence has been clear since the wars started in Syria in 2011. Not only does Moscow speak of the plight of the country's Orthodox Christians, but the Kremlim has an authority with the Asad regime in Damascus that no modern-day Great Power does.

Yet in spite of Russia's military strength and diplomatic adroitness, Russia's greatest impact on the Arab world came about in a way that was never intended.

Nineteenth-century Russia was home to over five million Jews. And nineteenth-century Russia was not a good place to be a Jew. Jews were restricted to living in the Pale of Settlement in western Russia. They were shut out of the state education system and subject to professional discrimination. Even worse, in 1827, under Nicholas I (r. 1825–55), Jewish men in the imperial army were liable to a staggering 25 years of military service.

Entitled to no legal protection whatsoever, Jews in Russia were subject to the mood swings of whichever tsar happened to be in power, which meant the rules could change at any time and for any given reason.[6]

Disaster struck Russia's Jews when Tsar Alexander II (r. 1855–81) was killed in 1881 after a bomb attack. Several of the tsar's attackers had Jewish names and the Jewish community as a whole were blamed. To make matters worse, the new tsar, Alexander III, passed a series of laws in May 1882, which effectively let the police take whatever action they wanted against Russian Jews. The attacks on Jews in 1881–2, known as *pogroms*, were on a horrific scale.

Russian Jews were no strangers to persecution, but what made these attacks worse than anything they had experienced before was the degree to which many Russians completely ignored what was going on. People looked the other way as Jewish homes were looted, Jewish women were raped, and Jewish men were murdered. For many Jews, this complacency—or complicity—made them reconsider their position in Russia. As a result, 1882 saw one of the biggest migrations of Jews in history as hundreds of thousands fled Russia to escape this persecution.

Most set sail for a new life in the New World. The more adventurous, the more religious, and the more desperate set sail for the old one. The Jewish Return to Palestine had begun. Years later, Russia, reborn as the Soviet Union, would be one of the first countries to officially recognize the State of Israel.

3

There had always been a Jewish presence in Palestine, especially in the Jewish Holy Cities of Hebron, Jerusalem, Safad, and Tiberias.

Neither the exile to Babylon nor the destruction of the temple in Jerusalem had broken the bond between Jews and their sacred cities. As well as these locally born Jews, many Jews from the Diaspora had found their way to their Holy Land over the centuries. But they were small in number and lived as much as possible within the confines of their own community.

In the nineteenth century, Palestine was a province of the Ottoman Empire. Islamic since the 630s, Ottoman since 1516, the majority community in Palestine were Arab Muslims. Christian Arabs were the largest minority. Under Islamic law, Jews and Christians are considered

"People of the Book" (*Ahl al-Kitab* in Arabic). They are believers in God who have received their own holy book: the Torah in the case of the Jews, the Gospels in the case of the Christians. As such, they are entitled to respect and legal protection. They are not considered equal to Muslims, but their status as People of the Book gives them a legally guaranteed place in Islamic society. While life has not always been plain sailing for Jews or Christians in the Muslim world—over the years, periodic bouts of communal tension have resulted in the death of members of minority communities—for Russian Jews arriving in Ottoman Palestine after the pogroms, their status as a protected community provided a safety net against the sort of state-sponsored persecution they had faced in tsarist Russia.[7]

The 1882 exodus of Jews from Russia to Palestine became known as the First *Aliyah*, or migration. The word comes from the Hebrew verb "to go up to higher ground" because for Jews moving to the Holy Land is seen as something good, something to aspire to. (Conversely, emigrating from it is seen as the reverse and comes from the Hebrew verb "to go down.") The numbers of Jewish immigrants were not on a scale that would significantly alter the population balance in Ottoman Palestine, but the migration tapped into a broader political trend that would have serious repercussions for the region: nationalism.

While the pogroms were happening in tsarist Russia, a well-heeled, well-connected young man from a well-off family in Budapest was studying for a law degree in Vienna. This young man—who now has a city on Israel's Mediterranean coast named after him—was Theodor Herzl.

The urbane and sophisticated Herzl was a world away from the archetypal religious Jew. Yet he, more than anyone else in the late nineteenth century, articulated the case for Jews to be considered a nation and, as such, to be given a national home. Herzl and those who shared his views argued that Jews had a collective, communal identity in the same way other peoples did. The nineteenth century had already seen the Germans and the Italians form their own nation-states, while the Greeks, the Serbs, the Bulgarians, and the Romanians had secured their independence. Why, argued Herzl, should the Jews be any different?

The difficulty for Herzl and his fellow Zionists was that the new nation-states of the nineteenth century were formed by people who already lived on the land that later became their nation. The Jews did not. And the land they wanted—Eretz Israel—was already inhabited. But Jews believed their historic and religious connection to Israel tied them to that land more than any other. They also believed that persecution, the like of which they were facing on a daily basis in tsarist Russia, made their case all the more urgent.

It was not just Jews who had a problem with tsarist Russia. A number of British politicians did too. Many members of parliament were not happy about Britain's alliance with Russia, and the harsh treatment of Russia's Jews had a lot to do with their unease. Even though the connection between Britain and Russia's royal families was close, there was little or no common ground politically between the two empires. In one, the tsar was an autocrat whose word was law. In the other, the king was little more than a country squire, a figurehead who spoke the words his government gave him. The tsar had political powers a medieval monarch would have envied. The king had no political power at all. The tsar had to answer to no one but God. The king had to answer to everyone from parliament to the people.

If the British and Russians were strange bedfellows, the French and the Russians were even stranger. Yet in 1893, France and Russia concluded an alliance. France was the spiritual home of anyone longing for liberty, equality, and fraternity. It was also a country where kings and emperors faced exile if they were lucky or the guillotine if they were not. Russia, by contrast, had only recently (1861) emancipated the millions of serfs who farmed the land, many of whom still lived in such abject poverty, their lives were little more than indentured slavery. For revolutionary, republican, rationalist France to make an alliance with autocratic, authoritarian, Orthodox Russia surprised many. But Paris had her reasons. Following the fiasco of the Franco-Prussian war in 1870–1, France desperately needed allies.

That alliance was the start of a diplomatic realignment across Europe. Britain and France fought against Russia in the Crimean War in the 1850s, but now the three empires were coming together. The 1893 Franco-Russian alliance, the 1904 Anglo-French Entente Cordiale, and the 1907 Anglo-Russian alliance put all three empires into the same camp: the Triple Entente.

The Triple Entente was an example of political pragmatism of the first order. It was an alliance born out of shared interests rather than shared values. And it was based on each country's deep desire to defend their spheres of interest, not only from each other but from the latecomer to Europe's imperial party: the bold, brash, and increasingly ambitious Kaiser Wilhelm II of Germany.

5

The German Empire and the Arab World: Family Feuds and Eastern Ambitions

1

For Kaiser Wilhelm II, the personal and the political were one and the same. And the reasons for it went back to his childhood.

Wilhelm was born of a union of two of the greatest powers in Europe. His father Frederick was heir to the Prussian throne. His mother Victoria (Vicky) was Britain's Princess Royal, the first-born child of Queen Victoria and Prince Albert. Frederick married Vicky when she was only 17. Behind the show and ceremony of their royal wedding was a very strategic political goal: Vicky's parents wanted to use her position as wife of the future Prussian king to cement relations between the two countries. Vicky's children would, after all, have a foot in both camps. They would be as much British as they were German.

In 1859, when only 18 years old, Vicky was pregnant with her first child. It was a difficult and dangerous birth. The baby was in the breech position. His arms were above his head, and there was no way to move him into the correct birthing position without causing serious harm either to him or his mother. Under normal circumstances, doctors might have opted for a caesarean even though that would have meant almost certain death for the mother. But these were not normal circumstances. Vicky was a royal mother. Born into one royal house, married into another, no doctor could take risks with her life.

The only remaining option was to force the baby's arms into position. But the cost of doing that was permanent disability for the young prince. Wilhelm was never able to use his left arm.

Vicky was distraught. The role of a royal wife was to produce healthy heirs, and she considered Wilhelm's disability her personal failure. Her family's behavior did little to persuade her otherwise. Showing an attitude that was breathtakingly callous, her father-in-law referred to his new grandson as "defective" and wondered if congratulations were really in order on the birth of such a child.

None of this should have mattered. But in nineteenth-century royal culture, it did. Ill health was nothing short of a catastrophe. (And remained so into the twentieth century: in England, King George V's son, John, born in 1905, suffered from epilepsy and was locked away from public view throughout his short life.) The culture of royalty was outdoorsy and involved men doing manly things like hunting, shooting, and riding. Royal culture was intrinsically martial and involved kings and kaisers donning uniforms to lead the troops on parade. All of these activities would be extremely difficult for the new German prince. And as European royalty, unlike Muslim monarchs, followed the principle of primogeniture, there was nothing anyone could do about it. Wilhelm was the first-born son and he would inherit the throne.

The stakes for Wilhelm were raised even higher in 1871 when the various German states united to become the German Empire. Germany was now a central European powerhouse stretching from France in the west to Russia in the east. Wilhelm would not grow up to be a king; he would grow up to be an emperor.

The combined effect of all these pressures was to push Vicky away from her first-born child. Barely an adult herself, she lacked the experience to deal with the situation. The young Wilhelm needed sympathy and understanding from his mother and he did not get it. Throughout his childhood, his mother seemed to be almost in a state of denial about his disability. She tried all sorts of ways to make him use his arm. When Wilhelm showed signs of leaning too heavily to one side, she had him spend hours at a time in a metal cage in an effort to straighten him out.

Little wonder, then, that Wilhelm grew up emotionally scarred. He had a revenge of sorts on his mother when he became kaiser in 1888. He humiliated her by confiscating all official papers in her possession, as if she were not to be trusted with the affairs of state. Vicky's brother Prince Albert (England's future Edward VII) never forgave him for it and harbored a life-long dislike of his nephew.

The loneliness of his childhood made Wilhelm impulsive and subject to mood swings. He could change his mind almost as soon as he made a decision. Perhaps the most psychologically interesting of European rulers of his era, he was not the most psychologically stable. And he was often his own worst enemy. An authoritarian streak masked his unmet craving for understanding and he could be cruel to the point of sadistic. A prig in public and a hedonist at home, he forced members of his inner circle to dress up in women's clothes and dance for him. Rumors swirled about the extravagances of his private life. He was married twice and had a string of mistresses. Wilhelm himself was only too aware of his emotional failings. In middle age, he confided to a close friend that there was something missing in him that other people had.

This close friend, Eulenberg, who was gay, was outed by the German press in 1908. Instead of standing by his friend, the kaiser caved to conservative public opinion and abandoned him. But the loneliness caused by separation from one of his closest friends cost Wilhelm dearly. He suffered a nervous breakdown.

Isolation was often an issue for the kaiser. He all too often felt like an outsider among Europe's royal elite. The British and Russian royal families holidayed together every summer in Denmark, but Wilhelm was not invited. The Danish wives of the English king and the Russian tsar never forgave Prussia for invading Denmark in 1864, even though Wilhelm himself was only a child at the time.

All of these slights, real or imagined, had political consequences. As kaiser, Wilhelm's personal life profoundly colored his political outlook, especially when it came to Britain. In the same way he both loved and loathed his mother, he both respected and reviled her home country. And just as he yearned for his mother's acceptance, he also yearned for the acceptance of his British cousins.

When he got neither, he took Germany on a different course. If Wilhelm's royal relatives in Britain did not respect him as an equal, they would have to take him seriously as a rival.

2

Germany was a young nation. Kaiser Wilhelm himself was older than the country he led. The unification of the various independent German states into the German Empire in 1871 unleashed a creative energy that launched the new nation on a trajectory of growth wholly different from anything it had known before.

The statistics speak for themselves.

Between 1870 and 1914, Germany's population doubled. Industrial output quadrupled. Illiteracy was virtually wiped out. University enrolment rocketed. German university students outnumbered their British counterparts by nearly seven to one. Thanks to the German education system's mix of *Gymnasien* (academic schools), *Realgymnasien* (technical schools), and *Technische Hochschulen* (technical academies), Germany quite literally progressed through technology.[1]

This increase in Germany's economic power had a knock-on effect on the country's military prowess. Imperial Germany followed Napoleon's example and had an army of the people: a conscript army. The country's population rose from 33 million to 65 million in the period from 1870 to 1914, which meant a vast increase in the number of men under arms. As a result, the German army was the biggest in Europe. It was more than double the size of France's and more than ten times the size of Britain's. For its part, France continued its Napoleonic tradition of having a conscript army, but as its population remained steady at 40 million, it could not compete with the German increase. As for Britain, its army was made up of volunteers, a fact which always put it at a numerical disadvantage.

It was not just the German army that rapidly increased in size. In 1897, Berlin took the decision to build a fleet of battleships. Little over a decade later, Germany's fleet had almost tripled in size (from 14 to 40) and was second only to Britain's, a state of affairs which seriously worried London. A powerful German navy threatened Britain's control of the seas and, by extension, Britain's far-flung empire.[2]

And that was the heart of the matter. The kaiser simultaneously admired and envied Britain's empire. He respected Britain's standing as an imperial nation, but he wanted Germany to be every bit as Great as Britain, if not Greater. All of which meant Germany had to have an empire, because, in the nineteenth century, empire was the measure of international power. No power could become a Great Power without one. But by the time Germany amassed the economic and military resources necessary to acquire one, all the best land had been taken.

Britain's empire included some of the most strategic shipping routes in the world and some of the most resource-rich land. France, too, had an enormous empire that took in nearly all of north-west Africa as well as chunks of south-east Asia. And Russia's territory stretched from Germany's doorstep in Europe right across Asia to the Pacific Ocean. Germany did succeed in conquering a number of territories: South-West Africa in 1884, Togoland the same year, and East Africa in 1886. But these conquests were before Wilhelm became kaiser in 1888, and he was eager to see Germany expand its territories under his leadership and take its place among the world's Great Powers.

In this, as with so much else in Kaiser Wilhelm's life, the personal influenced the political. Just as Wilhelm felt like the perennial outsider, the sidelined prince who was not invited on family holidays, the cousin who had to try harder than everyone else to be accepted by his royal relatives, he also felt his country had to try harder to secure its standing on the world stage.

Germany under Wilhelm was outpacing Britain economically, industrially, and militarily. British forces had not fought a battle on western European soil since Waterloo in 1815 when, alongside Prussian forces, they defeated Napoleon. Britain's other foray into war in Europe in the nineteenth century was in Crimea in the 1850s, a war remembered less in England for its military exploits than for the nursing skills of one Florence Nightingale. Britain's military campaigns during this era took place overseas. For the most part, they were unequal contests pitting the advanced weaponry of the developed world against indigenous people who had been happily minding their own business for generations. In stark contrast to Britain, Germany had taken on and soundly defeated a European equal in the war against France in 1870–1. Yet for all Germany's economic strengths and military successes, the country still lagged behind Britain, France, and Russia in international affairs.

Consequently, Germany looked elsewhere to exert its influence. In 1889, Kaiser Wilhelm visited the Ottoman capital to meet Sultan Abdulhamid II and strengthen ties between Berlin and Istanbul. The kaiser was the only European ruler the sultan ever met. The two had much to discuss. The Ottomans were in need of European technology and the Germans were happy to provide it. The culmination of this cooperation was to be the Berlin–Baghdad railway. Railways were revolutionizing traditional trade routes and travel patterns, and the construction of an overland route linking the German capital, the Ottoman capital, and the former capital of the Arab world was a way to undermine Britain's influence in the region by offering a land alternative to Britain's sea routes through Suez, the Red Sea, and the Persian Gulf. Work began in 1888. The kaiser's first visit to Istanbul followed swiftly afterwards.[3]

Wilhelm's second visit to the Ottoman Empire saw him visit Jerusalem as well as Istanbul. Dressed like a Crusader of old, the kaiser rode into the Holy City on the afternoon of October 29, 1898, on a white horse that matched his white uniform. The pomp and power of his visit might have been intended to invoke great German Crusaders of the past, like Frederick Barbarossa, but the irony was that the kaiser was no unwelcome infidel invader. He enjoyed good relations with the city's ruler, the Ottoman sultan, and was so well thought of by the Ottomans that he was given the nickname "Hajji Wilhelm.". If any ruler in Europe might be inclined to think of the sultan as an ally, it was Kaiser Wilhelm.

In March 1905, the kaiser was again riding through an Arab city on horseback. This time, it was Tangier in Morocco. France was in the process of conquering Morocco, but the outcome was not yet finalized. Enter the kaiser who turned up in the port city on a German cruise ship and proceeded to speak up for the sultan and for Moroccan independence. His real aim was to stop France securing one of the most strategic spots on the North African coast. Morocco's long Atlantic coastline on its west and the Mediterranean shore on its north give it a unique position on the corner of Africa and at the gateway to Europe. A country with a large navy could use it as a forward base to control Atlantic sea routes. The kaiser saw his chance. And for a period during 1905, all-out war between France and Germany seemed a very real possibility. Morocco's future was eventually sealed at the Algeciras conference in Spain in 1906 when Britain and Russia backed France's claim to the country and left Germany isolated.

The Moroccan crisis of 1905 showed the degree to which European rivalries were being played out on territory *outside* Europe. This rivalry reduced a country like Morocco, with a civilization and culture stretching back centuries, to little more than a square on the chessboard of the Great Game.

The crisis also showed how close to the brink of war European elites were prepared to go in the quest for empire. And regardless of the risks, that quest continued. The Moroccan crisis of 1905 was not the last one. Just over five years later, another one loomed.

3

This time, the flashpoint was the port of Agadir on Morocco's Atlantic coast. Nowadays, Agadir is a major tourist destination thanks to the startling beauty of its long, unspoilt beaches. The French, in particular, flock there in tens of thousands during the month of August. In 1911, it was the German navy that paid a visit when the warship *Panther* suddenly turned up in port. Officially, the reason was to protect German citizens from local unrest. In reality, the Germans were trying to gain leverage over the French. Once again, they failed. Once again, the kaiser backed down in the face of British support for France.

The two Moroccan crises showed how important the system of imperial alliances had become in international affairs. In 1905, and again in 1911, France had been able to withstand German pressure because Paris did not stand alone. Britain and Russia were hovering in support in the wings. That threat alone was enough to make the kaiser pause for thought.

He might have been confident about Germany's ability to fight France. But fighting on three fronts was a different matter. And in 1911, it was not an idea the kaiser was ready to explore.

That sense of Germany as a nation sandwiched between France on one side and Russia on the other had long been an issue for Berlin. It was at the heart of German foreign policy during the two decades of Bismarck's chancellorship (1871–90). To strengthen Germany's position, Bismarck made alliances with Germany's neighbors: the Dual Alliance with Austro-Hungary in 1879, which became the Triple Alliance when Italy joined in 1882. But these treaties did nothing to address the problem of Germany's geographical vulnerability to encirclement by France and Russia. If anything, they achieved the reverse. They pushed Paris and St. Petersburg closer together out of fear that a gigantic Germanic bloc was forming in the center of the continent.

In contrast to France and Russia, Britain had no land borders with Germany and was less vulnerable to fears of an invasion. In many ways, Germany seemed a more natural ally for Britain than either France or Russia. For one, Anglo-German history did not have the imperial baggage of Anglo-French history. From the Battle of the Nile in 1798 to the Battle of Fashoda in the Sudan a century later, the nineteenth century was a tale of Paris and London fighting like cat and dog for control of the world. Yet this period also saw Paris and London come together when it was mutually beneficial, as happened during the Crimean War in the 1850s and in Egypt in the 1880s.

That coming together happened again in the early twentieth century—helped, paradoxically, by the very intensity of Anglo-French rivalry that ended up becoming a bargaining chip in their negotiations. Germany, for all its economic and military might, still lacked an empire comparable to the British or French empires and, therefore, had no such bargaining power. Britain and France understood they had too much to lose by going to war against each other. By recognizing each other's spheres of influences, both kept what they already had. They might not gain any territory at the other's expense, but they would not lose any either.

And, perhaps most importantly of all, they could put up a united front against imperial newcomers like Germany and Italy. Italy had united as a kingdom in 1870, a year before German unification, and harbored similar dreams of empire. In 1911, Italian forces invaded Libya in a bid to build a new Roman Empire in the southern Mediterranean. But their ambition overreached their grasp. It took them nearly 20 years to conquer the country.

After the Agadir Incident in 1911, it looked as if Bismarck's fears of encirclement might become a reality for Germany. Luckily for the kaiser,

Germany enjoyed good relations with the empire whose lands were coveted by London, Paris, and St. Petersburg alike. Dismissed by Tsar Nicholas I of Russia as "The Sick Man of Europe," the Ottoman Empire's power had been in decline for years. Even so, the Ottoman sultan still held sway over large parts of the Arab world—that critical land mass between Europe and India. And so, Germany began to woo Istanbul.

6

The Ottoman Empire:
How the Arab World
Was Won and Lost

1

The Ottoman Empire was older than any of the European empires. Its origins went back to the dying days of the thirteenth century when an obscure Turkish tribal leader called Osman had a dream.

In Osman's dream, the moon leapt out of a holy man's breast and settled in Osman's. A tree then grew from Osman's navel and became so big that an entire ecosystem came to life under its shade. Mountains rose up. Rivers flowed. Plants grew. When he woke up, a bewildered Osman went to the holy man he saw in his dream and asked him what it all meant. The holy man was in no doubt. God had chosen Osman for divine favor. Osman and his sons would rule an empire. And to show how much he believed in his own power to predict the future, the holy man arranged for his daughter to marry Osman. The Ottoman dynasty was born.[1]

The reality of empire-building was much less mystic and much more mundane. But the fusion of faith and family at the heart of the dream did become the basis of Ottoman power. Along with one other critical element: fighting. The Ottoman Empire was born on the battlefield. At the turn of the fourteenth century, Osman was one of a number of tribal chiefs competing for control of what was essentially a lawless area south of the Black Sea in modern Turkey. He started with a stronghold several hundred miles south of the city of Iznik, famous to Christians the world over as Nicaea, home of the Nicene Creed.

From there, Osman's rule spread. By the end of the fourteenth century, Ottoman power was into its fourth generation and the family held much of modern Turkey and south-eastern Europe.

And so it continued. This was a conquest state whose rulers were enriched, whose armies were financed, and whose state coffers were filled by the spoils of war. And those armies were unstoppable. The march westward into Europe was relentless. The Ottoman state was a Muslim empire built on the soil of Christian Europe. Byzantine Constantinople became Ottoman Istanbul. Budapest, Belgrade, and Bucharest became Ottoman cities. The Black Sea became an Ottoman stronghold.

The Ottoman armies were not content to fight on just one front. They turned their attention eastward to take on their fellow Muslims: the Mamluk rulers of Syria and Egypt. The Mamluks fared no better against the Ottomans than the Christians of Europe. In 1516, the Syrian region became an Ottoman province and Jerusalem became an Ottoman city. A year later, it was the turn of Egypt. The Mamluk military oligarchs had ruled Egypt since 1250, but those centuries of power collapsed almost overnight in the face of superior Ottoman firepower and tactics.

For the Ottoman Sultan Selim I (r. 1512–20), Cairo brought a special treasure: the Muslim Holy Cities of Mecca and Medina. The Mamluks ruled these cities from their Egyptian powerbase and, now, they too fell under the sultan's sway. Eight generations on from the obscure tribal chief who dreamt of empire, the dynasty he founded had conquered the city of the Caesars, the city of Jesus, and the sacred cities of Islam.

Up to this point, the majority of the Ottoman conquests were in Europe, which meant the majority of the sultan's subjects were Christian. The sixteenth century saw that change as more and more Muslim lands were conquered by the armies from Istanbul. From the foothold in Egypt on the southern shores of the Mediterranean, Ottoman rule spread west across North Africa. Algiers became an Ottoman province in 1529, Tripoli in 1551, Tunis in 1574. Ottoman authority also spread east to encircle the Arabian peninsula. The port of Aden became a satellite of the sultan in 1547, Muscat in 1551, Yemen in 1568. And it was not just coastal cities that attracted the Ottomans' attention. They took the inland city of Baghdad from the Safavid rulers of Persia in 1534, then underlined their dominance of the Iraqi region by pressing to the sea and taking the port city of Basra in 1546. And on they went: into Arabia and down the eastern coast as far as the island of Bahrain in the Persian Gulf. By the end of the sixteenth century, the heart of the Arab world was theirs.[2]

To rule the provinces of this vast empire stretching from Budapest to Bahrain, the Ottomans usually relied on local men. Even former rulers defeated by Ottoman armies could find themselves retaining their position as long as they made sure taxes were paid and Ottoman sovereignty was acknowledged. The further a province was from the center of power, the more autonomy it enjoyed.

The very center of power, however, was reserved exclusively for the Ottoman family. The dynastic principle was popular among Muslim monarchs, even though it had no foundation in Islam. The Prophet Muhammad died in 632 without nominating any successor, let alone one from his own family. His immediate successors, known as the Rightly Guided Caliphs (r. 632–60), followed the Prophet's example and were equally averse to the dynastic principle.

The passage of power from father to son made its first appearance in the Muslim world several decades after the Prophet's death when the caliph Muawiya (r. 661–80) appointed his son Yazid (r. 680–4) to succeed him. The decision was not well received in the wider community because monarchy was an alien concept in Islam. Muslims believe majesty belongs to God alone. There was also the problem of Yazid himself. A gambler and a playboy, only his father seemed to have thought him the most suitable candidate to lead the Muslim community. His appointment as heir led to civil war. In the end, Yazid and his Umayyad family prevailed, not so much because of the power of their ideas but because of the unity of their family and the power of their army.[3]

It was a valuable lesson for the fledgling dynasty and for every dynasty that followed. A ruling family could not survive unless it was united and had a loyal army. As a result, every ruling family since the Umayyads ruled through an alliance of monarchy and military. The Ottomans were no exception.

Where they differed from their predecessors was how they chose *which* son should succeed and what happened to the sidelined sons. It came down to a problem of numbers. Islam allows a man to have four wives simultaneously. Given that divorce is incredibly straightforward—a man has only to say "I divorce you" three times in the presence of witnesses—a man may end up marrying many times during his life. Added to this was the complication of concubines. Sultans and caliphs kept a harem and many of their concubines became the mothers of royal babies.

The consequence of a sultan having so many women in his life was that he often had an unusually high number of sons. The first king of Saudi Arabia, for example, is said to have had 42 sons. (No one seems to have bothered to count the number of daughters—believed to be around 125.)[4] As there is no principle of primogeniture in Islam, all royal sons are technically eligible to rule. So, how did a ruler choose which son would succeed him? Previous dynasties left it to the ruler himself to decide. Sometimes, this system worked. Sometimes, it did not. Sometimes, sidelined siblings banded together against the favored son and took their differences to the battlefield, dragging the community into civil war. The Ottomans took a different route. They turned the succession into a contest, a kind of survival-of-the-fittest for royal sons. Whoever was strong enough to seize power earned the right to exercise it.

On the face of it, this system was fairer than relying solely on the whim of a ruler. But it also held the potential to be enormously divisive for the ruling family. In the beginning, seizing power meant little more than being the first to enter the capital after the sultan's death. But as the empire grew and the prizes of power became greater, that was no longer enough and Sultan Murad I (r. 1362–89) took an extraordinary step. (This was the same Murad who met his death at the hands of a Serb soldier in the Battle of Kosovo Polje in 1389, the anniversary of which was commemorated by Serbs every year on June 28.) When Murad became sultan, he decided to eliminate the competition. He killed every one of his brothers. In one fell swoop, he wiped out any threat from his family to his rule.

To the shocked public, this sibling slaughter was passed off as "God's will." As Ottoman power suffered no adverse consequences, the practice was judged not to have incurred God's wrath and was continued. Fratricide remained official Ottoman policy until 1595 when Mehmed III (r. 1595–1603) came to power. The new sultan had 19 brothers, some of whom were very young children. But that did not spare them the grisly fate that awaited a dead sultan's spare sons. All 19 were killed. The sight of so many coffins, particularly the small ones of the very young princes, provoked such a wave of weeping and wailing on the streets of Istanbul that Mehmed had to abandon the policy. From then on, power passed to the most senior member of the Ottoman family, regardless of whether or not he was up to the job.[5]

Not that anyone in the inner circles of power was anticipating any problems for the Ottoman state. At the end of the sixteenth century, the Ottomans were one of the wealthiest and most powerful families on the planet. When the Arab world joined their domains, they were masters of the Mediterranean, rulers of the Red Sea, and guardians of the trade routes between East and West. Many of the goods traveling from India and China to the markets of Europe had to pass through Ottoman lands and were liable to Ottoman taxes. It was a huge and enormously lucrative market and it provided one of the pillars of the Ottoman economy.

But it was all about to change.

2

The first sign that the tide was beginning to turn against the Ottomans was the war with the Habsburg Empire in 1593–1606. For 13 long years, the Ottomans fought the Austrians and for no obvious gain. They scored no significant victories. They conquered no new territory. They won no tangible booty.

For an empire built on the back of conquest, this was a disaster. The war cost so much and delivered so little, it caused a debt crisis. In 1600, the Ottoman currency, the *akche*, had to be devalued to finance the empire's debt.[6] Worse, though, than what the war inflicted on the imperial finances was what the war revealed about the empire's military. The Ottomans, so long used to setting the military pace, were now lagging behind their European enemies in tactics and technology. Their cavalry was simply no match for Austrian artillery.

For the Ottomans, it was not just on the battlefield that things were moving against them. The sixteenth century saw a seismic shift in trading patterns, which fundamentally redefined who held power in the world and why. It was all down to two men and their boats: Spain's Christopher Columbus and Portugal's Vasco da Gama. And between them, they inflicted serious damage on the Ottoman economy.

When Christopher Columbus set sail for India and discovered America by accident, the focus of the global economy shifted from the Old World to the New. When Vasco da Gama reached India in 1498 via the Cape of Good Hope, transport of the enormously profitable Indian spice trade shifted from land to sea. When the impact of these shifts became clear, it was all too obvious who benefited and who lost out. The Ottomans played no part in the voyages of discovery and made no conquests in the Americas. They spent the sixteenth century consolidating their Mediterranean base, while Spain and Portugal became super-rich on the wealth of the New World. That wealth, and those sea routes around Africa, enabled Portugal to challenge Ottoman control of the Persian Gulf. They never succeeded; a stalemate was reached, but for the Ottomans it was an alarming sign of European encroachment into their sphere of influence.

There would be more encroachments. The sixteenth century saw the rise of the sea-faring empires. Countries in northern Europe, such as Britain and the Netherlands, took advantage of their easy access to the Atlantic to set sail for new worlds and the wealth to be found in them. They set up trading companies (the English East India Company in 1600 and the Dutch East India Company in 1602) to finance their commercial ventures in India, a move which brought them into direct competition with the Ottomans for control of the trade routes between East and West. Suddenly, the Ottomans were fighting enemies in the East who were from the West. British interest in India was further piqued when Charles II (r. 1660–85) married the Portuguese princess Catherine of Braganza in 1661, and as part of her dowry, she brought the port of Bombay (now Mumbai).[7]

The Ottoman Empire possessed a huge internal market and, through the sixteenth and seventeenth centuries, the very size of this market served as a buffer against external changes and helped Istanbul maintain its place in the world. After 1683, however, no one could deny the Ottoman Empire was no longer a conquest state, ever on the offensive for new territories, ever confident of victory. That year saw the second, and final, Ottoman attempt to take Vienna. In defeat, the retreat became a rout. From then on, the Ottomans focused on holding what they had.

But even that proved increasingly difficult. Europe's empires were imperialist, expansionist, and ultraambitious. In the war of 1768–74, Catherine the Great's Russia dealt a death blow to Istanbul's control of the lands north of the Black Sea. Two decades later, it was the turn of Napoleon Bonaparte to stake his claim to part of the Ottoman Empire when he invaded Egypt. French rule was short-lived (1798–1801), but the Ottomans could not eject the revolutionary French forces by themselves and had to call in the British to help. The British were only too happy to do so. With huge swathes of India under their control, the British had even less desire to see Napoleon conquer Cairo than the Ottomans did. It risked bringing him too close to the subcontinent for London's comfort. The British preferred to defend an unlikely ally rather than see an imperial rival prosper.

The strategic calculation that led London to help Istanbul came to dominate the imperial politics of the nineteenth century, and there were many more unlikely alliances in the years ahead. The calculation centered on the contradiction at the heart of Europe's dealings with Istanbul: much as each European empire wanted to seize the sultan's realms for themselves, they were equally anxious to make sure none of their rivals profited from any sudden collapse of the empire. The strategy became known as "The Eastern Question" and was a pillar of British foreign policy during the 1800s. If it meant supporting the sultan in a war against one of their rivals, the British were quite prepared to do it.

In the meantime, all of Europe's empires circled like vultures over the sultan's vast territories and deployed every means at their disposal to undermine his rule.

3

The most potent weapon at the Europeans' disposal was not their military or their money. It was a series of seemingly obscure diplomatic arrangements made in the sixteenth century between Sultan Selim II (r. 1566–74) and the king of France. In 1569, the sultan decreed that any of the king's subjects traveling in Ottoman lands were liable to French rather than Ottoman law. In return, any of the sultan's subjects traveling in the French kingdom would remain under the sultan's jurisdiction. Once the French had secured these privileges, other European powers started to lobby for them too.[8]

On the face of it, these arrangements, or Capitulations as they came to be known, seemed fair to both parties. Selim II himself certainly saw no cause for concern. As Ottoman power was still expanding, he was negotiating from a position of strength and he granted them as a personal favor to the French king. But once the balance of power between East and West started to tip in favor of the latter, the Capitulations came to be used in a way the Ottomans never intended. They provided the platform for European intervention in the internal affairs of the Ottoman state.

The problem was that the Capitulations did not merely place a foreigner beyond Ottoman law; they placed him or her beyond Ottoman taxes and customs duties. This loophole was seized upon by foreigners wanting to do business in the Ottoman Empire. Like the global corporations of the twenty-first century that operate everywhere but seem to pay taxes nowhere, Europeans saw a chance to set up shop in the Ottoman Empire without having to pay any taxes to the local treasury.[9]

The Capitulations were deliberately manipulated to create an unequal playing field between local and foreign businesses. The end result was that a small foreign elite came to dominate certain sectors of the economy, especially those dealing with imports or exports to Europe. Local businessmen were effectively shut out of these lucrative markets. The impact this had on the Ottoman economy was far-reaching. The impact on the social fabric of Ottoman society was even more profound.

Ottoman society was a mosaic of religions, ethnicities, and languages, of which Turkish Muslims were the dominant group. It was their Islamic faith that shaped the state and defined the empire's worldview. Other groups had their place in that state—a place protected by Islamic law; but as non-Muslims in a Muslim state, they could never hope to enjoy equal rights with the Muslim community.

The Capitulations threatened this state of affairs. European empires used them not only to gain business leverage but also to set up spheres of influence within the Ottoman Empire. Catherine the Great blazed this trail when Russia became patron of the empire's Orthodox community following Russia's victory in the 1768–74 war. Others now followed in her footsteps. The French adopted the Maronite community in modern-day Lebanon. The British could not find many of their fellow Anglicans to defend, and not wanting to be outdone by their imperial rivals, they took it upon themselves to speak for the region's Jews. Even faraway America joined in. The nineteenth century saw the arrival of politically well-connected American missionaries who, with their schools and their churches, sought to bring the values of the New World to the Old.[10]

These two processes combined—the separate laws for foreigners and the adoption of non-Muslim minorities by outside powers—changed the character of the Ottoman Empire. Christian communities living in the heart of the empire increasingly came to be seen as a class apart who identified more with their co-religionists in Europe than with their Muslim neighbors. Meanwhile, Christian communities living on the fringes of empire in areas where they formed the majority community increasingly pushed for independence from Istanbul.[11]

They were encouraged in this by Britain, France, and Russia, who, for strategic reasons of their own, wanted to see the Ottoman Empire pushed out of Europe. The Balkan province of Serbia was the first to go, becoming autonomous in 1817. The provinces of Wallachia and Moldavia followed in 1829 (combining in 1861 to form Romania). And Greece became independent in 1830 after a War of Independence in the 1820s—made famous in Britain by the role played by the colorful English poet Lord Byron.

Throughout the nineteenth century, European elites were so heavily invested in the future of the Ottoman Empire that they were prepared to fight each other over it. In the middle of the century, what began as a spat over a star in Bethlehem ended up in all-out war with an unlikely alliance of Britain, France, and the Ottomans on one side and Russia on the other.

Just like the infamous fly whisk incident that led to a war between France and Algeria in 1830, the Crimean War also began with an incident that bordered on the ridiculous. In October 1847, the silver star on the floor of the Church of the Nativity in Bethlehem went missing. The star is meant to mark the spot where Jesus Christ was born. This particular one was donated by the French, and French monks immediately accused their Orthodox colleagues of stealing it. Christian fellowship flew out the window and a brawl ensued. (Strange as it sounds, this sort of thing is not as unusual as you might think in these sacred surroundings. To this day, the star can still bring out the less holy side of people. In their eagerness to kiss the sacred spot, worshipers often jump ahead in line and shove fellow worshipers out of the way.)

In 1847, Emperor Napoleon III of France and his Russian counterpart Tsar Nicholas I each claimed the right to replace the missing star. It was up to Sultan Abdulmajid to choose between them. To concentrate his mind, the French sent a gunboat to the region. Not surprisingly, the sultan sided with the French. The tsar was outraged and, reviving Catherine the Great's vision of a Russian-sponsored Christian Constantinople, he declared war on the sultan and ordered his troops to invade.[12]

On March 28, 1853, Protestant Britain sided with Catholic France and Muslim Istanbul to declare war on Orthodox Russia. The Crimean War (1853–6) was not Britain's finest fighting hour, but that was never the point. London's real aim was to prevent an outright Russian victory and preserve the status quo in the eastern Mediterranean. It was a strategic objective shared by the French.

Imperial overreach was another objective. If the Russians and Ottomans could be pushed to fight beyond their resources, then it did not matter who won on the battlefield. The real winners would be the British and the French.

That was exactly what happened. The Ottomans ended up on the winning side, but it came at a price they could not pay. The war cost the Ottomans so much, the sultan was obliged to take out the empire's first foreign loan. In 1854, the sultan became indebted to British and French banks.[13] It was a process, once started, that only led to more debt. And the Ottomans had neither the industry nor the resources to finance these mounting debts. Over the next 20 years, they took out one loan after another and on such unfavorable terms that there was no way to balance the books. By 1875, the Ottoman state was bankrupt. That bankruptcy opened the way for the Anglo-French takeover of the Middle East.

4

Within ten years of the Ottoman Empire going bankrupt, nearly all of Istanbul's territories in North Africa were in British or French hands. Nominally, these lands remained part of Istanbul's empire, but in reality, it was the British and French whose word was law.

European power did not stop at the outskirts of the empire. The extent of Ottoman debt allowed it to penetrate right to the heart of empire, to Istanbul itself. In 1881, the Public Debt Administration (PDA) was set up by the British and French to oversee the repayment of Ottoman debts. Just like a modern IMF bailout, the PDA operated in the interests of the creditors rather than those of the state whose finances they were restructuring. This loss of sovereignty was acutely felt across Ottoman society.

For many in Istanbul's intellectual elite, the bankruptcy showed how far the Ottoman Empire had fallen behind the European powers. In their opinion, there was only one answer to the crisis. The empire needed to modernize. And that meant being more like Europe. Inspired by the ideas and ideals of the French Revolution, they believed politics and power had to be opened up for public participation. It was a direct challenge to the absolute nature of the sultan's power.

It was not the first attempt to do so. In 1876, just a year after the bankruptcy was announced, the sultan's grand vizier Midhat Pasha set out a constitution to pave the way for a parliament. But the plan went nowhere. The sultan was less than happy about sharing his power with a parliament and used a legal loophole to quash the project.

The idea behind it proved much harder to quash, however. Throughout the 1880s, writers and journalists, academics and businessmen saw political change as essential if the Ottoman Empire aimed to close the technology gap and compete as an equal against the powers of Europe. In 1889, from the safety of faraway Paris, a group calling themselves the Young Turks demanded the reintroduction of the constitution and the establishment of a parliament in Istanbul.

By 1908, the Young Turks had had enough of waiting for the sultan to institute change voluntarily. They staged a coup and the 1876 constitution was reinstated. Sultan Abdulhamid II (r. 1876–1909) remained in power, but his authority was no longer absolute. What happened next was to become a pattern of politics in the Middle East during the twentieth century. Once in power, the Young Turks turned out to be no more tolerant of dissent than the sultan had been. They, too, set out to accumulate as much power as possible in their own hands.

Part of the problem was the very nature of political change in the Ottoman Empire. It was not organic. The Young Turks simply took the European political model of parliaments and constitutions and grafted it onto their own society—a society that was fundamentally different in outlook and experience from the nation-states of Europe. The European political model had grown out of the hopes and history of Europe's peoples. Often, it was the result of bitter and bloody wars. And within Europe itself, there were many different political models. Britain was a constitutional monarchy; France veered between republic and empire; Germany had a kaiser who wanted to ignore parliament; and Russia had a tsar who thought he was second only to God. There was no one size that fitted all. But rather than innovate and create a political model that suited their own society's needs, the Young Turks imitated aspects of European political culture and ended up alienating themselves from the mass of Ottoman society. They represented the urban elite to which they belonged but not the man in the market or the farmer in his field.

As a result, their revolution did little to address the yawning gap between power and the people. The average person remained as far from power as when the sultan had ruled alone. All of which meant that in 1914, when the time came to decide whether or not to fight in Europe's war, it was a decision that placed the ruling elite on the line. If they made the wrong decision and ended up on the losing side, they had no popular mandate to validate their decision.

Why they chose to side with Germany owed much to the Ottoman Empire's recent history. The links between Istanbul and Berlin were long-standing. As far back as the 1830s, the Ottomans turned to the Germans for help to reform their military along European lines. These military connections were accelerated during Abdulhamid's reign, particularly during the 1880s, with the German army training Ottoman officers in Germany as well as sending liaison officers to Istanbul.[14]

In the sultan's dealings with the kaiser, there was also an element of "my enemy's enemy is my friend." In Ottoman eyes, Germany did not have the imperial baggage of Britain or France or Russia. Germany did not appear to covet the Ottoman capital. Germany's banks did not control Ottoman debt. Germany did not occupy Cairo or Tunis or Algiers.

The structure for a German-Ottoman alliance was, therefore, already in place before the Young Turks staged their coup. What helped seal the alliance were the actions of the Allies themselves.

In the run-up to the war, Britain, France, and Russia made no significant diplomatic overtures to Istanbul. The truth was they did not rate the Ottomans as an enemy and did not value them as an ally. Then, on July 28, 1914, the First Lord of the Admiralty, a young Winston Churchill, confiscated two ships being built in Britain for the Ottoman navy. These ships, the *Reshadieh* and the *Sultan Osman I*, were no ordinary naval vessels. They were the foundation of the new Ottoman navy, designed to take on the Russian Black Sea Fleet. More than that, they were funded by public donation and, as such, were an emotional symbol of Ottoman identity. Children gave up their pocket money to help pay for them.[15]

In Istanbul, there was outrage at Churchill's actions. But even this was not enough to push the Ottomans into war against the Allies. Throughout the autumn, they continued to hedge their bets.

By November, they could no longer do so. On November 2, after the Germans shelled Russian Black Sea ports using Ottoman ships, Russia declared war on Istanbul. Britain and France followed three days later. On November 11, Sultan Mehmed V (r. 1909–18) responded by declaring war on Britain, France, and Russia.

Europe was split in two. Its fate hung in the balance. So too did the fate of the Middle East. The future of the Arab people now depended on what happened on the battlefields of Europe.

And it would fall to two Europeans—one English, the other French—to redraw the map of the Arab world and begin the process of making the modern Middle East. In doing so, they would play a critical role in laying the groundwork for nearly all of the wars raging across the region today.

Part II

Too Many Straight Lines on the Map: Where, When, and Why It Started to Go Wrong

7

London: Tuesday, December 21, 1915

The Englishman was Sir Mark Sykes. The Frenchman was François Georges Picot.[1]

And if you have ever looked at a map of the Middle East and wondered why so many of the borders in the region are so unnaturally straight, look to Sir Mark and Monsieur Picot for an explanation. The two men met in London on December 21, 1915, to discuss dividing the Ottoman Empire between Britain and France and, in the process, they laid the groundwork for the Middle East we know today.

Both men were bastions of their establishments. Even though France had given the vote to all adult men back in 1848 and Britain had a wide, if not universal, male franchise, the highest positions of power in both countries were still held by a small clique of men from a particular social background.

Thirty-six-year-old Sir Mark Sykes was born into a landed family in Yorkshire and grew up in a world of wealth and privilege. Like so many young men of his background, he trod the well-worn path from public school to Cambridge (although he did not complete his course) to the Palace of Westminster. In 1911, he was elected to the House of Commons as Conservative MP for the city of Hull in the north of England.

Sir Mark's conventional career path masked a childhood that was anything but. He was an only child and his parents, Sir Tatton and Lady Jessica, lived the kind of colorful life not uncommon among English aristocrats. A distant, aloof figure, Sir Tatton Sykes was more than twice his wife's age. For her part, lonely Lady Jessica drank too much and had a string of affairs, including one with a tour guide when the couple were on a family holiday.[2] "Warm-hearted but wanton" is how one historian describes her.[3] Ultimately, the facade could not be maintained and the couple's divorce in 1897 laid bare every detail of their marriage for public scrutiny.

Sir Mark Sykes's childhood left two enduring legacies, both of which had political consequences.[4] The first was religion. When Sykes was very young, his mother flouted convention and converted to Catholicism. She brought her son up in the faith, a course of action which destined him to be something of an outsider among England's Anglican elite. That did not deter him and, as an adult, he was an enthusiastic follower of his faith. When he was negotiating the future of the Ottoman Empire with the French, his Catholic faith helped him to understand, and sometimes even to sympathize with, France's plans.

The other legacy of Sir Mark Sykes's childhood was a fascination with the East. His family visited the region on a number of occasions, including the infamous holiday when his mother became intimately acquainted with their guide. For the young Sir Mark, the East became an obsession that would last for the rest of his life.[5] In this, he was not unusual. For well-heeled Europeans of his era with the resources to travel, the exotic East offered an escape from the restrictions and pressures of life at home. For Sir Mark, his childhood travels in the East were a welcome respite from the ups and downs of his parent's marriage.[6] As an adult, he was drawn to the region again and again. He traveled widely as a tourist and turned his experiences into travelogues-cum-popular histories. (Nowadays, he would blog.) Then, for four years, he worked at the British Embassy in Istanbul.[7]

His time in the Ottoman world served him well when he became an MP. He was almost unique among his peers in having traveled widely in the area. It mattered little that he spoke no Arabic or Turkish. It mattered even less that he had not studied the region, its religions, or its peoples in any in-depth or objective way. In an era long before universities had Middle East Departments or Oriental Institutes, a little knowledge of the Ottoman Empire went a long way. Sir Mark Sykes was considered an expert on the subject because he knew something about it when most of his colleagues knew nothing at all.

In April 1915 when British Prime Minister Herbert Asquith convened a committee of high-ranking officials from the Foreign Office and the War Office to draw up Britain's plans for the future of the Middle East, Sir Mark Sykes was part of the team. And not a junior member: he was there at the personal request of the man running the War Office, Lord Kitchener.[8] That committee, named after the diplomat Sir Maurice de Bunsen who headed it, met in the spring of 1915 and delivered its recommendations to the British government by June.

Those recommendations reflected the need to protect long-held British imperial interests. In other words: the route to India. Britain wanted nothing less than control of the land route through the Middle East from the Mediterranean to the Gulf. That meant taking everything from the coast of modern-day Israel through modern-day Jordan into central and southern Iraq with a slice of the eastern Persian Gulf coast thrown in too. Kaiser Wilhelm's plans to build the Berlin–Baghdad railway had seriously rattled the British. It risked bringing the Germans too close to the heart of the British Empire. One way to make sure it never happened was to control the land along the route and deny Germany access to it.

For Britain, controlling what would become Iraq was strategically important for another reason. In 1912, the Royal Navy launched its first oil-powered battleship: the HMS *Queen Elizabeth*.[9] It was the shape of things to come. Before then, royal navy vessels were coal-fired. Hence the British Empire's need for a string of coaling stations across the Mediterranean into the Gulf. Gibraltar, Malta, Cyprus, Suez, and Aden were all essential links in an imperial chain running from England to India. Without these ports, the Royal Navy could not refuel.

But change was afoot. The fuel of the future was oil. Iraq was believed to be full of it. And not only could Iraqi oil power the new Royal Navy vessels, it could also power the new weapons of war. The First World War, more than any previous conflict, witnessed a massive mechanization of warfare. Tanks, aircraft, and chemical weapons were the new normal. Britain's Royal Navy might still be the senior service, but from now on no war could be won without an air force, and an air force required fuel and forward bases. The British looked at Iraq and saw that Iraq could provide both. For the British, all that remained was to secure a port on the Mediterranean where oil could be shipped to the European market. Sir Mark Sykes lobbied for Haifa.

The British began negotiations with the French on Tuesday, November 23, 1915. At first, the meetings were led by Sir Arthur Nicolson of the Foreign Office, but by December 21, Sir Mark Sykes was in charge. Facing him across the negotiating table was the representative of the French government: François Georges Picot.

Forty-three-year-old François Georges Picot was an imperialist through and through. He was born into a family with sound imperial credentials. His father Georges was a leading light of one French imperial institution; his brother Charles a leading light of another. For the father, the main interest was French Africa. For the son, it was French Asia.[10] Career-wise, François Georges Picot followed in his father's footsteps and became a lawyer but then switched to diplomacy. Like his English counterpart Sir Mark Sykes, Picot had direct experience of living and working in the Ottoman Empire: he had served as French Consul in Beirut before the war.[11] As well as this knowledge and experience, Picot was also incredibly well connected. He was a member of the influential group, the

Comité de l'Asie Française, and came to the negotiations in London knowing exactly what the French colonial lobby expected him to deliver. He was not the man to let them down.

During the spring and summer of 1915, when the British were working out what they wanted from the Ottoman Empire, the French had not been idle either. They had been busy drawing up their own plans for a new Middle East. Just as the British plans centered on their imperial obsession in India, the French had an imperial obsession of their own: their historic civilizing mission. What the Crusaders started, what Napoleon continued, Picot and his colleagues were now determined to finish. Proof of just how much this meant to them was clear after the war when French General Henri Gouraud paid a visit in Damascus to the tomb of the Muslim hero Saladin whose armies had defeated the Crusaders in 1187 to bring Jerusalem back into the House of Islam. "We have returned," the soldier told Saladin (who had been dead since 1193).

In 1915, the French resolved to remake the Middle East in their image. Or, at the very least, to secure agribusinesses producing raw materials (such as Syrian silkworms) needed for the French textile industry. France had substantial financial investments in the region, and Paris wanted control of Greater Syria to safeguard those long-standing commercial interests. France also wanted to continue protecting the Maronite Christians in Mount Lebanon—a process begun in the 1860s and consolidated by the Jesuits and their missionary schools throughout the second half of the nineteenth century. For all France's revolutionary republican ideals, the Catholic Church was still strong in public and political life, and the Church was keen to maintain its connections so close to the Christian Holy Land. A Catholic himself, Sir Mark Sykes could understand their aspirations.[12]

More important, however, than Sir Mark's faith was the cold political reality of the situation. The British were not interested in Greater Syria. As far as London was concerned, France could have it. London was even prepared to cede to Paris the oil-rich region of Mosul in northern Iraq and parts of southern Turkey too. There was method in London's generous madness: Britain saw France as the first line of defense between Britain's interests in Iraq and Russia's to the north. If the Russians ever attacked, the British would not be first in the firing line. The French would block the way.[13]

One area, however, where Sykes and Picot could find no common ground was the Christian Holy Land. Both wanted it. Then, as now, the stakes were so high; no one could agree and no one would compromise. Then, as now, it became an issue of all or nothing. Then, as now, a solution of sorts was eventually ironed out that was not a solution at all.

The British claimed the Mediterranean ports but gave up their claims elsewhere in the land of Christ's birth. The French reciprocated and gave up their claims too. The future of the Holy Land would be internationalized. But this Wisdom-of-Solomon gesture by both parties was not what it seemed. The terms of the "internationalization" were deliberately vague and, in typical diplomatic doublespeak, open to contradictory interpretations. Both capitals were simply biding their time, waiting for the moment to secure by other means what they could not secure at the negotiating table. (The French did not wait long. They made a secret agreement with the Russians in the spring of 1916 to secure French control of Palestine.)[14]

Sykes and Picot finished their negotiations in January 1916, barely a month after the two men first met. The Sykes-Picot Agreement was ratified by London and Paris early the following month. It was officially signed on April 26, 1916.[15]

The breakneck pace of this behind-the-scenes diplomatic activity continued. An agreement was also reached with Russian Foreign Minister Sergei Sazanov, which ratified the Anglo-French deal and earmarked Istanbul and large chunks of eastern Turkey for Russia. The Italian Allies were not left out of this land-grab either. Southern Turkey was reserved for them. But it was the Sykes-Picot Agreement above all other agreements that became the blueprint for the postwar Middle East, and it is their names that have become synonymous with Western imperialism in the Arab world.[16] Nearly a century later, in the summer of 2012, the leader of al-Qaida in Iraq remembered the two men as he urged his followers to overturn "the borders implemented by the Sykes-Picot [Agreement]" and bring back "the Islamic state, the state that does not recognize artificial boundaries and does not believe in any nationality other than Islam."[17] Less than two years later, the man in question, Abu Bakr al-Baghdadi, had done just that and set himself up as the new caliph of the Islamic State.

The Sykes-Picot Agreement turned out to be almost prophetic in predicting what would happen to the Arab world after the war. Yet it was not at all clear at the time that events would turn out that way. In 1915, the war was still raging and an Allied victory was far from certain. The Germans were still deeply entrenched on French soil. The Russians were still bogged down on the Eastern front. The Turks, as the Allies had discovered to their cost at Gallipoli and would soon discover again at Kut, were a formidable foe. And the Americans, with their wealth of men and materiel, had not yet entered the war. Under such conditions, the Anglo-French decision to carve up an empire that had not yet collapsed appears to be an act of breathtaking diplomatic chutzpah.

Officially, London and Paris did it as a pre-emptive strike against Russia. Even though they were supposed to be allies, Britain and France were wary of Russia's Eastern ambitions. The British and French, with their own imperial obsessions, knew the Russians had one too: building a Russian Rome in Istanbul. If Russia capitalized on the war to secure a historic victory against the Turks in the eastern Mediterranean, the balance of power in the region would tip decisively in Petrograd's favor. A state of affairs neither Britain nor France wished to see. London and Paris were determined to limit the fallout of any potential Russian victory against the Ottomans. The Eastern Question had dominated foreign relations among the Great Powers in the last half of the nineteenth century. Sykes-Picot was a twentieth-century response to that nineteenth-century question: a means of ensuring that whatever outcome prevailed, Britain and France would not lose out.

There was another reason the British and French were so keen to make gains in the Arab world after the war. They had to justify the sacrifice their men were making. No one had expected the war to last so long, be so bloody, and cost so much in blood and treasure. The price for all those lost lives had to be paid somehow.

The death toll from the First World War still has the power to shock. Britain lost more than 700,000 men in the course of the conflict. The French lost 300,000 men in 1914 *alone*.[18] By the end of the war, they had lost another million. Russia lost even more and in even less time (they left the war in 1917): one million and seven hundred thousand men. In total, the Allies lost 5,100,000 men to win the war—more than 1,600,000 than their opponents.[19] These figures do not include the wounded, the captured, or the missing in action. The Allies had to have something to show for all that loss.

The idea of finding compensation in the East for losses in the West was not new. At the Congress of Berlin in 1878, the Great Powers agreed that France should have Tunisia as compensation for losing Alsace-Lorraine to the Germans in the Franco-Prussian war of 1870–1. On a similar theme, at a conference in Algeciras in Spain in early 1906, the British and French sealed the fate of Egypt and Morocco as a way of preserving the balance of power in Europe.[20]

At the Congress of Berlin and, again, at the conference in Algeciras, the Great Powers did not consider the wishes of Tunisians, Egyptians, or Moroccans. Likewise, Sykes-Picot took no account of the hopes and aspirations of the people whose lives they were about to turn upside down. Imperialism fostered a sense of entitlement that enabled diplomats from Europe to sit at a desk with a map and a ruler and draw lines through historic heartlands, sacred cities, and family farms without a second thought for the long-term implications. In Europe's corridors of power, the Middle East was a blank space waiting to be remade. Even the term "Middle East" reflects this line of thinking. It is not a local term. It does not come from any of the many languages of the region. It was the brainchild of an American naval strategist, Alfred Taylor Mahan, who came up with it in 1902 when he was advising British strategists how to protect the sea routes to India. The name neatly encapsulates how the area fitted into imperial strategic thinking: it was in the "middle." It had no intrinsic value of or by itself. Its value lay in its position on the way to somewhere else.[21]

There was, however, a major miscalculation in this line of thinking: one that would reverberate through the rest of the century and into the next. What the Allies wanted in the Middle East—what the Sykes-Picot Agreement laid the groundwork for achieving—bore absolutely no relation to the facts on the ground.

8

The Arab World before the War: The Facts on the Ground

1

The Ottoman Empire in the early twentieth century shared a strong sense of historical continuity with the Islamic caliphates of the past. Under the Ottoman dynasty, as under previous Islamic dynasties, communal reference points and definitions of identity dated back centuries: to the life and times of the Prophet Muhammad.

The Prophet Muhammad's message was truly revolutionary. Islam fundamentally altered how people saw themselves and how they defined their place in the world. It created a whole new form of identity that, in turn, became the framework for a whole new type of society. Such radical redefinition of what a society is, and who its members are, is difficult to achieve at any time or any place. In the twentieth century, the leaders of the Soviet Union did their level best to remake Russians into Communists. But even with all the technology the modern world has to offer and all the coercive power of the Soviet state at their disposal, they still could not achieve it. The pull of Mother Russia was too strong. Russians remained indisputably Russian.

Back in the seventh century, the Prophet Muhammad succeeded in remaking his world. And he did so not only for his own time and place. He created an identity and a community that transcended the immediate environment and has withstood the test of time. Recent surveys illustrate just how enduring that sense of identity has proven to be.

As recently as 2006, a Pew survey of German Muslims showed that two-thirds of those polled saw themselves as Muslim first and German second. (By comparison, of the German Christians polled, only 13 percent saw themselves as Christian first, German second.) The figures for the United Kingdom are even more striking. Of the British Muslims polled, 81 percent saw themselves as Muslim first, British second. (By comparison, of the British Christians polled, only 7 percent saw themselves as Christian first, British second.)[1]

The results of another survey are equally enlightening. In 2009, Gallup asked a sample of British Muslims if religion was important in their daily lives. Seventy percent responded yes. (By comparison, of the British Christians polled, only 29 percent answered yes.) Gallup also asked a sample of German Muslims the same question. Eighty-two percent responded yes. (By comparison, of the German Christians polled, only 33 percent answered yes.)[2]

The nature of the Islamic faith helps explain why Islam's reach is so wide and why the Prophet Muhammad was so successful in building a community based on it. Islam is a public religion. Its defining characteristics are the five pillars of the faith: the statement of belief, daily prayer, almsgiving, fasting during the holy month of Ramadan, and the pilgrimage to Mecca. These are community-based activities that are less concerned with individual morality or theology than with a shared experience of the faith. Islam is not a religion where, if you are a believer, you stay home to work on your personal relationship with God or wrestle privately with your doubts and inner demons. Islam is a religion that requires you to go to the mosque, pray as part of the community, and live your faith on a daily basis. Nowhere is this sense of Islam as a community more visible than in Mecca during the pilgrimage. Nowadays, two million pilgrims make the journey.[3]

Like any revolutionary way of living, Islam was—and still is—universal in its application. Anyone can be a believer. Because of this, when the Muslim armies left Arabia not long after the Prophet's death in 632 and conquered much of the known world, the conquered peoples had a way "in" to the new order, if they chose to take it. There were also safeguards if they did not. Conversions were not forced. The Quran stipulates, "There is no compulsion in religion."[4] In fact, Christians and Jews were often encouraged *not* to convert as they paid a poll-tax (*jizya*), which was a valuable source of revenue for the nascent Islamic state. But as time passed and as Arab armies won more territory, conversions grew. Within a century of the Prophet's death, the Islamic call to prayer echoed from Afghanistan in the east to the Atlantic in the west and to the foothills of the Pyrenees in Europe. The Muslim community of believers had become truly transnational. Its members came from groups as diverse as Arab and Armenian, Spanish and Syrian, Turk and Tuareg, Kurd and Circassian. The House of Islam had room for all of them.

For those who were not believers, particularly the Jewish and Christian communities across the Middle East, the jizya was the price they had to pay for securing their place in society. Never equal to Muslims, the best they could hope for was a protected position in the Islamic order. For the most part, they got it. There were, however, sporadic eruptions of intercommunal violence. One of the most notorious examples of which was the massacre of over 10,000 Christians by Druzes in Mount Lebanon in 1860.

There were also occasional bouts of state-sponsored discrimination although these were not of the same caliber of persecution that Jews and Muslims experienced in medieval Europe.[5] The reign of the Fatimid caliph al-Hakim in Egypt (r. 996–1021) is one example. Al-Hakim was slightly unhinged—the historian Philip Hitti calls him "deranged"—and he made Christians and Jews wear black so they could be identified in public.[6] He also had them wear crosses or bells around their necks in the public baths for the same reason. It was not just minorities, however, who felt the full force of al-Hakim's instability. He introduced measures that affected everyone in the community, such as when he banned certain foodstuffs for no apparent reason. In his treatment of religious minorities, this caliph was the exception rather than the rule, and his son and successor al-Zahir (r. 1021–35) took immediate steps upon his succession to reassure Jews and Christians.[7]

In the Muslim world, Islam clearly was—and still is—the dominant identity. Faith marks the border of belonging. But that faith is not static. It is constantly evolving. Within Islam itself, there are countless groups and sub-groups claiming people's allegiance and defining their identity. The two best known are the Sunnis and the Shi'is, and these, too, contain many groups and sub-groups.

Within Sunni Islam, there are four main schools of religious thought named after the theologians who founded them: the Hanbali, the Hanafi, the Maliki, and the Shafi. In Shi'i Islam, there are also various sub-groups such as the Seveners and the Twelvers. The numbers represent the generations descended from Ali, the Prophet's cousin and son-in-law, and father of the martyr al-Husayn. Shi'is believe the Hidden Imam, the Redeemer figure who will usher in an era of divinely inspired justice, will come from one of these lines of the Prophet's family. These sub-groups, in turn, have sub-groups that branch off into what almost amounts to a different religion, such as the Alawi or the Druze.

There are also faith-based movements that combine religion and activism like the Sufis with their whirling dervishes and their revolutionaries who fought the French in Algeria and the Italians in Libya. Then there are the Wahhabi zealots with their austere brand of militant Islam who joined forces with a little-known family in eighteenth-century Arabia and later created the Kingdom of Saudi Arabia.[8]

While Islam is the primary identity for Muslims, it is not the only one. This is a culturally complex, multilayered community and people have a number of secondary identities, one of the most important of which is the tribe. Before Islam, the great tribal rivalry in Arabia was between the Qays tribal federation in the north of the peninsula and the Yaman in the south. Islam superseded this tribal rivalry but never entirely eradicated it.[9]

One of the reasons the tribe survived as a communal unit was due to the nature of the early Islamic conquests. When the Muslim armies swept out of Arabia and swept all before them in the 630s and 640s, they built garrisons in the areas they conquered. These military camps (*amsar* in Arabic) were situated in key strategic locations close to good transport links, such as al-Jabiya in the Golan Heights, Fustat on the Nile (later to grow into Cairo), Basra near the Persian Gulf, and Kufa on the Euphrates. They were initially intended as forward bases for the next phase of military expansion, but they soon developed into bustling cities.

Because the armies fought in tribal units, land in these cities was allocated by tribe and each quarter was settled exclusively by the members of one tribe. In this way, not only was the strength of the tribe retained; so too was the link between the tribe and the military. This, in turn, meant the tribal loyalties of Arabia fanned out across the empire. Wherever the armies won new territory, that new territory was settled by the tribe who conquered it.

With tribal identities remaining so strong among the conquerors, the conquered people kept their own tribal relationships and affiliated, often en bloc, with the tribes from Arabia. As a result, the tribe as a unit of social organization retained its importance in the Islamic world and never lost it. Tribal rivalries became so much of an issue in the late seventh and early eighth centuries; they helped bring down Islam's first dynasty, the Umayyads, in 750.[10]

Throughout the history of the Islamic caliphate, regional and urban identities also retained their hold on people's loyalties. The people of great cities like Jerusalem and Damascus had a sense of history stretching far back in time which they managed to fuse with their Islamic identity. In places like Egypt and Iran, home to great civilizations predating Islam, a multilayered sense of identity was common. An Egyptian living in Alexander's city on Africa's Mediterranean coast could be proud of Egypt's Hellenistic, Roman, and Pharaonic past and be no less a Muslim for it. Equally, an Iranian living in the imperial city of Isfahan could be proud of Cyrus the Great for making Persia the greatest country on earth in the sixth century BC and, likewise, be no less a Muslim for it.

Different races and regions, different cities and tribes: the Islamic world from the Prophet to the dawn of the twentieth century was a mish-mash of peoples and places, cultures and languages. But the glue that held it all together was Islam. Muhammad's message succeeded in holding his community together for centuries, regardless of whether the caliphate was led by the Rightly Guided Caliphs in Arabia (632–61), the Umayyads in Damascus (661–750), the Abbasids in Baghdad (750–1258), the Fatimids in Cairo (969–1171), or the Ottomans in Istanbul.[11]

Sykes and Picot were about to change all that. They aimed to do nothing less than overturn thirteen centuries of history and introduce the nation-state to the Middle East. To understand just how difficult a task that was going to be, you have only to look at Greater Syria.

2

Greater Syria was no ordinary part of the Muslim world. It was a super-province whose territories covered modern Syria, Lebanon, Israel, Jordan, and parts of Iraq and Turkey. Damascus was its political center, Jerusalem its spiritual anchor.

Greater Syria was conquered by the Muslim armies between 633 and 641. In the early days of the caliphate when power was exercised from Medina in Arabia (632–61), caliphs were so concerned about the potential of this region to become a state within a state; they divided it into four (later five) administrative districts (*ajnad*) to prevent its governor from becoming too powerful. But it happened anyway. In 661, the governor of Greater Syria, Muawiya bin Sufyan, a former citizen of Mecca and one-time opponent of the Prophet, emerged as the victor in Islam's first civil war and claimed the caliphate as his.

His victory was due in no small measure to the vast resources of Greater Syria. It was a cultural, economic, and military powerhouse. Blessed by geography, this was a fertile region with agricultural techniques far ahead of Europe's. Its cities were hubs along east-west trade routes. Its soldiers were the shock troops of the Islamic empire.

For the best part of a century, Muawiya's Umayyad family drew on these resources and ruled the Islamic world from their Syrian strong-hold.[12] It was from here that the high watermark of imperial expansion was reached when Muslim forces conquered Spain in 711 and reached France in 732. And it was from here that many of the recognizable symbols of Islamic civilization—the magnificent mosque architecture, for example—first took shape.

Damascus lost its political pole position when the Umayyad dynasty fell in 750. But the memory of its greatness lingered. Political geography might change, but basic geography does not. Greater Syria still sat at the very heart of the Arab Muslim world. In the world before air travel, this was still the crossroads between East and West.

In Arabic, the region was known as *al-Sham*. Al-Sham is sometimes loosely translated as "Syria," but this Syria does not have the same borders as the modern Arab Republic of Syria. In fact, it does not have any borders at all. People could travel and trade freely throughout this vast region, just as they could throughout the Islamic empire. This idea of an Islamic world without borders is still relevant today. The Islamic State of Syria and the Levant (ISIL) use al-Sham in the Arabic version of their name: *al-dawla al-islamiyya f'il-'Iraq wa'l-Sham* (DA'ISH for short). They do so to show their rejection of the Middle East's nation-state system with its artificially created borders and artificially created national identities.

Historically, al-Sham corresponds to the territory of the region's original administrative sub-districts, most of which were in place from Roman times. Running north to south along the Mediterranean coast, these districts were Qinnasrin, Homs, Damascus, Jordan, and Palestine.[13] Like historic Syria, these districts do not correspond to the same territory as their modern namesakes. The Damascus region, for example, took in practically all of modern Lebanon. The Jordan region took in all of the north of modern Israel. Qinnasrin took in parts of modern Turkey.

This system of governing the region through sub-districts had deep roots in history. Whichever caliph ruled Greater Syria would appoint governors to the major cities and/or sub-governors to the outlying provinces. There were periods when this pattern was interrupted—at times of weak central authority and during the Crusader era—but for much of the Islamic era, Greater Syria was ruled by governors appointed by the caliph in Baghdad or Cairo and, from the sixteenth century to the twentieth, by the sultan in Istanbul. The region's sub-districts were known as *wilaya*s in Arabic or *vilayet*s in Turkish.

Sykes-Picot proposed drawing lines through the wilayas where previously none had existed. These lines severed communities who had lived side by side for centuries and they partnered others who had no wish to be neighbors. They upset the regional economy and disrupted long-established trade and farming patterns. They relegated religion as a form of identity and imposed a new one, the nation, on people who had no wish for it. And perhaps most importantly of all, they created internal borders in a world that had no experience of them.

In doing so, the Sykes-Picot Agreement wove intercommunal tension into the fabric of the states they created and stored up problems for the future. France's principal aim in creating Lebanon was to protect France's overseas trade network and the Maronite Christians. To do this, the new state had to contain the thriving cosmopolitan port of Beirut and the Maronite heartland of Mount Lebanon, autonomous since 1860. Such a country would have been tiny in comparison to its neighbors and its size would have left it vulnerable. To avoid such a scenario, additional parts of the Damascus region of Greater Syria were added to Lebanon: the port cities of Tripoli, Tyre, and Sidon, along with the Biqa Valley.

In the wake of these changes, Lebanon bore more than a passing resemblance to the French Crusader kingdoms of old. And while the country was certainly larger, it now contained the seeds of its own destruction. The Lebanese population was made up of a large community of Muslims split between Shi'is in the south and the Biqa Valley, and Sunnis in the rest of the country. It also contained a sizable community of Maronites and a considerable number of the Maronites' long-term rivals, the Druzes. The Maronites and the Druzes had gone to war on at least three occasions in the nineteenth century (1838, 1841–2, and 1845) followed by a wave of tit-for-tat sectarian killings culminating in the 1860 massacre of the Maronites.

This ethnic make-up was too diverse for a small country lacking any sense of national identity, any national infrastructure, any national institutions, and where intercommunal competition for limited state resources would be fierce. It also made no allowances for the impact of changing demography: the birth rate was much higher among Muslims than Christians—a state of affairs that would, over time, undermine the French-sponsored plan for Christian hegemony of the country.

Lebanon was not the only new country affected by Sykes and Picot. Lebanon's newly created neighbor, Syria, was not immune to the long-term negative effects of their plans. Syria was sundered of most of its southern territories, and Damascus, capital of the new country, was completely severed from its western hinterland (now in Lebanon). Beirut, the main port in the region, had been the gateway for Syrian exports to Europe. Not anymore: the truncated version of Syria had no access to it.

Syria's loss of size and status cast a long shadow over the wider region. And just as France had a historic mission in the region, so too did the new Syria. Once independent, the rulers of Damascus were determined to reclaim the city's historic hinterland, an objective that prompted Syria to intervene in Lebanon's civil war (1975–90), to ally with the Shi'i group Hizbullah, and stay on as an occupation force until they were forced out early in the twenty-first century following the assassination of former Lebanese prime minister, Rafiq Hariri, on Valentine's Day 2005.

Internally, Syria had problems too. The country's ethnic mix is even more heterogeneous than Lebanon's. Greater Syria was a crossroads civilization and the new Syria, formed from its predecessor's geographical core, became predominantly Arab but with significant minorities of Armenians, Circassians, Kurds, and Turkomen. Religiously, the majority of the population is overwhelmingly Sunni Muslim with an Alawi minority concentrated in the north-west around Latakia on the Mediterranean coast. Significant minorities of Druzes, Shi'is, and Christians make up the rest of the population.[14] Under the Sykes-Picot Agreement, all of these religions and races, like the ones in Lebanon, had to set aside their previous terms of communal reference and redefine themselves in accordance with the lines drawn on the map at the request of the French Republic.

But if the French could be accused of willfully ignoring history, so too could their allies, the British. The main British proxy state in the Middle East, Iraq, was just as hastily cobbled together with just as little regard for history.

3

For the British, Iraq started off as a tale of two cities: Baghdad and Basra.

These cities and the famously fertile land between them (known as the *Sawad* or "black," referring to the color of the soil) gave the British what they needed to secure their strategic objectives in the Middle East. Baghdad, in the center, was the gateway to Transjordan and the land link west to Palestine. Basra, in the south, was the gateway to the Gulf and the sea route east to India.

There was, however, a major problem. Baghdad and Basra had very little in common. They had developed along completely different religious and political trajectories and they belonged to completely different economic and geographical spheres of influence. These differences were manageable within the broader, regional framework of the Ottoman Empire. But within the narrower, nationalist construct of a nation-state, they would be much harder, perhaps impossible, to manage. The new Iraq was, therefore, a forced political marriage on a grand scale.

The differences between the two cities date back centuries: to Islam's arrival in Iraq in the seventh century. In 637, Muslim armies fought a decisive battle against the Persians at al-Qadisiyya near al-Hira on the Euphrates. Within days, they had moved upstream to one of the wealthiest cities in the world, the Persian capital Ctesiphon, and taken it too. By 641, Mosul in the north was theirs.[15]

Basra in the south was an early example of Islamic town planning and was built as a forward base for the Muslim armies. Basra, together with

Kufa further north and Bahrain to the south in the Persian Gulf, became the launch pads for the Islamic conquest of Iran. Basra, Bahrain, and Kufa shared something else in common: all would later become bastions of Shi'i Islam.

The Sunni–Shi'i split in Islam is not theological. It is political. But it has religious consequences. In Christianity, Roman Catholics and Protestants spent the Middle Ages fighting wars over fundamental points of doctrine. Who, for example, has the right to remit sins? A specially ordained priest or only God Himself? For medieval Christians, these were not insignificant matters. Salvation was at stake. In Islam, Sunnis and Shi'is have fought wars over who has the right to lead the community. Any suitably qualified Muslim, as Sunnis believe, or a member of the Prophet's family, as Shi'is do? For Muslims, salvation was also at stake. It was the community's leader who led them in prayer and in whose name prayers were said in the mosque on Fridays. If that leader is not legitimate, neither are the prayers.

In the first Islamic civil war (656–61), Kufa and Basra came out strongly on the side of the Prophet's family. Even though they lost, it did not dent their enthusiasm for the cause. Or for rebellion. A pattern soon emerged of brief but brilliant rebellions by members of the Prophet's family against the ruling Umayyad dynasty (r. 661–750). These rebellions did not amount to much in military terms, but they had strong emotional pull and won the hearts and minds of many in the community, particularly in southern Iraq and the Gulf.

The most famous of these dramatic but doomed bids for power was launched by the Prophet's grandson al-Husayn in 680 at Karbala, 25 miles north-west of Kufa. Al-Husayn's woefully small but loyal band of 80 followers was no match for the massed ranks of the army of the Umayyad caliph, Yazid (r. 680–4). In the one-sided battle that followed, Umayyad soldiers slaughtered dozens of members of the Prophet's family including al-Husayn.[16]

For Shi'is, this is no remote historical event. To this day, they commemorate the events at Karbala and reenact them with intense emotion in an annual passion play. But at the time, the people of Kufa and Basra, under virtual house arrest by the Umayyad governor, did not come out in support of al-Husayn. And the lingering guilt over leaving him to his tragic fate only deepened their veneration for the Prophet's family, their suspicion of Sunni central authority, and their tendency to rebel against it.[17] This loyalty to the Prophet's family has stood the test of time. Southern Iraq remains a stronghold of Shi'i Islam.

This Shi'i connection put the south at odds with northern and central Iraq, which were predominantly Sunni, and pulled southern Iraq into the cultural orbit of the Gulf, a large proportion of whose people were—and still are—also Shi'i. Iran, to the east, officially became a Shi'i state under the Safavid dynasty (r. 1501–1722) when Shah Ismail declared he was the hidden member of the Prophet's family they had all been waiting for.[18] Kuwait, to the west of Basra, also has a sizeable Shi'i community. To the south, the oil-rich province of al-Hasa on the eastern coast of Arabia is overwhelmingly Shi'i, as is the population of the island kingdom of Bahrain.

Baghdad, by contrast, was built to be a bastion of the establishment. And that establishment was Sunni. The city did not even exist at the time of the conquest of Iraq, but in 762, it was earmarked to be the future political capital of the Islamic world. Designed to be a clean break with the past, the city was the brainchild of the Abbasid caliph al-Mansur (r. 754–75) whose name means "the victorious." He was a ruthless political operator not averse to having the head of friend as well as foe lopped off, if the political need arose. Everyone from members of the Prophet's family to members of al-Mansur's *own* family, even members of his army, including the soldier who led the revolution that brought him to power, suffered the deadly consequences of falling under this caliph's suspicions.[19]

Clean breaks were this family's style. When they overthrew the Umayyad dynasty, they held a banquet near Jaffa in modern Israel for surviving members of the deposed ruling family. The Umayyads saw the invitation as an olive branch and agreed to turn up. They should not have. As soon as they entered the dining hall, the doors were locked behind them and a massacre ensued. By the end of the evening, there were no Umayyads left in Greater Syria who could launch a rebellion against the new rulers of the Arab world. Amidst the carnage, the banquet did not go to waste. Leather mats were thrown over the bodies and the executioners, with their work done, sat on top of the dead and the dying and polished off the food.[20]

This rupture with the past was underlined by another one, although one that was much less bloody: the decision to sideline Syria and move the caliphate to Iraq. There was no Iraqi city suitable to be the new capital— Kufa and Basra were too rebellious—so al-Mansur built his own. Not far from the former Persian capital, Ctesiphon, he found the little village of Baghdad. Here, on the River Tigris, surrounded by the rich agricultural land of the Sawad that would ensure the capital's food supplies, al-Mansur built his circular City of Peace (*Madinat al-Salam*).[21]

Baghdad was a giant exercise in town planning, land speculation, and social engineering. A city of royalty and religion, power and pleasure, soldiers and scholars, this was the empire in miniature. And right at the center of it was the caliph's palace with its green dome visible from afar.

While Basra—the soldiers' city—was settled by tribe, Baghdad—the royal city—was settled by the peoples and professions of the empire. Whole streets were assigned to different trades or crafts. Butchers occupied one street; booksellers another. Goods from all over the empire were traded in the caliph's city. Religious minorities found a home here too. Baghdad became home to a large number of Jews—the descendants of the Babylonian exile—as well as a large community of Nestorian Christians. Later immortalized in the *Arabian Nights*, Baghdad acted as a magnet drawing in the riches of the empire as well as attracting people from every corner of the Islamic world who dreamt of a better life. In its prime, it was the wealthiest city on the planet.

It was also indisputably Sunni. Al-Mansur, like the Umayyad caliphs before him, did not think twice about using overwhelming force to crush Shi'i rebellions. In later years, the city would have a large Shi'i population (now mostly situated in the northern suburb of Sadr City), but from its birth and throughout its history, Baghdad was predominantly Sunni.

Baghdad remained the center of the Abbasid caliphate until the Mongols sacked the city in 1258 and the dynasty fell. The city's glory days, however, had long since passed. In the ninth and tenth centuries, regional governors flexed their muscles against the central authority in Baghdad to claim greater autonomy. They carved out mini-fiefdoms in the regions they ruled but still pledged allegiance to the caliph in Baghdad. The result was a looser, more federated system with the caliph acting as a unifying figurehead, while the governors, out in the provinces, wielded the real power. Baghdad's once-all-powerful sway weakened to such a degree that there were even competitor caliphates: one in Cordoba and one in Cairo.[22]

The different historical experiences of Baghdad and Basra—one a city of power, the other a city of protest—gave them contrasting communal identities. This, in turn, gave them a different experience of how power was exercised. As a provincial city, Basra was run by a governor appointed by the central authority. Baghdad, for a large part of its history, was that central authority.

At the beginning of the twentieth century, these historical differences were not obscure facts of interest only to scholars and specialists. They were very real fault lines and had every potential, if mishandled, to rip the new country apart. And the British plan for Iraq, whether by accident or design, was bent on doing exactly that. The new Iraq was to have Baghdad, the former seat of the caliphate, as its capital. But Baghdad was a Sunni city in a country whose population was overwhelmingly Shi'i—an anomaly that bothered Britain's man in Baghdad, Colonel Arnold Wilson, after the war. He expressed doubts about the country's long-term viability if a Sunni minority in Baghdad continuously exercised power over a Shi'i majority elsewhere in the country. [23] (Wilson favored direct rule.) London rejected his concerns. In doing so, they ended up doing what the French had done in Lebanon and Syria and wove sectarianism into the fabric of their proxy state.

As if the historical and political differences between Baghdad and Basra were not enough to place a question mark over the new state, the two cities had completely different economic orbits. Basra, in the south, looked to the Gulf for commercial opportunities. Baghdad, landlocked in the center, looked to the neighboring towns and provinces.

To put two cities with such different historical experiences together and expect them to function as a coherent political unit was a tall order. Almost like building a nation around Paris and Geneva and hoping the fact they both are European, French-speaking, and historically Christian would be enough to forge a shared sense of national identity and establish a functioning government.

To add Mosul to the Iraqi mix—as happened after the war—made the nation-building project an even more complicated task. Mosul, unlike Baghdad and Basra, was a frontier province. For most of Mosul's history, it was a martial city, governed by military men and garrisoned by soldiers trained to fend off a Byzantine invasion.

To complicate matters further, Mosul itself was far from united. It was Sunni like Baghdad, but its population was an ethnic mix of Arab and Kurd. And the Kurds, an independent mountain people with a strong sense of cultural identity, had no wish to be part of this new country. They wanted one of their own.

In the early twentieth century, a new army was poised to invade Mosul: prospectors looking for oil. Britain and France believed the city sat on top of an untapped reservoir of oil—a commodity they needed to rebuild their economies after the war. That sealed the city's fate, drew it into the Sykes-Picot framework and eventually into the British sphere of influence.

In creating Iraq, Britain stitched together a state out of three disparate regions that had very different histories. In creating Lebanon and Syria, France did the opposite and carved up a region that had functioned as a political unit for centuries. In doing so, Paris and London took a process of nation-building that, in their own continent, had taken centuries, tele-scoped it into a matter of months, then imposed it on people who had not asked for it. And they did it to satisfy their own imperial interests.

From the outset, the flagship states of the Anglo-French Middle East were artificial constructs. They were nations in name only.

9

The Remaking of the Middle East: Enter the Nation-State

The nation-state was a European idea.

And it was a relatively recent one. As Professor David Reynolds points out in his award-winning book *The Long Shadow*, the nineteenth century was the era when this idea took flight. In 1800, there were around 500 political entities in Europe. By 1900, there were around 20.[1]

Italy and Germany were prime examples of this political consolidation. Italy started the nineteenth century as a collection of city-states and ended it as a unified nation-state. Germany started the century as a collection of duchies and principalities and ended it as the biggest nation-state in central Europe. These new states linked land and language, race and religion, to create a nation and a nationality out of a multiplicity of regional identities that had existed in the past. The structure of the nation-state also revolutionized the economy. With national unity came economic unity: internal taxes and tariffs were abolished, making the new nation-state one vast, free-trading area. Germany, for one, soared economically postunification.

The political dynamic behind the emergence of nation-states came from the French Revolution. After 1789, the "people" were a factor in politics. No longer did kings have a divine right to rule. No longer did the clergy hold a monopoly on morality. No longer did power belong to the privileged few. Once the Terror subsided, freedom and fraternity were France's ideological gifts to the world.

In the Napoleonic wars that followed the Revolution, Europeans became more aware of themselves as "people." And many of them demanded the right to be citizens rather than subjects. Citizenship meant participation. Participation meant voting. And voting meant public ownership of the state in a way that had never happened before. The cumulative effect of these changes was to revolutionize how people saw their country and their place in it.

The ideals of the French Revolution held a particular appeal for Europeans living in the Ottoman Empire. People like the Greeks, Romanians, and Serbs shared neither religion nor race with the Ottoman Turks who ruled over them. The idea of the people as a "nation" and of that people's right to self-determination became a rallying cry for independence from Istanbul. Wars of national liberation ensued. People felt a sense of ownership, of involvement, in the process of building their nation-state. The Great Powers were only too happy to help them in their struggles. Anything that reduced the power of the sultan was welcomed by London, Paris, and St. Petersburg.

The Great Powers had, in fact, been trying to disrupt the social fabric of the Ottoman Empire for years. The process began in earnest in the late eighteenth century when Russia's Catherine the Great stretched a minor clause in the Treaty of Küçük Kaynarca (1774) to the limit and virtually adopted the Ottomans' Orthodox Christians as surrogate Russians. By the nineteenth century, Europe's economic and military power had grown to such an extent that the continent's Great Powers could intervene more directly in Ottoman affairs. The effects were soon seen in changes to Ottoman law.

Under European pressure, Sultan Abdulmajid I (r. 1839–61) introduced a series of laws that fundamentally altered the legal basis of citizenship in the Ottoman Empire. These laws were known as the Imperial Rescripts. The first, the Imperial Rescript of Gülhane, was brought in 1839. It was controversial because it introduced the idea of equality between all religions. As the Quran stipulates that Muslims and non-Muslims are *not* equal, many Muslims believed the sultan's law contravened Islamic law. Many non-Muslims were not too happy about it either. One of the advantages of being a non-Muslim in a Muslim empire was exemption from military service. (The reliability and loyalty of non-Muslims was questioned.) Equality changed all that. Thousands of Christians voted with their feet and left for pastures new, usually the United States.

The second Rescript, brought in 1856, took the process a stage further and made all (male) subjects of the Ottoman Empire equal. This, too, appeared to contravene Islamic law as it recognized no difference between Muslims and peoples of other faiths.

For Muslims, the Rescripts were problematic because they challenged the very basis of what it was to be a Muslim in a Muslim state. Religion was relegated to second place. Rather than privileging Islam, the Rescripts privileged European ideas of citizenship and nationality. Intercommunal tensions rose across the Ottoman Empire throughout the nineteenth century. In Damascus in 1840, for example, Jews were accused of a blood libel after a Capuchin monk disappeared and the blame was placed on a local Jew. The incident set off a wave of similar accusations across the region.[2] Before the nineteenth century, such accusations, while common in Europe, were practically unheard of in the Arab world. In the nineteenth century, the problem reached what Professor Bernard Lewis calls "epidemic proportions."[3] Insecurity was spreading. Muslims felt their dominant position in society was under threat from Great Power patronage of religious minorities, from the commercial advantages minorities gained from that patronage, and from all-round European meddling in Istanbul's internal affairs.

For the vast majority of Muslims, the Rescripts and the European ideas they represented had little or no impact on their self-identity. But for Istanbul's cultured elite, Europe and Europe alone had the answers to the economic and political problems facing the Ottoman Empire. In 1889, a group of exiled intellectuals, writers, and journalists met in Paris, the ideological heartland of nineteenth-century people power, and set up the Ottoman Society for Union and Progress (better known as the Young Turks). They wanted the 1876 Constitution restored. They called for political reform and participatory government but did not go so far as to call for the end of the sultan's rule.[4]

Given the febrile atmosphere in Istanbul at the time, clandestine (or exiled) organizations were the order of the day. Even the supposedly loyal military were not immune. Like Istanbul's intelligentsia, the Ottoman military were used to European ideas. From the mid-nineteenth century, Ottoman soldiers were trained by European instructors in the use of European-made weapons. In the late nineteenth and early twentieth centuries, secret societies sprang up in army garrisons across the empire. One of them, the Fatherland Society, was set up in 1905 by none other than the future father of the Turks, Mustapha Kemal. The word "fatherland" (*watan*) was less overtly nationalist than its equivalent in Europe. In the Turkish context, it embraced the idea of Islamic as well as Ottoman identity.[5]

Over time, it was through these two channels—the literary elite and the officer class—that the idea of Turkish national identity took root. Before the war, it remained an elite movement. The groundswell of support that would transform it into a mass movement did not come until the end of the war and the collapse of the Ottoman Empire. Turkey's national consciousness was forged, as was the case with so many of the postwar nation-states in Europe, in blood on the battlefield.

Turkish nationalism, however, presented problems for the Arabs of the Ottoman Empire who shared a religion with the Turks but not a language or a land. In the Arab provinces, the idea of nationalism gained traction in certain circles before the First World War, but here, too, it was an elite movement, drawing support mostly from the class of notables in major cities like Damascus. It did not have widespread support in the community, the majority of whom saw it as an alien concept.

In Europe, the nation-state as a political unit met a political need that already existed. In the Middle East, it was a different story. Beirut and Baghdad were not clamoring for independence from the Ottoman Empire. Damascus was not a hotbed of insurrection against Istanbul.[6] Instead of the grassroots movement it was in Europe, and later in Turkey, nation-building in the Arab Middle East was a top-down process imposed by outsiders. Right from the outset, it lacked legitimacy among the people who would have to live with the consequences of it.

That lack of legitimacy did not deter the British or the French. They had won the war, and validated by that victory, they could now impose their terms and remake the Middle East as they saw fit.

10

From Sykes-Picot to the Treaty of Sèvres: Betrayals, Backstabbing, and Broken Promises

1

There is a saying that history belongs to the winners. The victors do not just win the war on the battlefield. They win the war of narratives that follows. Their view of history becomes *the* view of history.

Even more importantly, geography belongs to the winners. And after the armistice of November 11, 1918, the victors quickly set about remaking the world in their own image. In 1919, against the breathtaking backdrop of the Hall of Mirrors in the Palace of Versailles, the Allies dismembered the Austro-Hungarian and German Empires and redrew the map of Europe. A year later, the diplomatic action turned to the Italian Rivera resort of San Remo, then to the Parisian suburb of Sèvres where the Allies dismembered the Ottoman Empire and redrew the map of the Middle East.

In the end, the Treaty of Sèvres of August 10, 1920, echoed the aspirations of Sykes-Picot. At Sèvres, France got Lebanon and Syria. Britain got Iraq, Palestine, and Transjordan. In addition, London kept Egypt, the ports along the Arabian coast, and retained a controlling influence in Arabia. The Ottoman Empire was reduced to a rump state in its heartland of Anatolia.

The reason Britain and France were able to secure their objectives so successfully at Sèvres was very simple. There was no one to stop them. Of the other Allies, Russia had left the war in 1917 following the Revolution and the collapse of the Romanov Empire. The United States and Italy, each for different domestic reasons, had dropped out of the negotiations before Sèvres reached a conclusion.[1] And the Ottomans, as the defeated power, were in no position to negotiate.

Yet the almost uncanny similarity between Sykes-Picot and Sèvres made the process of remapping the Middle East seem a lot smoother than it actually was. Beneath the surface harmony of the peace conferences, the reality was very different. Betrayals, backstabbing, and broken promises were the order of the day. The Allies had little compunction about lying to each other and even less about lying to the people of the Middle East.[2]

The fate of Greater Syria was a perfect illustration of this. France wanted it. Picot thought he had secured it. But his negotiations with his English counterpart in 1915–6 made no allowance for what Britain was up to in Arabia and the effect those actions would have in Greater Syria.

Britain's interest in Arabia dated back centuries and London's strategy had not changed in all that time. In the twentieth century, as in the nineteenth, Britain focused on developing relationships with a small number of influential ruling families. At the turn of the twentieth century, three rival families were competing for control of the vast arid territory of Arabia: the Rasheeds in the north, the Saudis in the center, and the Hashemis in the west. The Hashemis had a special prestige as they claimed descent from the Prophet's family, and their leader, Sharif Husayn, was in charge of Islam's Holy Cities of Mecca and Medina.

In Sharif Husayn, London saw an opportunity. If he could be persuaded to use his prestige as a descendant of the Prophet and as guardian of the Holy Cities to launch a holy war against the Ottoman sultan, it could turn the course of the war in the Middle East.

Promises were made to the sharif. The British would provide the logistical support for him to stage a revolt against Ottoman rule. In return, when the war was over, Husayn would be given a kingdom. Precisely where that kingdom would be was never specified. In October 1915, not long before Sykes and Picot first met, Sir Henry McMahon, British High Commissioner in Egypt, sent the by-now-infamous letter to the sharif in which he told him he would be given the entire region except for the parts of Greater Syria the French wanted. But Sir Henry, based as he was in Cairo, made his promise without authorization from London. And London remained deliberately vague. That vagueness encouraged the sharif to believe what he wanted to believe and he wanted Greater Syria as part of his kingdom.

The Arab Revolt went ahead in 1916. Made famous by the involvement of T. E. Lawrence, the Revolt secured some of Britain's military objectives in the Middle East but by no means all of them. From early on, it was clear the sharif's ambition did not match his popularity, and the Arab Revolt was not the mass uprising the British had hoped for. Even though people in the Arab provinces of the Ottoman Empire had much to complain of when it came to Istanbul's handling of the war—dissent was mercilessly crushed; harvests and animals were routinely requisitioned by the sultan's army without a thought for how the local population were to be fed, so famine became rife (the older generation in Lebanon still recall those days with a shudder when they think of what people were forced to do to buy even the smallest amounts of food)—it was a step too far for most Muslims to turn against fellow Muslims and side with Europeans who were currently occupying most of Muslim North Africa.

By July 1917, Lawrence and the sharif's men had captured Aqaba on the Red Sea coast. The year 1917 was good for British forces in the Middle East. Imperial troops (mostly Indian) captured Iraq in March. In December, General Sir Edmund Allenby's army broke through into Palestine from Egypt and made it to Jerusalem in time for Christmas. In a deliberate contrast to the kaiser's grand entry into the Old City on horseback in 1898, Allenby strolled through the Jaffa Gate on foot.

The next goal for the British was Damascus. From Palestine, British forces set out for central Syria in 1918, and in October, they captured it. Here, too, the Allied entry into the city was deliberately choreographed. Faysal, the sharif of Mecca's son, was to lead the troops into the city that had once ruled the Arab world. That way, the Allied arrival looked less of a foreign invasion than a local liberation.[3]

It did not go to plan. Faysal and his men arrived too late, and Allenby's army had to take the city themselves. But this delay was the least of Britain's—or Faysal's—problems. The battle for Greater Syria now began in earnest. The French insisted Sykes-Picot be honored and claimed Syria as theirs. Faysal insisted otherwise. He tried to gather nationalist support for an independent Syria and proclaimed himself king. In the ensuing political chaos, law and order fell apart.

The British, with nearly all of the Ottoman provinces of the Middle East under their military command, saw no reason to assist French imperial ambitions and looked for ways to wriggle out of Sykes-Picot. Faysal was a useful pawn in their greater game. As such, he was the only Arab invited to speak at the Paris peace conferences and he was invited purely because it suited British interests. The British were far less accommodating of other Arabs who wanted to make their case at Paris. They banned the Egyptian delegation (the *Wafd)* from attending and sent the leader of the delegation, Sad Zaghlul, into exile in Malta. When Egyptians launched a popular uprising in March 1919 against the decision, Britain deployed the army and appointed General (now Lord) Allenby to run the country.

Within Greater Syria, Faysal was able to garner a degree of support for his claims to be king. People who had previously shown little enthusiasm for nationalism changed their position when it meant independence from a European power rather than from the Muslim Ottomans. Faysal's appeal, however, was limited by the fact he was not Syrian himself.

The turbulent situation in Greater Syria was eventually settled in the summer of 1920, and it was settled in a way that would become a fixture of politics in the Middle East in the twentieth century: by the use of force. On July 24, 1920, French forces attacked Faysal's supporters at Maysaloun just outside Damascus. They used every weapon at their disposal from air power to heavy shelling. The residents of Damascus were left stunned by the bombardment. Faysal's men were outgunned, outnumbered, and very quickly defeated. He fled south to the British zone. It was upon arriving in Damascus on July 26 that French General (and hero of the Great War) Henri Gouraud made straight for Saladin's tomb and declared to the long-dead conqueror of Jerusalem: "We have returned."

In the struggle for Syria, the British made conflicting promises both to France and to Faysal. When it suited them, they said France should have Syria. When it suited them otherwise, they said Faysal should have it. In the end, when London had to decide one way or the other, the British did what they always did in the Middle East and sided with their fellow imperial power.

Faysal, however, was not abandoned by his British allies. He was given a kingdom after all. Just not the one he expected. He was made king of the newly created Iraq. After three years of British military occupation, Iraq was rebellious. A tribal uprising in the summer of 1920 proved difficult to quell and left thousands dead. Given the tense atmosphere in the country, the British were keen to install a puppet ruler through whom they could exercise power.

Faysal fitted the bill perfectly. London quickly set about securing public support for Faysal's "election" as king—a process that involved a number of dubious practices, including Britain's man in Baghdad, Sir Percy Cox, inviting a rival of Faysal to tea and having him arrested as he left and deported to the British colony of Ceylon, now Sri Lanka.[4]

In August 1921, in what would become another fixture of politics in the Middle East in the twentieth century, Faysal "won" just short of 100 percent of the vote and was duly declared king. The writer-cum-diplomat-cum-kingmaker Gertrude Bell, Cox's cohort in arranging Faysal's ascent to the throne, declared afterwards that she would never again be involved in such a process. It was too exhausting.

While Bell and Cox publicly succeeded in making Faysal king, the country's real rulers were the British. The Anglo-Iraqi Treaty of 1922 made sure of it. Everything from finance to foreign affairs remained under London's control. Faysal's new kingdom was independent in name only. Faysal himself did not appear to mind. British support suited him. It suited his brother too. Abdullah, the sharif of Mecca's favorite son, was also given a kingdom by the British. In 1922 the province of Palestine was split in two and Abdullah was made *amir* (prince or ruler) of the newly created Transjordan, which became the Hashemite Kingdom of Jordan in 1946.

Through the sharif's two sons, Britain secured their interests in the center of the Middle East. Abdullah remained in control of Jordan until his death in 1951. The country's current king, also called Abdullah, is his great-grandson. Faysal's family, however, did not fare so well. Faysal remained on the throne until his death in 1933, when he was succeeded by his son, Ghazi. But in 1958, Ghazi's son, another Faysal, was overthrown and killed in a military coup that brought the *Baath* Party (and eventually Saddam Hussein) to power.

As for the sharif, he remained a king without a kingdom. He lost the battle for Arabia to the Saudi family who unified their various domains into the Kingdom of Saudi Arabia in 1932—making the country the first in history to be named after the family who founded it. The discovery of oil would, in time, make that family one of the richest in the world.

2

The regional repercussions of the Anglo-French carve-up of Greater Syria show how complicated the process of nation-building could become when the main players made conflicting promises to each other and to the other parties involved. An even more complicated example of this kind of diplomatic doublespeak happened over the Ottoman province of Palestine or, as it came to be known, The Twice Promised Land.

Both Britain and France wanted it. Sykes and Picot could not come up with an answer, so they shelved it. The ink was barely dry on their arrangement when Paris made a backdoor deal with the Russians to secure French control over the Christian Holy Land.[5]

London's diplomats had also been trying to woo the Russians. In November 1917, Britain issued the Balfour Declaration, which outlined London's view on the future of Palestine. Britain mistakenly assumed Russian Jews wielded great, if unseen, influence in Petrograd and London wanted to show support for Zionism in the hope of keeping Russia in the war. [6] The Balfour Declaration appeared in *The Times* on November 9, just a day after the Russia's Provisional Government fell.[7] The new revolutionary rulers of Russia paid no heed to Balfour and proceeded with their plans to leave the war.[8]

For some in the British elite, there was more to the Balfour Declaration than the power politics of the war. The British Prime Minister, David Lloyd George, had been sympathetic to the Zionist cause for the best part of 20 years—as a lawyer, he was the British representative of Theodor Herzl's Zionist movement—and was personally acquainted with Dr. Chaim Weizmann, President of the British Zionist Federation. (Weizmann was a chemist who discovered an alternative method of producing acetone, a key component in explosives. He gave his work away free to the British government to help the war effort. He would later become Israel's first president.)[9]

Religion also played a role in attracting support for Zionism among the British political elite. In an age when people grew up reading the Bible (in many homes, it was the only book), the prospect of a Jewish home in the Holy Land appealed to many revivalist Protestants on a very deep level. They were not necessarily interested in supporting the rights of Jews per se, but they were interested in the Jewish Return to Zion because in that they saw fulfillment of the prophecies of the Last Days in the Book of Revelations. Only when the Jews were gathered in the Holy Land would the Messiah reappear. Decades later, the religious right in the United States would take the same view and make the same political conclusions.

The Balfour Declaration was named after British Foreign Secretary Lord Balfour. Now notorious as the document that made one of the most contradictory promises in the history of the Middle East, the Balfour Declaration promised British support for the establishment of a Jewish home in Palestine—as long as any such home did not impinge on the rights of the Christians and Muslims already living there.[10] Such a promise was clearly going to be impossible to implement. Worse, it satisfied no one. For Arabs, it went too far. For Zionists, it did not go far enough.

After Sèvres, the King-Crane Commission was set up to look into the problem of Palestine. Dr. Henry King was head of Oberlin College in Ohio, and Charles Crane was a trustee of Roberts College in Istanbul. Both men were politically well connected in Washington and were the personal appointees of US President Wilson. The two men traveled tirelessly round the region canvassing the views of people directly affected by the proposed changes in Palestine. But their efforts were to be in vain. Once again, Britain and France joined forces to make sure the report was left to gather dust on a shelf deep in bureaucratic oblivion.

With King-Crane out of the way, it fell to Britain, as the occupying power on the ground, to take control of the land of Christ's birth. London had, at last, got what it wanted.

3

The Treaty of Sèvres made the aspirations of Sykes-Picot a political reality.

Under the terms of the treaty, the new states—Lebanon and Syria, Iraq and Jordan—were to become independent and members of the newly formed League of Nations. In theory, it was the responsibility of the mandated powers (Britain for Iraq and Jordan; France for Lebanon and Syria) to prepare them for independence.

The reality was very different. Neither London nor Paris had any intention of ceding control of their proxy states. The French, in a contradictory blend of missionary zeal and revolutionary fervor, pursued a policy of direct rule in Lebanon and Syria. The British, in an equally contradictory blend of pragmatism and elitism, pursued a policy of indirect rule in Iraq and Jordan through the kings they had handpicked for the job.

The result was that the Treaty of Sèvres did not abolish the idea of empire in the Middle East. It entrenched it. In doing so, Sèvres raised more questions than it answered: questions that, over the course of the twentieth century and into the twenty-first, would become ever more urgently in need of answers.

11

The Poisoned Legacy and the War's Unanswered Questions

The Treaty of Sèvres created a whole new reality in the Middle East.

The people of the region were now citizens of nation-states. Their identity was based on their nationality, no longer their faith. Muslims were no longer the favored majority; Jews and Christians no longer the protected minority. In the new nation-states, all citizens were equal. All had the same rights and responsibilities before the law. Which raises the question: where did Islam fit into this new reality?

For the French, the answer was simple. It did not. Under French control, Lebanon and Syria were put on the path toward the secular model of the French state. The French Revolution separated Church and State—in theory, if not always in practice—and that same separation was now to take place in Lebanon and Syria. In the French worldview, religion belonged in the private realm, not the public arena. To them, the secular and the sacred did not mix.

The British also adopted a separation of Church and State, although their approach was more hands-off. The British had no interest in remaking Muslim society. Their primary concern was strategic: the maintenance of their empire. In the countries they controlled, the British ruled through kings and let these kings speak for Islam. The crowned heads of the new Middle East thus became symbols of the country's religious identity, while, behind the scenes, the British were the ones really in control.

In the Sèvres states of the new Middle East, Islam no longer touched upon every aspect of a believer's life. In the French-sponsored states, it was pushed to the margins of public life (it certainly had no place in politics). And in the British ones, it became a useful tool to legitimize the British-backed ruling families.

The relegation of religion to the background of public and political life was good news for the religious minorities in the region. They were now on an equal footing with everyone else. But it left many Muslims with an acute sense of dislocation. The ground had quite literally shifted beneath them. With the Ottoman Empire carved up, the caliphate was consigned to memory. For centuries, it had signified the unity of the Muslim community and provided a powerful link to the earliest days of the Islamic community and to the Prophet's first successors. That was now over and there was nothing to replace it.

The First World War left the Arab Muslim world defeated and dismembered. It was a searing blow and many found it hard to come to terms with the new reality. They needed an outlet to express their sense of brotherhood as Muslims; something to show that, for them, Islam is more than a religion; it is a way of life.

The British and French were oblivious to this sense of dislocation. They were also oblivious to the potential consequences of it. Namely that European attempts to de-Islamize the public-political arena were leaving a vacuum that would achieve the exact opposite of what London and Paris wanted. The French policy of secularization and the British policy of promoting puppet kings to speak for Islam would, over time, encourage many Muslims to rediscover Islam in a new, politicized form. Because, for a large number of Muslims, the sacred and the secular *did* mix.

None of this was relevant to Britain and France. For London and Paris, the new Middle East was an opportunity to entrench their interests and achieve their strategic objectives. Both kept substantial deployments of troops in the region. Both blocked attempts to open up the political process to anyone who might challenge their interests. And both remained absolutely committed to maintaining the order they created. From now on, the watchword was stability.

As a result, the Middle East became less of a region, more of a sphere of interest. For the Great Powers of the West, the new status quo had to be upheld at all costs—because it was *their* status quo. Which meant the new system became equal in its inequality. Instead of abolishing the second-class status of non-Muslims and making all citizens equal, *everyone* now came second to European interests. Exactly how tenable this situation was over the long term was open to question. But, again, the British and French seemed to have no answer, no strategy, and no real grasp of what was going on. They seemed to believe they could indefinitely stand, King Canute-like, against the wishes of local people and fend off calls for independence.

The League of Nations assigned the Sèvres states to London and Paris on the grounds that they would prepare them for independence. There were people in the Middle East, Muslims as well as members of other faiths, who initially welcomed British and French involvement in nation-building, seeing it as an opportunity to develop business links, secure investment, and arrange technology transfers. But they welcomed the Europeans on the understanding they would be true to their word and leave when the job was done.

British and French actions throughout the 1920s and 1930s suggested otherwise. The British, for example, said of Iraq after the "election" of Faysal as king that the country "was to be administered according to the wishes of the inhabitants of the country *insofar as they coincided with strict British... control.*"[1] This was almost an exact echo of the words Lord Cromer used when he ruled Egypt in the nineteenth century. His spirit was clearly alive and well because nothing had changed in the new century. The French took a similar view. Professor David Fromkin in his magisterial work on the creation of the modern Middle East, *A Peace to End All Peace*, shows how the French paid no attention to their obligation to the League of Nations to set Syria and Lebanon on the path to self-governance. Quite the opposite: Paris viewed the commitment as "window-dressing, and approached Syria and Lebanon in an annexationist spirit."[2]

As the years passed, the British and French dug deeper into their new territories and responded to any political opposition to their rule by criminalizing it as a security threat. Given the asymmetric balance of power between the rulers and ruled, there was little local people could do about it. In the end, it would take another world war to make the British and French go.

All of this left a legacy. It was during this era that many people first experienced the contradictions between what the West says and what it does. During the interwar years, the Great Powers repeatedly demonstrated a tendency in the Middle East to say one thing and do another. If, nowadays, there is a barrier of mistrust between East and West, much of it goes back to what went on during this period.

This mistrust was further fueled by the nature of state creation in the Middle East. It lacked legitimacy from the start. And this left a huge question mark hanging over the Anglo-French Middle East: just how viable were the states created by the Treaty of Sèvres in the long term? Iraq, Syria, and Lebanon were not ethnically united. Such states are hard, if not impossible, to govern. In the absence of a shared sense of nationhood upon which to build the new nation, politics coalesce around issues of identity. Politics based on identity distort the political arena and turn it into a sectarian fight for survival. When different groups compete for state resources under these circumstances, victory for one group is seen as defeat for another. Elections, if they are held at all, turn into little more than mini-censuses or sectarian headcounts. People from one community simply do not vote for representatives from another. Even if you passionately disagree with what "your" group is doing, it is not possible to vote against them. To do so would be a step too far, seen as selling out or, worse, as betrayal.

Identity politics are the most dangerous form of us-and-them politics. States where they are the norm are like tinderboxes waiting to explode. All they need is a spark. And what nation-states of this kind have in common, whether they are in the Middle East or in Europe, is how they were created. In almost all cases, they were put together by outsiders with no regard to their internal fault lines. In some cases, as with the British in Iraq or the French in Syria, those fault lines were deliberately manipulated to make a policy of divide-and-rule easier.

In the short term, such a strategy might work. But in the long run, it cannot. Communal tension is always too close to the surface. And the longer it festers, the more dangerous the eventual explosion will be. This kind of nation-building is not the road to consensus politics, good governance, or long-term stability. It is the road to civil war.

Looking at the Middle East a century on from Sykes-Picot, the consequences of the lines they drew on the map are painfully clear. The internal contradictions of these states are pulling them apart before our eyes. The current crisis facing Iraq, Syria, and Lebanon is existential. When the dust eventually settles and the wars eventually end, these states will no longer exist in their present form. And such is the severity of this crisis that Jordan may not prove immune and may yet be sucked into the quagmire too. Yet all of this was avoidable. The Arab provinces of the Ottoman Empire had very strong regional and tribal identities. In the long run, those regional and tribal loyalties would have provided a better basis for the boundaries of the new nation-states of the Middle East than the imperial ambitions of London or Paris. And it would have been a better idea to leave it to the citizens of these new states to work out what role religion should have in the public space for themselves rather than create countries with sectarianism at their core.

In the wake of the First World War, the Middle East was not the only part of the world to suffer from lines drawn in the wrong places on the map. The Treaty of Versailles did for Europe what the Treaty of Sèvres would do for the Middle East. US President Woodrow Wilson's Fourteen Points supporting the principle of self-determination inspired people across Europe to seize the moment and claim their independence. Representatives of the Czechs, the Poles, and others turned up at the Paris peace conferences to lobby for their right to national self-determination.

The fact that many of them had fought alongside the Allies during the war strengthened their position.

The main difference between the new Europe and the new Middle East, however, was that the Allies had no intention of running the new nation-states of Europe. You might think that would have made the process of nation-building in Europe more straightforward than it was in the Middle East. But it did not. Here too, the Great Powers made a mess of it. Across Europe, new nations emerged from the dismembered Habsburg and Hohenzollern Empires. Czechoslovakia, Hungary, Poland appeared on the map as newly independent countries. Romania doubled in size. The German city of Danzig became a Free City. Serbia and Montenegro merged with a huge chunk of the former Austro-Hungarian Empire to become the Kingdom of the Serbs, Croats, and Slovenes. Imperial Austria became a rump state, a shadow of its Habsburg glory. Elsewhere, Estonia, Latvia, Lithuania, and Finland emerged as new nations from the remains of the Romanov Empire.

And as happened with the new nations of the Middle East, these new European nations had borders that did not correspond with their histories or their regional identities. Large populations of Germans found themselves living beyond German or Austrian borders. The newly created nations of Poland and Czechoslovakia had large populations of ethnic Germans—a fact that would have devastating consequences for both countries, for the rest of the continent, and for the rest of the world less than 20 years later when Adolf Hitler sent his storm troops in to reclaim them for the German Fatherland. It would take another world war followed by a very long Cold War followed by a catastrophic civil war in the Balkans before the map of Europe would more accurately reflect the wishes of the people who lived on the continent.

The cost of those wars is beyond measure. New words and new phrases came into the language—Holocaust, Final Solution, ethnic cleansing, genocide, Weapons of Mass Destruction, Mutually Assured Destruction—to describe entirely new horrors. The history of Europe in the twentieth century is a stark lesson in what can go wrong when lines are drawn on the wrong part of the map and when politics fails (or is denied the chance) to offer an answer. It also shows how easily demagogues and dictators can manipulate the genuine grievances of the situation to push their own cynical advantage. What is happening now in the Middle East is a similar process: lines in the wrong place on the map and the failure of politics have led to a series of wars that are redrawing the map with the aim of creating a new political order.

One part of the Ottoman world that did manage to find a way through the Paris peace conferences was the future Turkish Republic. Under the leadership of one of their greatest soldiers, Mustapha Kemal, the Turks fought their way to independence. The Turkish Republic was recognized at the Treaty of Lausanne in 1923.

Other people were not so lucky. The Treaty of Sèvres promised autonomy for Armenia. The Armenians suffered unimaginable losses in the massacres of 1915–6 when it is said that as many as one-and-a-half million of their people were killed by the Ottomans. (These figures are accepted in the West but are seriously questioned by Turkey.) After the war, Armenia declared independence in 1918, but that independence was short-lived. The new country was swallowed up by Bolshevik Russia in 1920 and did not achieve independence again until 1990.

The Treaty of Sèvres also promised autonomy to the Kurds. Unlike the Armenians, the Kurds did not get their state after the war. And they still have not.

The Treaty of Sèvres left two other groups of people without a country. And the story of those two peoples—and their struggle over the same piece of land—has proven to be one of the Middle East's most dangerous fault lines and one of its most intractable problems. It was the question Sykes and Picot could not answer and the question that, today, still eludes an answer.

And the failure to answer that question has turned the conflict over the land that is holy to Jew, Christian, and Muslim into an all-or-nothing battle for survival with repercussions far beyond the Middle East.

Part III

All or Nothing: Why All Roads Lead to Jerusalem

12

Where to Begin?

In a region beset by wars, one war in the Middle East has lasted longer than any other: the war between the Israelis and the Palestinians. But when it comes to setting this long-running conflict in its historical context, where should you begin?

In 1967 when Israel won the Six-Day War and, later, claimed Jerusalem as the country's capital?

In 1948 when the State of Israel was created after the British left?

In 1917 when Britain took Palestine from the Ottomans and ended nearly 1,300 years of Islamic rule?

Or do you begin further back?

In 1516 when the Ottomans won Palestine from its Egyptian rulers?

In 1187 when the legendary Saladin defeated the Crusaders and brought Jerusalem back into the Islamic fold?

In 1099 when the Crusaders seized Jerusalem from its Muslim rulers and slaughtered the city's Jewish and Muslim inhabitants?

Or do you begin even further back?

In 638 when Muslim armies won Jerusalem from the Byzantines?

In 70 when the Romans, led by Titus, destroyed Herod's Temple in Jerusalem and exiled the Jews from their Holiest City?

Or do you go right back to 586 BC when Nebuchadnezzar invaded Jerusalem, destroyed the Temple, the Holy City, and sent the Jews into exile in Babylon?

Where you begin is important for a number of reasons, not least because your choice of starting point can be interpreted as endorsing one side's position over the other. The conflict between the Israelis and the Palestinians is one of the most contentious issues in the world today. It is so contentious that it has become almost impossible to write about it without offending someone or without your comments being misinterpreted. Now that social media has made it so effortlessly easy to heap anonymous abuse on anyone who endorses one view over another; some historians and writers choose to save themselves the hassle and ignore the subject altogether. As for teaching the subject, that in itself has become so much of a challenge, *how* the subject is taught has become an object of study.

All of this matters because this conflict is no longer about land and land alone. It is a battle of narratives between two competing versions of history, between two competing legitimacies. Under these circumstances, history becomes a battleground, a frontline, an alternative form of propaganda, where the pen can indeed be mightier than the sword.

This presents a serious challenge for historians who, by training, are supposed to be neutral and whose allegiance is supposed to be to the facts and the accurate and fair representation of them. But if the facts themselves are under dispute, the accurate and fair representation of anything is no easy matter. The names you use become overloaded with significance. The same goes for the dates you choose to frame your narrative. In this minefield, whatever you say and however you say it will be interpreted by someone, somewhere, as taking a side.

Take, for example, events in 1948. Israelis refer to the war that led to the foundation of the State of Israel as the War of Independence. Palestinians call it the Catastrophe (*al-Nakba* in Arabic). There is not much common ground between the two.

So, if you are a historian, which term do you use? If you call it the War of Independence, Palestinians and their supporters think you have taken Israel's side. And if you call it the Catastrophe, Israelis and their supporters see it as a negative judgment on Israel's right to exist.

Another example comes from another war: the Arab-Israeli War in 1973. It happened during the Jewish High Holiday of Yom Kippur, so in Israel it is called the Yom Kippur War. In this particular year, Yom Kippur happened to fall at the same time as the Muslim Holy Month of Ramadan (the Islamic calendar is lunar and is 11 days shorter than the calendar used in the West), so in the Arab world, the war is called the Ramadan War.

Because the use of either term may be seen as endorsing one version of events over the other (even if that is not the intention), historians tend to use the more neutral term "October War." But even an attempt to be neutral will not stop accusations of bias. In this battle of competing legitimacies, where one man's terrorist is another man's freedom fighter, where one man's defense force is another man's army of occupation, where one people's triumph is another people's tragedy, the refusal to wholeheartedly endorse one point of view over another can still be seen as closet support for the "other" side.

This is more than a debate over semantics. For Israelis and Palestinians alike, the stakes could not be higher. For them, it is a matter of life and death. The day-to-day realities of their lives are the headlines the rest of the world can switch off if the conflict becomes too much to bear. Israelis and Palestinians do not have that luxury. So, if an outside observer of the conflict appears to privilege one side over the other, it provokes a reaction because it looks as if one side's suffering is more important than the other, as if some lives matter more than others.

In a conflict that has spread far, far beyond conventional warfare, where the battle lines are so blurred that no one is safe and where, in 2014, people as uninvolved in armed combat as teenagers hiking on a summer day, young boys playing on the beach, a teenager on his way to early morning prayer at the mosque, commuters waiting for a train, children sleeping in their beds, and men praying in a synagogue—all became fatalities of this conflict; how do you begin to tell this story in a way that adequately reflects the complex histories of Israeli *and* Palestinian? Because without that, there is no chance of understanding what is really going on in this conflict or what might happen in future. And without that, you cannot begin to understand the modern Middle East.

Perhaps history can offer an answer.

Over a thousand years ago, one of the greatest historians who ever lived, a man named Abu Jafar Muhammad bin Jarir al-Tabari (838–932), produced a monumental work called *The History of Prophets and Kings*. The English translation runs to 38 volumes. Al-Tabari was a meticulous historian so devoted to his craft that he once sold the sleeves of his shirt to buy bread so he could keep working.[1] The scope of his *History* is proof of that devotion. It stretches from creation right up to the year 915 and is widely regarded as the most universal history of the Islamic world. Its influence is such that it became the model for subsequent histories of Islam.

Al-Tabari is little known outside the Arab Islamic world, yet his contribution to history is enormous. More than that, he wrote with a freshness that gives immediacy to the events he describes. Everything from the fate of the Prophet's nail clippings to a caliph's inconsolable grief over the death of his favorite slave girl, no detail is overlooked or omitted in his *History*.[2] His account of the harrowing martyrdom of the Prophet's grandson al-Husayn—the event reenacted every year by Shi'is—is so poignant; it is hard not to be moved by it.

From a modern standpoint, what is particularly interesting about al-Tabari is *how* he chose to tell history. He checked his sources and he cited those sources. But if his sources disagreed; if, for example, he unearthed several different versions of the same event, al-Tabari did not ditch one version in preference for another. Nor did he try to mold them into one comprehensive narrative. He simply gave all sides of the story and let the reader decide. Often finishing the account with a philosophical "Allah knows best."

So, in what follows, we will take the Tabari route. There will be no attempt to create an overarching narrative of the Israeli–Palestinian conflict. No attempt to take sides. No attempt to offer easy answers. The history of this conflict is too complicated for that. Instead, both sides of the story are presented, starting with the Israelis. This is not to give the Israelis the first word—or, for that matter, to give the Palestinians the last word—but for the very simple reason that "I" comes before "P" in the English alphabet. And since it is so difficult to find a noncontentious date to start with, we will start with a place—one that is revered and respected by Jew, Christian, and Muslim alike: the Holy City of Jerusalem.

13

Jerusalem: The Temple Mount

1

In the Old City of Jerusalem is the Temple Mount.

Known as *Har ha-Bayit* in Hebrew, this is the beating heart of Jewish religious life. Here is the home of the Ark of the Covenant. Here is the Temple of Solomon. Here is the Holy of Holies: the place so sacred no human foot may touch it because it is the earthly home of God.

Nearly two thousand years ago, in the year 70, the Temple built on this sacred spot by Herod was destroyed by a Roman army led by the emperor's son, Titus. All that was left was the Western (or Wailing) Wall. Following the destruction of the Temple, slaughter or slavery was the fate of nearly all Jerusalem's Jews. Thousands were killed. A small group resisted and staged a suicidal, and now legendary, last stand at the fortress of Masada in the desert outside the city. It took the Romans three years to bring the siege of Masada to an end, and, when they did, they also ended Jewish rebellions against their rule for the time being. Elsewhere in the Roman-ruled province of Judaea, life went on pretty much as normal for most Jews.[1]

Sixty years later, in the 130s, Jewish resistance to Rome reemerged in the form of Simon bar Kochba, otherwise known as the Son of the Star. He was incensed by Emperor Hadrian's decision to flatten what was left of Jerusalem and build a Roman city on the ruins named Aelia Capitolina, complete with a temple to the empire's very own god Jupiter.[2]

Simon bar Kochba launched a ruthless but ultimately doomed rebellion. Fighting against the greatest empire on earth, the odds were stacked against him. In victory, Hadrian was merciless. He upheld his recently imposed ban on circumcision, the sacred ritual that proved Jewish men's obedience to their God. By doing so, Hadrian threatened the future of the Jewish community.

Jerusalem itself effectively ceased to exist. As did Jewish Judaea. And this is where the name "Palestine" enters the story. Hadrian renamed Judaea "Palaestina." It was a name deliberately chosen to wound, as it derived from the name of the Jews' Biblical enemies, the Philistines.[3] The Jewish exile from Jerusalem now began in earnest. It became a capital offence for Jews to go anywhere near their Holy City.

It was not the first time the Jewish Temple had been destroyed. The Babylonians had done the same thing when they invaded the Kingdom of Judah seven centuries earlier. But within five decades, the Jews had recovered, rebuilt, and reclaimed power. Nor was it the first time Jews had been banned from Jerusalem. The Babylonian exile following the destruction of the Temple must have seemed just as catastrophic to the people who endured it. But in exile, the Jews regrouped and recovered and, eventually, thrived. Babylon became an important center of Jewish life and learning—it even produced its own Talmud; and right up to the middle of the twentieth century, Baghdad was home to a large and prosperous Jewish community.

There was also the fact that not every Jew lived in Jerusalem or chose to make the Holy City the physical focus of his or her daily life. There were substantial Jewish communities throughout the Roman Empire, including a large one in Alexandria in Egypt, and the lives of these Jews were largely unaffected by events in Jerusalem.

For Jews, however, Jerusalem is more than a place. It is almost an article of faith.[4] The city is their House of God and the symbol of their covenant with the Almighty. Losing access to the city is, therefore, like losing a link with God. To be deprived of the possibility of praying there was a devastating blow for Jews regardless of whether or not they lived in the city.

Such an intense spiritual connection to one place does not exist to the same degree in Christianity. Christians, consequently, do not have quite the same sense of sacred geography. Jesus is their Jerusalem, their link to God, their spiritual center of gravity. Muslims, by contrast, know all about sacred geography. The meaning that Mecca has for Muslims is the same that Jerusalem has for Jews. And Muslims, as well as revering Mecca, also share the Jewish reverence for Jerusalem: before they turned to Mecca in prayer, Muslims turned to Jerusalem. The city was the original *qibla*, the direction of prayer, in the early days of Islam. These cities, therefore, do not just exist on the map. They exist within the hearts and minds of the faithful. And this invests them with enormous power, both religious and political. This is because the best way—sometimes the *only* way—to fulfill your sacred covenant with God by praying in the Holy City sanctified by His presence is to make sure you control it.

For Jews, then, *any* exile from Jerusalem was hard to bear.

What, however, would make *this* exile so uniquely devastating and make its consequences reverberate through the centuries up to the present day was what happened in a small town in Asia Minor named Nicaea two centuries after the Son of the Star's ill-fated rebellion. In Nicaea, in 325, Emperor Constantine decided to rewrite history and make the Jews responsible for Christ's death.[5]

2

Constantine's Road-to-Damascus moment is the stuff of legend.

In 312, the future ruler of the pagan Roman Empire saw the sign of the cross in the sky the night before he was to go into battle. Alongside the cross were the words "By this sign you will conquer." Constantine took heed and the rest is history. The next day, he won the Battle of Milvian Bridge, and the Roman Empire would never be the same again. Under Constantine, Christ was Rome's redeemer. (But Constantine himself, wily operator that he was, hedged his bets right to the very end and left it until he was on his deathbed in 337 to seal the deal with his God and become a Christian.)

Under Constantine's rule, Christianity was no longer a persecuted cult. The followers of Jesus were no longer mocked and thrown to the lions for the amusement of the citizens of Rome. Under Constantine, Christianity enjoyed imperial patronage. But at the time of his epiphany, the faith was far from united. A ferocious debate was waging over the nature of Christ. Was he divine or was he human? Was he both? If so, how could a man be God? How could the Son also be the Father?

One school of thought, known as Arianism after Bishop Arius of Alexandria, believed the Father and the Son were not the same.[6] Others disagreed and believed Jesus was coeternal with God. The debate was intense and threatened to pull the church apart. Constantine convened a Council of Bishops at Nicaea in 325 to decide the matter.

At the Council, the bishops ruled against Arius and issued a statement of belief (a creed). Known as the Nicene Creed, it put the Father, the Son, and the Holy Spirit on an equal footing. Jesus was now God. Amended slightly in 381, the Creed became a key part of the liturgy during the Middle Ages and is still recited in services today. As for Arius, he came to an unusual end. While walking through Constantinople, his insides—bowels, intestines, liver, the lot—suddenly fell out of him. To say his opponents were beside themselves with glee at the horrible nature of his death would be an understatement. They saw it as divine judgment.

What, you might well be wondering, has any of this got to do with the Jews? In theory: absolutely nothing. But in reality, the Nicene Creed changed everything. Now that Constantine had endorsed Christianity and now that Jesus was God, the crucifixion was recast in a whole new light and the Jews became the villains of the piece. They were now "Christ-killers." Barnet Litvinoff explains the effect the Creed had in his seminal study of anti-Semitism, *The Burning Bush: Antisemitism and World History*: "The Nicene Creed thus laid the crime of deicide upon the Jews, a stigma that would survive the current of centuries."[7]

In many ways, the groundwork for blaming Jews for Christ's death had actually been done long before Nicaea. According to award-winning historian Dairmaid MacCulloch, an expert on the history of Christianity, the early Christians had no wish to find themselves on the wrong side of Roman imperial power. Yet the Romans had killed their savior. How were they to square that circle? If the Romans could not be held responsible for Christ's death, then who could?

Early Christians found their answer by foisting "the blame on to the Jewish authorities."[8] In his bestselling *A History of Christianity*, Professor MacCulloch refers to two Gospel accounts of the crucifixion. In one, the Gospel of John has the Jews actively seeking the death penalty for Jesus.[9] The Gospel of Matthew has them go even further. They appear to know perfectly well what they are doing—they seem almost to relish it—and they also appear to know the repercussions their actions will have for future generations of their faith.[10] These accounts clearly set the Jews up as the fall guys for Christ's crucifixion. By contrast, Pontius Pilate, the representative of the most powerful empire on the planet and a man with legions at his disposal, appears powerless in the face of the baying Jewish mob and is therefore absolved of all blame.

All of this had serious long-term consequences. Constantine used Christianity to buttress his political power, and after Nicaea the Jews found themselves on the wrong side of that power. Laws against Jews had been relaxed since the days of Hadrian and a small number were now allowed to live in Jerusalem. Not any longer. Constantine reintroduced the discriminatory laws. And like Hadrian two centuries earlier, Constantine knew where to hit the Jews where it would hurt the most: Jerusalem. The Roman city of Aelia Capitolina underwent another transformation. Jupiter was cast aside for Jesus. The New Jerusalem was the City of Christ.[11]

Nicaea brought two different processes together and molded them into one narrative. The first was the decision by early Christians to align with Rome, as demonstrated by the Gospel accounts of the Crucifixion. The second was Rome's subsequent alignment with Christianity, as demonstrated by Constantine's conversion. Taken together, these meant Church and State were now one.

Nicaea then gave that Church and State a powerful legitimizing device: their own God. And it placed the blame for the earthly death of that God squarely on the shoulders of one community. All of which meant that as Christianity spread across the Roman Empire, Jews were sometimes tolerated, sometimes not; sometimes persecuted, sometimes not. But there was always one constant: the Jew was always vulnerable, always the outsider, always carrying the burden of Christ's crucifixion.

The post-Nicene narrative of the Jews as Christ-killers would frame Judaeo-Christian relations for the next 17 centuries. In fact, it did much more than that. It poisoned them. Anyone wishing to discriminate against Jews could, with a considerable degree of justification, claim scriptural sanction for doing so. Centuries later, in the 1090s, when the Crusaders set off from France at the Pope's behest to free Christ's city from the "infidel" Muslim, their first victims were the Jews they met along the way. Right across Europe, from Speyer to Prague via Worms and Mainz, the armies of the cross slaughtered Jews in their thousands. And they did not stop when they reached Jerusalem. The Crusader conquest of the Holy City was marked by a massacre of its Jewish and Muslim inhabitants. Jews were burnt alive as they sought refuge in their synagogue. This was not Christianity's finest hour.

Worse was to come. Scripturally sanctioned persecution of Jews became a recurring theme of the Middle Ages in the Christian West. Wherever religious righteousness and political power came together, it was almost a certainty that Jews would bear the brunt of it.

When Ferdinand and Isabella completed the Reconquista of Spain with the conquest of Muslim Granada in 1492 and united the country under Catholic control, it was not only the defeated Muslims who suffered, the Jews did too. Their status as the perennial outsider left them defenseless against a state power determined to make them suffer for a crime-cum-sin they had never committed. The Dominican Tomás de Torquemada had occupied the office of Grand Inquisitor since 1483 and he set about making the lives of Jews hell. And he did so with the full backing of the church, the state, and the papacy. Successive popes not only endorsed the Inquisition, they encouraged it. Pope Innocent VIII, for example, sought to deny Jews safe haven anywhere in the Christian world. According to him, Christian rulers across the continent had a duty to return to Spain any Jews fleeing the Inquisition who entered their jurisdiction—even though any such return meant certain death.[12]

For Jews, facing death at the stake, exile was the least worst option. The Middle Ages, therefore, saw massive shifts in population as the long-established Sephardi Jewish community of Iberia moved, on pain of death, from Spain in 1492 and from Portugal in 1496 to the less hostile environments of the Netherlands, Morocco, or the Turkish heartlands of the Ottoman Empire. In the long run, those who wound up in Morocco and Istanbul did better. In the Islamic world, where Jews were protected under Muslim law, their descendants would be spared the fate of Europe's Jews in the twentieth century.

In Europe, even when the Middle Ages ended, the persecution went on. The Inquisition itself did not end until 1834. But prejudice and persecution were not confined to Spain. In the self-styled New Rome of the New Caesars—the Russian Empire of the Romanovs—Jews again found themselves cast in the role of outsiders in a Christian kingdom. Their outsider status was confirmed by banishment to the Pale of Settlement. But life in the Pale and the social and economic restrictions that went with it were not the worst of the Jews' problems. The pogroms of the 1880s, followed by those in the first decade of the 1900s, left thousands dead. From Kiev to Kishinev, no Jew was safe from the rampaging mob.

The fact that some of these pogroms happened at Easter, the festival commemorating the crucifixion, showed how enduring the link between the Gospel interpretations of that event and state-sponsored anti-Semitism had become. For Jewish communities in this part of Europe, Easter was the most dreaded time of year because of the religiously inspired anger it could unleash.[13]

The Jewish High Holiday of Pesach (Passover), which sometimes fell at the same time as Easter, was another occasion that could give rise to that same form of religiously inspired anger. The idea of a ritual murder or blood sacrifice had somehow seeped into the European cultural Zeitgeist, and Jews were periodically accused of murdering a Christian (usually a child) to use the blood to make the unleavened bread eaten during the Passover meal or *seder*.

No matter how unlikely these accusations turned out to be (in some cases the child who was said to have disappeared did not even exist, as happened near Toledo in Spain in 1488), they nevertheless led to collective punishment of the local Jewish community, many of whom would be burned at the stake for a crime that no one could prove had actually been committed.[14] Accusations of ritual murder persisted into the early twentieth century.

Over the years, the idea of the Jew as an outsider in Christian Europe became such a powerful cultural undercurrent in society that it persisted even when the link between Church and State had officially been broken. Even free-thinking France, where Jews had been granted equality in 1791, was not immune to it.[15] Almost a century after the Revolution, a court case split fin-de-siècle Paris in two and showed the power that religiously inspired ideas still wielded in the secular French Republic.

In 1894, Captain Alfred Dreyfus, a Jew from a wealthy family in Alsace (then under German control after Germany's victory in the war of 1870–1), was accused and convicted of treason for selling state secrets to Germany and Italy even though German and Italian Intelligence said they had never heard of him. Stripped of his rank and his freedom, Dreyfus was sentenced to life on the penal colony of Devil's Island.

The case raised all sorts of questions about the place of Jews in French society. It also profoundly influenced the journalist Theodor Herzl, who was covering the trial, in his move toward Zionism.[16] Supporters of Dreyfus claimed (rightly, as it turned out) that he was a scapegoat. Opponents claimed the case showed Jews could not be trusted as Frenchmen because their loyalties lay elsewhere. It took 12 years for Dreyfus to clear his name. And to do it, he had to take on the combined forces of the French military, the Catholic Church, and large sections of public opinion. Decades later, in the 1930s, anti-Semitism still lurked not too far beneath the surface of the French establishment. When Léon Blum became prime minister in 1936, he was openly taunted in the press for being Jewish.[17]

Against the backdrop of this persecution, there was also progress. Jews flourished in the liberal atmosphere and religious tolerance of the Netherlands. Prussia's Jews had enjoyed citizenship since 1812. Postunification, German Jews were the most assimilated Jewish community on the continent. And in the United Kingdom, Benjamin Disraeli, a baptized Jew who never forgot his Sephardi origins, held the highest office in the land not once but twice. Disraeli was Conservative prime minister in 1868 and, again, from 1874 to 1880.

But in spite of this progress, persecution persisted. And in spite of all the horrors the Jews had endured in the past—whether at the hands of the Caesars or the tsars, the Crusaders or the inquisitors, the mobs or the militias—worse was to come. Nothing could have prepared Europe's Jewish community for the horror they would face in the twentieth century at the hands of one of the most civilized countries in the world.

3

Award-winning author Aharon Appelfeld was eight years old when he was sent to a concentration camp by the Nazis.

He escaped and spent three years hiding in the Ukrainian country-side before joining the Russian army at the age of 11. He later became an Israeli. In his novel *The Age of Wonders* he tells the story of Bruno, a young Jewish boy growing up in 1930s' Austria, as the world around him slowly but systematically collapses. One of the reasons the story is so compelling is that the reader knows only too well the awful fate awaiting Bruno and his family and desperately wants them to avoid it. Part One of *The Age of Wonders* ends with the ominous words, "By the next day we were on the cattle train hurtling south."[18]

Then Appelfeld shows his genius and his mastery of the craft of storytelling. On the horrors of the Holocaust, he is silent. After Part One ends, you turn the page and Part Two begins: "At the end of April Bruno returned to the town of his birth."[19] It is spring, the season of rebirth and renewal, many years later "when everything was over" and Bruno has come back alive.[20] He, like the Jewish people, has faced annihilation and he has survived.

Appelfeld's silence on the *Shoah*, as it is called in Hebrew, can be read on many levels. A searing indictment on events and those who made them happen. An echo of the silence of those who could have stopped them but did not. A refusal to trivialize human suffering by turning it into literary voyeurism. Or it may be that Aharon Appelfeld simply did not think the words existed to describe what he went through.

Whatever Appelfeld's motivation, *The Age of Wonders* is one of the most powerful, poignant, and personal accounts of the Holocaust. And it is precisely because of that carefully calibrated silence that sits right at the heart of the book.

Appelfeld recognized that the nature of the Holocaust robs words of their power. Nothing on this scale had happened before. The nearest analogy was the massacre of the Armenians in 1915–6 by the Ottomans when, according to Armenian accounts, one-and-a-half million people were killed. Four times as many Jews were killed in the Nazi extermination camps. To put the scale of these fatalities in context: throughout 2014, events were held across Europe to commemorate the beginning of the First World War. The death toll from the trenches was staggering, and in the coverage of the commemorations, you could see that the enormity of these losses had lost none of its power to shock. The *Blood Swept Lands and Seas of Red* installation at the Tower of London where each poppy marked a British loss became a must-see destination—the modern equivalent of a pilgrimage site. The muted, yet emotional, nature of the public's response suggested the war was a wound that had not yet healed. In the First World War, the British lost nearly three-quarters of a million men. The combined total of Allied fatalities was five million, one hundred thousand men. In the Holocaust, the Jews lost six million people: nearly one million more people than the *combined* Allied fatalities in the First World War. Three-quarters of a million more people than the *entire* population of a country the size of Scotland. All of whom were civilians. All of whom were unarmed. All of whom were deliberately targeted for death. A quarter of whom were children.

How did it happen? Adolf Hitler became Chancellor of Germany on January 30, 1933. He had not won the position outright—his National Socialist Party had no overall majority—but his party enjoyed massive popular support. Since 1920, it had consistently won more votes than any other party.[21] The doors to power were opened for Hitler by Germany's aristocratic old guard who thought he could control the unsettled German masses and they could control him. Had any of them labored through the turgid, rambling prose of *Mein Kampf*, published nearly a decade earlier, they would have known exactly what kind of character they were dealing with. The day after becoming chancellor, Hitler dissolved parliament. Less than two months later, on March 21, 1933, he opened the Dachau concentration camp to "retrain" opponents.

As it began, so it continued. Day by day, the chip-chip-chipping away of individual rights and liberties in the name of the collective greater good, the German Fatherland, gathered pace. As Robert Gellately demonstrates in his ground-breaking book *Backing Hitler: Consent and Coercion in Nazi Germany*, not only was this creeping takeover of the state *not* a secret but sizeable parts of the population actively supported it.[22] Many Germans went along with Hitler's dictatorship because, as part of the collective, they were safe. They were not on the margins of society. They were not outsiders. So they were not targets.

For German Jews, it was a different story. For them, it began with a boycott and ended with the Final Solution. The initial reaction to the discrimination was disbelief. German Jews were patriotic and proud of their country and many had fought at the front in the First World War.[23] The officer who recommended Hitler for the Iron Cross, First Class, which Hitler was so proud of that he wore it every day for the rest of his life, was Jewish: Captain Hugo Guttman. (Captain Guttman left for Canada after Hitler came to power.)[24]

On Saturday, April 1, 1933, only days after Dachau was opened, the first boycott of Jewish businesses took place. A Jewish war veteran and store-owner named Edwin Landau decided to stage a personal show of defiance. He put on his war medals, kept his store open, and visited other Jewish businesses in the local area as a public gesture of solidarity with their owners. But even though Landau received support from his regular customers, he was farsighted enough to read events for what they were. He was under no illusions about what would happen next. As a Jew, he knew he had no future in Hitler's Fatherland.[25]

Less than a week later, on April 7, Hitler brought in the Civil Service Law, which banned Jewish professors from teaching in German universities. From the boycott in April to the burning of books on *Kristallnacht* in November, the first year of Hitler's chancellorship saw Jews pushed to the margins of society. Blamed for everything from Germany's defeat in the First World War, to Marxism, to the parlous state of German finances, to the age-old crime of killing Christ, German Jews witnessed the rolling back of rights that had taken centuries to win. And it all happened within a matter of months.

The Nuremberg Laws of 1935 sealed the process by depriving German Jews of their citizenship. From then on, Germany's Jews effectively lost control of their own lives. If you were a Jew, everything from where you worked and lived, to who you could marry, to whether you could own a business or a pet, even the name you called yourself and the food you ate (ginger and chocolate, for unspecified reasons, were among many foodstuffs forbidden to Jews)—every aspect of your life was now dictated by the state.

From delegitimization, it was a short step to dehumanization. And to the cattle train hurtling south.

4

One of the most startling aspects of the Holocaust is how much was known about what was going on and how little was done to stop it.

The smoke from Auschwitz could be seen as far away as the Russian front. Thanks to intelligence from escaped prisoners, its exact location was known by the Allies early in 1944. Much earlier than that, Europe's Jewish communities were inexplicably disappearing from public view, sometimes with the connivance of governments and local people. Latent anti-Semitism often helped the German forces carry out their work. Vichy France actively collaborated with the Nazi policy of deporting Jews.[26] Irène Némirovsky's bestselling novel, *Suite Française* (which became a major motion picture in 2015 starring Kristen Scott Thomas), was written against the backdrop of the German occupation of France but not published until nearly seven decades later. It shows how, even post-Dreyfus, there was still a sense in some quarters in France that Jews were not quite part of the *patrie*. They were still outsiders. In the novel, one of the French characters has the same emotional response to anti-Semitism as she does to patriotism.[27] Némirovsky herself would feel the full force of Nazi anti-Semitism. She was killed in Auschwitz in August 1942 just a month after being arrested by French police and deported. The author's young daughters, Denise and Elisabeth, spent the rest of the war in hiding, on the run from the French police who would have sent them to the same fate as their mother.

During this time, there were countless individual acts of heroism: the ones we know about, such as Sir Nicholas Winton's *Kindertransport* and Oskar Schindler's list, and ones we do not. But at a national level, with the exception of Denmark whose government refused to hand over Danish Jews to the occupying German army, there was not a great deal done to help Europe's Jewish community. The train lines were not bombed. Borders were not opened. Refugees were not welcomed. Conferences were convened to discuss the crisis—at Lake Evian in 1938 and in Bermuda in 1943—and still nothing was done. Although the fate of Europe's Jews is often cited as a reason justifying Allied involvement in the Second World War, that was not the case at the time. For the Allies, stretched to breaking point and battling on many fronts, saving Europe's Jews was not the priority. A rescue was launched late in the day for Hungary's Jews when the combined efforts of the Red Cross, the papacy, and Portugal, Spain, Sweden, and Switzerland (all neutral countries) saved tens of thousands from certain death in 1944. But for the rest of Europe's Jews, with nowhere to go and no one to save them, there was no such escape.

Watching these events unfold with increasing horror and desperation was the Jewish community in Palestine. According to them, there *was* somewhere for Europe's Jews to go: to Zion, their historical homeland, now the province of Palestine under British rule since 1917.

After the exile from Jerusalem in 70, Jews had continued to live in the renamed province of Palestine in the Roman era, mostly in the north and along the Mediterranean coast. They were still there after the Muslim takeover in the 630s. If anything, Islamic rule made their lives easier as they enjoyed state protection as People of the Book.

The numbers of Jewish migrants to Palestine increased dramatically during the 1880s, partly as a result of the pogroms in Russia and partly as a result of the growing idea of Jewish nationalism or Zionism. In 1882—the year of some of the worst pogroms in Russia—a bookish young Lithuanian named Eliezer Perlmann arrived in Palestine, promptly declared his old self dead, renamed himself Ben Yehuda, and set about resurrecting the Hebrew language. Almost single-handedly, Ben Yehuda gave the Jewish migrants what a new nation cannot function without: a common language. With a shared language, the Jewish migrants were no longer a random group of individuals speaking a Babel of languages. They were slowly becoming a community, a nation in waiting.[28] In recognition of his efforts to achieve this, one of the main streets in downtown Jerusalem now bears Ben Yehuda's name.

In the Balfour Declaration of 1917, Britain recognized the legitimacy of this community to a homeland in Palestine. Even though the British declaration did so in terms that were deliberately ambiguous, thousands of Jews who supported the idea of a homeland in Biblical Zion (as well as many who did not) took advantage of it and migrated to Palestine. The pace of this migration increased rapidly in the 1930s for obvious reasons. Between 1932 and 1938, nearly 200,000 Jews migrated to Palestine, many of them from Germany. This was more than the number of arrivals (190,000) during the 50 years from 1881 to 1931.[29] The fact that more migrants arrived in Palestine during the 1930s as during the previous 50 years shows how desperate Jews were to escape Europe.

Another 140,000 arrived in Palestine between 1938 and 1948.[30] Much of this migration was illegal as the British imposed tighter restrictions after the Arab Uprising of 1936–9. During the Uprising, Palestinian protests over the rising number of Jewish migrants put increasing pressure on British forces. Palestinians feared Jewish migration was creating facts on the ground that would change the character of their land and tip the population balance against them. Britain's inability to come up with a strategy that addressed the concerns of both parties revealed the contradictions inherent in the Balfour Declaration from the beginning.

For Jews, the timing of Britain's decision to curb migration to Palestine could not have been worse. At the very time Hitler was accelerating the systematic persecution of Jews toward the Final Solution, Britain closed their last remaining escape route. It was seen as a betrayal of the worst kind, condemning untold numbers to death, and it shaped the attitudes of many Zionists toward Britain for years to come.

Even when the war ended, the question of where Europe's Jews should go remained unanswered. After everything that had happened, many survivors had no wish to return to their former homes. In the upheaval and chaos after the war, many had no homes to return to. About a quarter of a million survivors of the Nazi death camps now found themselves in camps again, this time for Displaced Persons. Again, the Jewish community in Palestine called for them to be allowed to come and join them. Again, Britain refused citing the need not to alter the population balance between Palestine's Jewish community (the *Yishuv* in Hebrew) and the Arabs.

The British, however, had not taken into account how much the Jewish community had changed. The experience of the Holocaust had steeled something inside them. Even those who had not experienced it directly, for example in the United States, changed. Too many had lost too much. Too many had glaring gaps in their family trees. The effect of that change was immediate. Never again would Jews wait for other people to rescue them. From now on, they would rescue themselves.[31]

In the 1940s, militant Zionists took matters into their own hands and waged a campaign against the British Mandatory authorities in Palestine. The British saw the campaign as terrorism. These Zionists saw it as a liberation struggle. Two future prime ministers of Israel, Menachem Begin and Yitzhak Shamir, were involved in the campaign at the highest level: Begin in the Irgun and Shamir in the Stern Gang. Their groups were ruthless but effective. The Stern Gang assassinated British Colonial Secretary, Lord Moyne, in Cairo in November 1944. The Irgun blew up Jerusalem's iconic King David Hotel, home to the British administration, killing 91 people on July 22, 1946. The bombers got past the rigid British security by hiding the explosives in milk churns and placing them in the nightclub in the hotel's basement. The dead included Jews as well as Arabs and British.

For the men and women of the Irgun and the Stern Gang, the use of violence was justified as a means to a political end. They did not see themselves as terrorists. They saw themselves as fighting for their freedom against an army of occupation—the same argument that years later Izz al-Din al-Qassam, the armed wing of the Islamic Resistance Movement Hamas, would use against Israel.

The violence of the Irgun and the Stern Gang had the desired effect. Faced with a problem that defied solution and increasingly fed up with being caught in the crossfire, war-weary Britain gave up and handed the question of Palestine over to the newly formed United Nations. Britain then prepared to leave.

The UN established a Special Commission to come up with a solution. Made up of 11 members, the Commission recommended by a majority of four that Palestine should be split in two with Jerusalem as an international city. The seven states in favor of the two-state solution were Canada, Czechoslovakia, Guatemala, the Netherlands, Peru, Sweden, and Uruguay. India, Iran, and Yugoslavia favored a federal state. Australia abstained. The UN General Assembly accepted the majority decision and adopted it as a resolution on November 29, 1947.[32] Jews were jubilant. Their right to their own state had received international recognition. For them, there was no turning back.

In a museum in Tel Aviv on the night before the British Mandate was due to end, David Ben-Gurion declared the creation of the State of Israel. It was May 14, 1948. Within minutes, the world's two superpowers, the United States and the Soviet Union, recognized the new Israeli nation. For Jews, it was a moment to savor.

They did not have long to enjoy it. Egypt, Lebanon, Syria, Transjordan, and Iraq immediately declared war on the fledgling state. But the Jews, reborn as Israelis, were ready. They knew what was at stake. They knew they were fighting for more than their state. They were fighting for their survival. For them, the country they ultimately won in the war against the Arabs in 1948—and have had to defend in the many wars since—was more than a state. It was a sanctuary. Under the Law of Return, Jews everywhere have a right to residence in Israel. For them, this was the ultimate protection from persecution and the first and last line of defense: the ability to defend *yourself.*

The citizens of the new state knew only too well that had Israel existed ten years earlier, many of the lives lost in the death camps of Europe would have been saved. Take Edwin Landau as an example. The German war veteran and store-owner who staged his show of defiance on the day of the boycott in April 1933 left soon afterward for Palestine. He was lucky. He had the resources to get out. Had he stayed in Germany, he would almost certainly have been killed. Millions of others were not so fortunate.

Critics of Israel often accuse the country's politicians of using the Holocaust to justify Israel's actions against the Palestinians, as if the experience of suffering on such a massive scale gives Israel a blank cheque to do what it wants; as if that suffering places the country above international law and can be used to guilt the Western world into silence. For many politicians—and especially those responsible for the safety of Israel's citizens—the effects of the Holocaust go much, much deeper. Events in Europe in the 1930s and 1940s marked the collective Israeli psyche on the most profound level. The memory of millions of men, women, and children being systemically dehumanized until they were labeled *Untermenschen* (sub-human) and then sent to their deaths in the gas chambers while the rest of the world stood by has taught the State of Israel the true value of independence. It is not that Israeli politicians and the Israeli people do not care what the rest of the world thinks. It is that history has taught them they cannot afford to care too much. They have other priorities. First and foremost of which is the protection of their fellow citizens. And if they tend to react to any threat against their nation as if it is an existential one, it is—again—because history has taught them to expect nothing else. The Holocaust did not happen in a vacuum. Europe's Jews endured centuries as the perennial outsider, always reliant on the kindness of strangers for their safety and their survival. At least one senior soldier in the Israeli army has been known to hang a photograph of Auschwitz in his office as a reminder of what happened to Jews when they did not have their own state.[33]

For Jews, the creation of the State of Israel only three years after the near-annihilation of their people was nothing short of miraculous. That victory was underlined by another one 19 years later. In June 1967, Israel faced invasion on three fronts: from Syria in the north, Jordan in the east, and Egypt in the south.

For Israel, the Six-Day War was an all-or-nothing battle for survival. The threat to the nation's existence was so severe that the man in charge of the military, Chief of Staff (and future prime minister) General Yitzhak Rabin, worked himself to the verge of a nervous breakdown. Just days before the war started, Rabin was so overwrought that he had to be sedated.[34]

One of the most iconic images of the war is of Israeli paratroopers praying at the Western Wall on the morning of June 7. For centuries, Jews had kept the dream of Jerusalem alive by ending the Passover dinner with the words "Next Year in Jerusalem." Now they had done it. For them, it was an epic tale of triumph over adversity, a fairy tale come true. But every fairy tale has a dark forest. And this one is no exception.

Jews were not alone in venerating Jerusalem. Christians did too. For them, it was the city of Christ's death and resurrection. Muslims also venerated this Holy City. For them, it was their Noble Sanctuary. And just as Jews never gave up the dream of return to their sacred city, neither would they.

14

Jerusalem: The Noble Sanctuary

1

The name Abd al-Malik is barely known in the West.

Literally, it means Slave of the King, the king in this case being God. Islam recognizes no other. Abd al-Malik was caliph from 685 to 705. He belonged to Islam's first ruling family, the Umayyad dynasty, who ruled the Arab world for the best part of a century.[1] A man of great energy, Abd al-Malik spent his first decade in power fighting (and winning) a civil war. He spent the next decade building an empire. It was Abd al-Malik who took the disparate provinces of the Arab conquests and united them into a cohesive, cultural unit. Nowadays, when we talk of the "Arab world," it was Abd al-Malik who created it. To do it, he made Arabic the language of the imperial administration and introduced a single currency. These changes might not sound revolutionary, but their long-term effect was. They radically altered the way people lived their lives. From this point on, everyone in the caliphate spoke the same language and used the same money. This was political and economic integration on a grand scale.

As well as winning wars and building empires, Abd al-Malik also found the time to enjoy a hectic private life. Married at least six times (he might have married three more times, but the sources cannot agree), he had nine legitimate sons—four of whom succeeded him as caliph— and three daughters. He had another seven sons by his harem of slave girls.[2] Given the dangerous domestic politics of the harem, Abd al-Malik did well to avoid the fate of his father, the caliph Marwan (r. 684–5). He was smothered to death by a pillow-wielding wife whose son Marwan had ousted from the succession in favor of Abd al-Malik.[3]

The reason history remembers Abd al-Malik is not his administrative reforms or his busy private life; it is because of what he did in Jerusalem.

Even if you have never heard of him, you will know his legacy. You see it every time you see a news report from the Old City of Jerusalem. Abd al-Malik built one of the most iconic buildings in the world: the Dome of the Rock. And in doing so, he turned Constantine's City of the Cross into Islam's City of the Crescent. Even now, the Dome of the Rock remains so central to the city's Islamic identity that a massive photograph of it forms the backdrop to Hamas press conferences, no matter where in the world those press conferences are held.

The Dome's origins are shrouded in speculation and mystery. Built against the backdrop of war, the reasons for its construction were for a long time obscured by the fog of that war. Abd al-Malik commissioned it while he was fighting a man named Abdullah ibn al-Zubayr.[4] Abdullah ibn al-Zubayr lived in Medina and came from a family with impeccable Islamic credentials. His parents were early converts to Islam who stood by the Prophet Muhammad when others (like Abd al-Malik's Umayyad family) had scorned him. He was fighting to take power away from the Umayyad monarchy in Greater Syria and bring it back to the people in the Islamic heartlands of the Holy Cities.

For much of the war, Abdullah ibn al-Zubayr controlled Mecca and Medina, which meant he also controlled the pilgrimage. This gave him a powerful propaganda weapon and it was one he wielded to great effect. During prayers in Mecca, he made pilgrims from Abd al-Malik's Syrian powerbase give him the oath of allegiance as caliph. When Abd al-Malik heard about this, he was furious and hit back by banning his Syrian supporters from going near Mecca. In response, Abd al-Malik's Syrian supporters raised quite a "hue and cry."[5] Performing the pilgrimage is the fifth and final pillar of Islam. An obligatory religious rite, it is a duty to God that must be carried out at least once in a believer's lifetime. For Muslims, the pilgrimage is the spiritual highpoint of their lives. Their salvation is at stake. If the Syrian pilgrims could not go to Mecca, where could they go?

The timing of the Dome's construction in the late 680s and early 690s (it was finished in 692) along with the suggestion by an early and usually reliable source that the Syrian pilgrims needed somewhere else to go led some scholars to speculate that the Dome was built as an alternative to the Kabah in Mecca.[6] But given the unique importance of Mecca for Muslims, that seems unlikely. It also ignores the ferocious, and ultimately successful, efforts Abd al-Malik made to reclaim Mecca. As a Muslim, he knew *nowhere* could replace Mecca. But in the short term, while the war against Abdullah ibn al-Zubayr raged on, Syrian pilgrims could go to Jerusalem not as an alternative to Mecca but as a temporary substitute. Known as *al-Quds* (the Holy) in Arabic, Jerusalem is one of the most sacred cities for Muslims. Jerusalem, like Mecca, is a *Haram al-Sharif*, a Noble Sanctuary.

Jerusalem's sanctity for Muslims dates from the beginning of the Prophet Muhammad's mission, and the city occupies a unique place in the development of Islamic ritual. It was, in fact, Islam's first Holy City. When Muslims were first commanded to pray to their God, it was to Jerusalem they turned. It was not until 623, the year after the Prophet escaped Mecca for the safety of Medina and more than a decade after he had received his first revelation in 610, that the qibla, the direction of prayer, was changed to Mecca.[7]

Jerusalem's position at the heart of Islam was integral to Muhammad's mission because of the critical role the city played in the prophetic traditions that preceded him. Muhammad never claimed to be proclaiming a "new" religion. He saw himself as the restorer of an old one: the belief in One God that was first revealed to Abraham.[8]

According to Islam, that message needed to be restored because the Jews and the Christians, who received it previously, had mishandled it. The Jews made the mistake of breaking their covenant with God by worshiping the calf.[9] In disobeying God, they were guilty of ingratitude, and in seeing themselves as God's Chosen People, they denied the rest of humanity access to God's message and were, therefore, guilty of arrogance.[10] The Christians, for their part, made the mistake of attributing partners to God. In seeing the Father, the Son, and the Holy Spirit as one and the same, the Christians were little better than pagans and were guilty of *shirk* (idolatry).[11]

Muslims believe that in 610, God gave His final message to mankind via Muhammad and, in doing so, made Muhammad the "Seal of the Prophets." There would be none after him. This was humanity's last chance to get it right. The belief that Muhammad was the "Seal" profoundly shaped how Islam viewed the two monotheistic religions that came before it. It also shaped how Islam viewed the city—Jerusalem—holy to both religions.

Because Islam was the last in the line of revelations from the Almighty, Muhammad's message acknowledged what had come before. Without Judaism and Christianity, there would be no Islam. The One God of the Jews and the Christians was the One God of the Muslims. The prophets of the Jews and the Christians were the prophets of the Muslims.[12] The Holy City of the Jews and Christians in Jerusalem was also the Holy City of the Muslims.

That sense of continuity meant Muslims were duty-bound to respect the religions and the religious geography that came before Islam, even if, according to Islamic tradition, those religions had strayed from the straight path and garbled the message God gave them. In the Islamic world, Jews and Christians were, therefore, allotted special status as

People of the Book, that is, people with their own scripture. This, in turn, led Islam to adopt a completely different attitude to Judaism and Christianity than Christianity did to either Judaism or Islam. Not for Islam was the scripturally sanctioned persecution of Jews as Christ-killers. Islam did not consider Jesus to be Christ. In Islam, Jesus is a prophet and a man to be respected like all other prophets of God, but he is not God Himself. Because of this, in the Arab Islamic East, there was space in society for the Jewish community in a way that was not always the case in the European Christian West. While Jews in the East were never equal to Muslims and the Quran often refers to them with derision or contempt for mishandling the message God gave them, they were largely left alone to live their own lives.[13] Frequently, they were patronized. Less frequently they were persecuted. The Holocaust could not have happened in the medieval Islamic world.

But that does not mean everything between the two religions was uncomplicated. Some of the Quranic statements on interfaith relations are not always easy to understand. In places, the Quran veers between a positive attitude of the Jews and a negative one—sometimes in the same verse.[14] This, for example, is verse thirteen from *sura* (chapter) five of the Quran. Here, God tells Muhammad how the Children of Israel suffered the consequences for failing to heed His word:

> Because of their breaking their covenant,
> We cursed them and made their hearts hard.
> They changed words from their places; and
> they have forgotten a part of that by which they were reminded.
> You will continue to observe treachery from them
> —except for a few of them.

Yet immediately after this, the verse changes tone completely: "But pardon them and forgive. God loves those who do good." [15] Then, later in the same chapter (verse 51), the tone changes again, and Muslims are warned not to take Jews or Christians as friends.

Prior to the present day, one of the most turbulent periods in Jewish-Muslim relations was in the early days of Islam. There was a sizeable Jewish community in Arabia, especially in the city of Yathrib (later *Madina al-Nabi*, the City of the Prophet, or Medina for short), and Muhammad hoped the Jews, as the original recipients of God's message, would recognize his revelation. He was disappointed when they did not. Relations between Muslims and Jews broke down after Muhammad's flight, or *hijra*, to Medina in 622. The reasons for this had nothing to do with religion and everything to do with politics.

In Medina, Muhammad and the Muslims were still at risk from revenge attacks by the authorities in Mecca. Because of that, before Muhammad arrived in Medina, an agreement had been reached with the host community, including the Jewish tribes of Nadir, Qaynuqa, and Qurayzah, over security in the event of an attack from Mecca. The Treaty of Hudaybiyah was a mutual defense pact in which an attack on anyone was seen as an attack on everyone and each community guaranteed the safety of the other communities.

What happened in reality was different. The Jewish tribes had long-standing connections with Mecca and they did not see Muhammad's battles as theirs. In short, they became "a security risk."[16] They broke the terms of the treaty, turned against Muhammad, and colluded with his Meccan opponents. Faced with this threat, Muhammad acted to protect his people. The Nadir and Qaynuqa tribes were given the choice of conversion or exile. They chose exile. The fate of the Qurayzah tribe was much more severe: their men were killed and their women and children sold into slavery.

The slaughter and slavery of this tribe is often cited nowadays, along with some of the seemingly mixed messages in the Quran, as proof of Muhammad's anti-Jewish tendencies and Islam's inherent hostility to Judaism. But it was not Muhammad who condemned the Jews to this fate. When they surrendered, he asked them to appoint an arbitrator to decide their punishment, and it was this man, Sad ibn Muadh, who decreed what should happen to them, not the Prophet.[17]

The incident was not the start of a campaign against Jews.[18] Nor did it have any long-term impact on relations between Jews and Muslims in the Islamic world. As eminent historian Bernard Lewis explains in *The Jews of Islam*, his study of Jewish-Muslim relations: "There is little sign (in Islam) of any deep-rooted emotional hostility directed against Jews—or for that matter any other group such as the anti-Semitism of the Christian world."[19] An example of Islam's attitude to Jews is what happened when the Muslim armies took over Palestine in the 630s: the Jews, as People of the Book, were granted greater rights than they had ever enjoyed under the Romans and Byzantines.[20]

As for Islam's relationship with Christianity, it was similar to Islam's relationship with Judaism: a mixture of disdain and indifference but little or no persecution. In the Islamic East, Christians were often subject to mockery for confusing Jesus with God. But Christians did not find themselves subject to the religiously sanctioned hostility that Christianity inflicted on the religion that preceded it. Many Christians in Palestine were not even sorry to see the Byzantines go. At the time of the Muslim conquest, Eastern Christianity was divided by reruns of the Arian controversy on the nature (human, divine, or both) of Jesus. Some of these groups took the opposite view from Constantinople and were not well treated by the Byzantine authorities. As a result, while some Eastern Christians did not exactly welcome the Muslim armies, they did not exactly oppose them either.

But if Islam tolerated the religious messages that preceded it, Christianity, particularly Western Christianity, was not so accommodating of the religion that came after it. At times, its relationship with Islam has been only marginally less fraught than its relationship with Judaism. From the birth of Islam until relatively recently, Christianity has viewed Islam with outright suspicion, if not hostility. (Many would say it still does.) That suspicion has often found expression in vitriolic attacks on the Prophet Muhammad. In the medieval era, Christianity viewed Muhammad as nothing less than the Anti-Christ because his teaching reduced their Christ to a mere prophet.

Not surprisingly, then, it was in Jerusalem, the city of the Jews and of Jesus (and, at one stage, of Jupiter too), that Abd al-Malik chose to seal Islam's position as the last of God's revelations and to celebrate the faith's success in becoming a world power. The Dome of the Rock was deliberately designed to dominate the city's landscape and to eclipse everything around it. Nothing about its location or decoration was accidental. Everything about this building was intended to make a statement about power and victory: the power of God and the victory of the Muslim armies over their Byzantine (i.e., Christian) rivals. Built on the site of Solomon's Temple, the Dome's location lets everyone know Islam has overtaken Judaism. Built in the style of a Byzantine church but covered in verses from the Quran referring to God's unity (*tawhid*) rather than the Christian trinity, its decoration is a public statement that Islam has overtaken Christianity too.

The site itself is also hugely significant within the Muslim tradition. The rock is where Muhammad is said to have ascended into heaven and met God during his famous Night Journey. Awakened one night by the angel Gabriel, Muhammad was taken from Mecca on a miraculous journey to Jerusalem on a winged horse with a human face called Buraq. In Jerusalem, Muhammad and Gabriel were greeted by previous prophets including Abraham and Moses. Jesus was also present. Muhammad then traveled up through the seven levels of heaven to meet God. (It was during this meeting that God commanded Muhammad to have Muslims to pray 50 times a day. On the advice of Moses who was concerned that praying 50 times a day might be too much for mere mortals, Muhammad managed to get it down to five.)

With its golden dome reflecting the sun and its deep-sea blue tiles shimmering in the light, the Dome is a stunning representation of heaven on earth. It draws your eyes like a magnet. In an era long before mass media, this was visual propaganda of the first order. And it was all the more effective because it is permanent. Caliphs and Crusaders could come and go. Dynasties could rise and fall. Empires could wax and wane. But with the Dome of the Rock sitting right in the center of this sacred city, Abd al-Malik's legacy is a declaration that Jerusalem, or at least this part of it, belongs to Islam.

2

Dynasties did indeed rise and fall. But Jerusalem remained at the heart of Islam.

Under Islamic rule, the city was part of the province of Palestine, which was a sub-province of Greater Syria. During the Umayyad era, Greater Syria was the center of the caliphate, and Palestine was of such strategic importance to the ruling family that it was often governed by no less a figure than the heir apparent. The importance of the province was due in no small measure to the sanctity of Jerusalem. The Umayyads were aware of the city's symbolism and did not hesitate to use it to sacralize their power. It was in Jerusalem that the Umayyad era officially began. The founder of the dynasty, Muawiya (r. 661–80), received the oath of allegiance as caliph there.[21]

As time passed, increasing numbers of local people embraced the religion of the conquerors. Islam was no longer the faith of the ruling elite and their armies. It became the faith of the masses. Jerusalem then went through one of its periodic reinventions and became a Muslim city. The Jewish and Christian residents who did not convert were left alone to worship and live in their own way. As long as they paid their poll tax (the jizya) and did not build their synagogues and churches higher than the mosques, they were protected by the state.

When the Umayyads fell from power in 750 and were all but wiped out in the meal-cum-massacre at Jaffa that same year, the new ruling family, the Abbasids, showed just as much reverence toward the Holy City as their predecessors had done. Even though the center of power shifted to Iraq, Jerusalem remained an integral part of the Islamic empire and the new caliphs were keen to show how much the city meant to them. Al-Mansur (r. 754–75) performed the pilgrimage to Mecca in 758, then went to Medina and onto Jerusalem. This was quite an arduous journey in the heat of early summer, but the caliph understood the value of being seen in all three of Islam's Holy Cities.[22] His son, the caliph al-Mahdi (r. 775–85), also made the journey to Jerusalem and took a significant entourage with him.[23]

The caliph al-Mamun (r. 813–33) went even further. Pomp and patronage were not enough for him. His plan was much grander. He tried to rewrite history. Literally. He, like Abd al-Malik, had fought and won a civil war. His, though, was against his brother, and the double shadow of regicide-fratricide hung over his rule. Such was the importance of the Dome of the Rock in Islam that al-Mamun decided to use it to legitimize his rule. He sponsored a renovation program and had his name inscribed on the foundation stone to make it look as if he, rather than Abd al-Malik, had commissioned its construction. He might have got away with it if the stone mason had not forgotten to change the date of the Dome's construction.[24]

Al-Mamun was one of the last Abbasid caliphs to wield absolute authority. Officially, the family held power until 1258, but from the ninth century onward, they functioned more as figureheads than as Commanders of the Faithful. During this time, a strategic realignment took place within the caliphate. The era of conquest was over. The vast wealth of conquered countries no longer flowed into the caliph's exchequer and the imperial capital was no longer able to support itself financially. So power shifted to the regions. This process gained more momentum during the tenth century when successor states and competitor caliphates became the norm.[25]

This decentralization of power would turn out to be disastrous for Jerusalem. With a caliph in Cordoba, another in Baghdad, and sultans springing up across Syria, the House of Islam was a house divided. In the summer of 1099, that division worked to the advantage of the Christian armies of the Crusaders. As they laid siege to Jerusalem, no one came to help the city's beleaguered inhabitants. On July 15, 1099, after nearly five hundred years of Islamic rule, the city fell to the Christians.

A bloodbath followed. For two days, the Christian Crusaders murdered every Muslim they met. The few to whom mercy was granted were made to bury the dead in unmarked graves and were then sold into slavery. The city's Jewish community sought refuge in their synagogue. But they were no safer there than they would have been out on the streets. The invaders blocked the exits, surrounded the building with flammable material, then set fire to it. Few survived. Those lucky enough to escape did not survive for long. They were killed by the soldiers waiting outside.[26]

Muslims were stunned by the loss of Jerusalem.[27] Bitterly divided, it took the Arab world nearly 50 years to coordinate a fight back. In the meantime, the Crusaders were not idle. They held Jerusalem for nearly a century and carved out principalities and kingdoms in cities along the Mediterranean coast.

The First Crusade is a grim tale and its effects are still with us. For people in the West today, it is a remote story and one that most of us do not know about in any great detail. Yet it has soured relations between the Christian world (i.e., the West) and the Muslim world in ways the modern West does not always appreciate or understand. Before the Crusades, the Arab world was self-contained, self-confident, and self-sufficient. The loss of Jerusalem was, therefore, a crushing blow to the community's collective self-esteem. It laid bare the caliphate's internal political weaknesses for all to see and revealed that the Muslim community was not as united as it had once been. Petty rivalries and political power plays were the order of the day. Squabbling sultans were more concerned with their own interests than with those of the community. Reclaiming Jerusalem came way down their list of priorities.

Over the long term, what made the loss of Jerusalem so much worse for Arabs was the manner of the Christian victory. The Crusader army acted with the backing of the church and enjoyed the full blessing of the pope. For such an army to behave with such brutality in the City of Christ was a contradiction in terms for many of the city's inhabitants.

In time, the massacre of the city's population would be woven into a solid anti-Western narrative. It was the Arab Muslim world's first experience of invasion from the West and, in time, the Crusades would be recast as a lens through which to see all future invasions, particularly the colonial invasions of the nineteenth and twentieth centuries. If you have ever wondered where everything started to go wrong between the West and Islam, this is it. It was not immediately recognized at the time—the great shifts of history rarely are; but for many in the Arab world, this is the moment when the West showed its true colors. After the Crusades, Jerusalem, a city already burdened with too much history, became much more than a place of prayer. It became a fault line between East and West.

On October 2, 1187, the armies of Saladin reclaimed Jerusalem. The date was auspicious. In the Islamic calendar, it was the twenty-seventh of Rajab: the anniversary of the Prophet's Night Journey from Jerusalem to heaven.[28] As conqueror, Saladin was very different from the crusading conquerors of 88 years earlier. Not for him was a massacre of the city's Christians. He allowed his defeated opponents to ransom themselves and gave them safe passage out of the city. His actions were brought to the attention of a wider audience in the Ridley Scott motion picture *Kingdom of Heaven*. In one of the most memorable scenes, Balian the Christian defender of Jerusalem (played by Orlando Bloom) asks Saladin why he is showing mercy to Christians when none was shown to the Muslims. Saladin's response is simple: he is not those men.

Saladin's victory brought Jerusalem under the control of his Ayyubid family who also ruled Egypt and Greater Syria, and Jerusalem was, once again, within the House of Islam. But that house remained bitterly divided. And those divisions again threatened Jerusalem.

In 1229, Ayyubid Sultan al-Kamil (Saladin's nephew) did something that seems almost unbelievable given his uncle's efforts to win back Jerusalem. Al-Kamil handed the city over to the Crusaders without an arrow being fired. He made a secret treaty with Frederick II giving him control of the city in return for Frederick's military support against al-Kamil's (Muslim) enemies. It was not until 1244—when al-Kamil was long gone—that one of his successors reclaimed the city.[29]

From then on, ruling families came and went, but Jerusalem remained a Muslim city. The Ayyubids held power until 1250 when they were ousted by a corps of slave soldiers known as Mamluks, from the Arabic word for "owned." This was Egypt's first encounter with rule by the military. It lasted until 1516-7 when the Mamluks were defeated by the Ottomans on the battlefield and Egypt and Greater Syria were added to Istanbul's growing list of conquests.

The Mamluks and the Ottomans understood Jerusalem's importance to Islam. The Mamluk sultan Qaitbay (r. 1468–96) built and endowed a *madrasa* (school) in the enclosure where the Dome of the Rock stands. Qaitbay also built extensively in Mecca and Medina and the work in Jerusalem was part of a wider program of patronage in Islam's Holy Cities. It was appropriate too: this sultan's honorific title was *al-Ashraf* (the most noble), which comes from the word *sharif*, the noble in Noble Sanctuary (Haram al-Sharif).[30] The madrasa's fountain still stands. The Ottoman sultan Suleyman the Magnificent (r. 1520–66) was also busy in Jerusalem. He, too, was linked to the city by his name, which is Arabic for Solomon. He refurbished the Dome of the Rock using tiles from Iznik (the Byzantine Nicaea of the Nicene Creed) and went as far as to have his own tomb designed in the same style as the Dome.[31]

For any sultan, these projects were an unrivalled opportunity to project power. More than that, they provided a platform to proclaim a ruler's Islamic credentials. Where better for a sultan to show himself as a good Muslim than in one of Islam's Holiest Cities?

At the beginning of the twentieth century, Ottoman rule in Palestine had lasted nearly four centuries. The province itself and the Holy City at the heart of it had been Islamic for nearly thirteen centuries. And then everything changed.

3

On November 9, 1917, *The Times* of London published the Balfour Declaration. In it, Britain declared its support for a Jewish homeland in

Palestine as long as any such homeland did not prejudice the rights of the province's non-Jewish communities in any way.[32]

The Balfour Declaration was an astonishing document for the British to issue. At the time it was published, Palestine was part of the Ottoman Empire. It was not Britain's to dispose of, one way or another. There was also the question of the document's contents: the idea that substantial migration to Palestine could take place without altering the population balance between Arab and Jew. How the British thought that circle could ever be squared was never explained. Building a Jewish homeland in Palestine would, by its very definition, involve levels of immigration that would alter the population balance. For Zionists and their supporters, that was the whole point. The reason for building their state was to go and live in it. But for Arabs, Balfour was a disaster. It threatened the loss of the land they had lived on for centuries.

The British, however, were not used to taking the views of Arabs into consideration and Balfour is no exception. The declaration did not happen in isolation. It fell within the framework of the Anglo-French carve-up of the Middle East outlined in the Sykes-Picot Agreement. That, too, did not happen in isolation but was part of the wider Anglo-French imperial project for the region. Palestine was just another piece in this grand imperial puzzle.

It cost the British nothing to support Jewish claims to a homeland in Palestine. If anything, Britain hoped to benefit from it, believing it would help the Allied effort by keeping Russia in the war. It is even possible the British did not anticipate substantial Jewish migration or any potential population shift. That might sound unlikely, but so much of British strategy at this time was based on what the British foreign policy establishment wanted to see rather than what was actually going on, so it is possible they miscalculated here too. As for the Arabs, the British did not factor them into the equation in any meaningful way until the Arab Uprising in the 1930s.

Balfour became a reality when Britain occupied Palestine in December 1917, and it soon affected population numbers. Fewer than 30,000 Jews lived in Palestine before 1900. That figure rose to 61,000 by 1920, a tenth of the province's total population of 601,000. After Balfour, it kept on rising. The 1931 British census has the Jewish community at 175,000 with the Arab population at 880,000. Throughout the 1930s, the number of Jews arriving in Palestine continued to rise. This was partly due to Balfour's recognition of the Jewish right to a homeland in Palestine, but it was mainly due to events in Europe and the urgent need for Jews to flee German-occupied lands. Nearly 150,000 Jewish immigrants arrived in Palestine between 1933 (the year Hitler took power) and 1935 (the year of the Nuremberg Laws).[33]

This was the moment Britain chose to act to preserve what remained of the population balance between Arab and Jew. The violence of the Arab Uprising of 1936–9, and the widespread social discontent behind it, made the British authorities take steps to curb migration. For Jews, facing annihilation in Europe, it could not have come at a worse time. For Arabs, it was arguably too late. Palestine's population had already changed radically.

Caught between the competing demands of Arab and Jew, the British set up a Royal Commission to work out what to do with Palestine. Known as the Peel Commission after the lord who led it, it published a weighty 400-page report in July 1937 and recommended dividing the province in two. It turned out to be another example of imperial short-sight. Yet again, the British failed to grasp the reality that in this kind of all-or-nothing struggle, giving something to one group (even if it is not everything they want) is automatically taken as a loss by the other side. The report was eventually shelved.

But nothing, it seemed, could stop Jewish migration and the population of Palestine continued to change. On the eve of the creation of the State of Israel, Jews made up nearly 40 percent of the overall population.[34] It did not help the Palestinian cause that a number of Arab landowners, many of whom lived outside the province in what had once been Greater Syria, were willing to sell land to the Jewish Agency.

There was no such lack of coordination on the Jewish side. They were organized, effective, and, after the trauma of the Holocaust, they were ready to do whatever needed to be done to secure their state. The Arabs, by contrast, were pushed onto the defensive from the start. From their point of view, the Zionists had everything to gain and they had everything to lose. Attempts by the outside world to solve the problem through a two-state solution were not, to Arab eyes, impartial because they gave too much to the Jews and asked the Arabs to give up too much. Arabs rejected the UN plan, not because they were unwilling to find a solution but because they could not willingly agree to give up so much of their own land.

When the crisis culminated in the war of 1948, the word Catastrophe barely begins to cover events from the Palestinian point of view. It was not just land they lost. Although that was hard enough to bear: a society, a way of life, a culture—all these were lost too. Families were broken up. The Catastrophe hit men particularly hard. Deprived of the means to earn their living and provide for their families, a terrible sort of limbo and inertia set in.[35] People did not know how long the situation would last and many kept their house keys as a sign of their confidence that they would, one day, return home. To this day, people still keep them, even though the houses no longer exist. The key remains a powerful symbol for Palestinians, proof they have not given up. Palestinian politician Dr. Mustafa Barghouti often wears one on his lapel.

After the 1948 war, the issue of refugees and their Right to Return became one of the major fault lines in this conflict. Even the reasons why Palestinians left in the first place are a source of contention and are treated very differently in the two competing narratives. For years, the Israeli narrative had the Palestinians packing up their bags and running—almost through choice. Palestinians, on the other hand, call what happened to them ethnic cleansing and, as proof, cite events in the village of Deir Yassin, outside Jerusalem, on April 10, 1948, when the forces of the Irgun, the Stern, and the Haganah killed around 250 men, women, and children. News of Deir Yassin spread and fear of a possible repeat prompted Palestinian communities to flee before the advancing Zionist armies.

UN Resolution 194 affirms the Right of Return and Arab leaders refer to it as the reason they have not given citizenship to the Palestinian refugees scattered across the Middle East, believing that if they do, Israel will consider the problem solved. For Israel, the Right of Return threatens the very existence of the Jewish state. Over 20 percent of Israel's population is Arab, descended from people living there pre-1948. If every Palestinian refugee (and his/her descendants) is allowed to return, the population balance in Israel would be so radically altered that Jewish Israelis would become a minority in the country—a situation not unlike the one Arabs feared happening to them in the 1930s and 1940s.

For Palestinians, the Right of Return is an article of faith. It goes directly to the legitimacy of their argument that Palestine is their home. And they find it hard to understand why Western leaders side so openly with Israel when, from the Palestinian point of view, Israel is the colonial settler state that drove them from their homes in the first place. In this regard, many Palestinians believe they are paying the price for Europe's treatment of the Jews during the 1930s and 1940s. The Holocaust was an indictment not only of Germany but also of the culture that let it happen. And from the Palestinian point of view, Western powers have compensated for it ever since with their almost total support of Israel and, once again, the cost of a war in Europe is compensated for in the East. Israelis see it differently: for them, the right of their state to exist is legitimate in and of itself. The Holocaust showed what could happen in the absence of a Jewish state, but it is not, and never could be, the country's raison d'être.

The gap between these two points of view is enormous and provides yet another example of how far from resolution this conflict is. But perhaps the biggest fault line in this conflict and, therefore, the one with the least amount of room for compromise is the area sacred to Judaism, Christianity, and Islam: Jerusalem.

Following Israel's victory in the Six-Day War, the city was later annexed to become the country's capital. Although not universally recognized as such—nearly all foreign embassies remain in Tel Aviv—for Israelis, there is no question that Jerusalem is their capital. After so many centuries in exile, during which Jerusalem served as the focus of the community's longing to return, it is highly unlikely any Israeli prime minister will ever agree to cede control and share the city's sovereignty.

But it is equally unlikely Palestinians will ever give up their longing for their own state with Jerusalem as their capital. For Palestinians, the loss of Jerusalem in 1967 compounded the losses of 1948. In one war, they lost their land. In the other, they lost their liberty. They call the Six-Day War the *Naksa*, or Setback. In the wake of that war, new resolutions were passed at the UN—242 and 338—and "land-for-peace" became a much used phrase. But in the short term, no land was given back and there has been no peace.

What *has* happened in the decades since 1967 is a significant shift in the nature of this conflict. The early Jewish pioneers were militant about their Zionism, much less militant about their Judaism. Politics were dominated by secular parties (the Labor Party in particular) and the conflict with the Palestinians was seen as a battle over land between two competing national identities. After 1967, that changed. With the Israeli occupation of the West Bank came the dream of a Greater Israel, and a new wave of religiously motivated immigrants arrived in the country on a mission to resurrect the Zion of the Bible.

Given the multiparty nature of Israeli politics and the frequency of coalition governments, smaller religious parties often wield disproportionate influence over the secular majority. For that reason, Israel is sometimes called a "minoritocracy." And religion has changed Israeli politics from within. If you believe you are doing God's work, compromise—the very essence of politics—becomes impossible and, in the minds of some, a betrayal. Nowhere is this clearer than in the issue of land. Yitzhak Rabin, Nobel Laureate, prime minister, and Chief of Staff in the Six-Day War, was killed in November 1995 by a religiously motivated settler opposed to his peace deal with the PLO the year before.

The rise of religion in Israeli politics has been mirrored by a similar process in Palestinian politics. In the Arab world, many saw the humiliation of the Six-Day War as a damning indictment of the secular, nationalist policies of Egypt's Nasser. For many of the disappointed and dispossessed, there was only one answer: Islam. The rise of Islamist politics and of parties like the Muslim Brotherhood dates from this period.

For Islamists, Jerusalem is just as important as it is for religious Zionists and that makes the possibility of compromise just as difficult.

Jerusalem has come to signify the all-or-nothing nature of this struggle. It is now a barometer of how the role of religion has evolved in the course of the conflict and how, in turn, that has changed the nature of the conflict itself, making it much more difficult to resolve. Religion is no longer simply an issue of communal identity. Which was a tangled enough web to unweave. Religion has become an issue of political *ideology*. That risks turning the conflict into something it was not: a religious war between Jews and Muslims. Which risks the conflict spreading far beyond the region.

Nowhere is that more obvious—and more dangerous—than in Jerusalem. In 2000, a visit by former defense minister (and future prime minister) Ariel Sharon to what he called the Temple Mount and what Arabs call the Haram al-Sharif started a riot and led to the Second Intifada. Sharon was a particularly controversial figure for Palestinians because of his role in the Lebanon War in 1982 when Israel's Lebanese Phalangist allies massacred nearly three thousand Palestinian civilians, many of whom were women, in the Sabra and Shatila refugee camps that summer. He was banned from holding public office in Israel for years afterward.

The Second Intifada was much more violent than the first and was disastrous for Israelis and Palestinians alike. Sharon's visit was an example of how, in the highly charged and divisive atmosphere of Jerusalem, events can spiral quickly out of control and neither side is left unaffected.

Jerusalem is no ordinary city. And because it means so much to so many, neither side can give it up. In this increasingly divisive and dangerous conflict, it is the one thing both sides have in common.

*   *   *

But what the two sides do not have in common is any balance of power.

Right now, one side has it all. The other has none.

On a political level, the State of Israel enjoys the enthusiastic support of the political institutions of the most powerful country in the world. As Prime Minister Binyamin Netanyahu said in his address to the US Congress on March 3, 2015, the bond between the United States and Israel is so close they are like "family." As a result, Israel enjoys the protection of the United States and its veto at the UN Security Council. Israel also enjoys the almost unqualified support of most of the leaders and governments of the Western world.

The Palestinians, by contrast, find themselves standing where so many Arabs have stood before them: on the wrong side of global power. While they enjoy the support of large numbers of people in the West, that has not translated into support for their cause at government level. That is because Israel also enjoys popular support in the West, particularly among the governments who see democratic Israel as one of their own: part of the Western establishment, part of Western culture, part of the global (i.e., Western-dominated) economy.

There is, however, one area where the Palestinians enjoy total support: among the people of the Arab world. The near three hundred million people in this region wholeheartedly back the Palestinians' quest for an independent state.

Yet that popular people-based support has failed to translate into support at government level. Which leads to one of the great conundrums of the modern Middle East: why are leaders of the Arab world *not* doing what members of the Jewish Diaspora do so effectively on behalf of Israel and using their collective assets—in the Arabs' case, their diplomatic leverage, their oil wealth, and their considerable commercial clout—to help the Palestinians achieve their goal of statehood?

The answer to that question goes directly to the heart of what's really going on in the Middle East: to the question of who holds power and why.

Part IV

Kings, Colonels, and Coups: Why There Is a Democratic Deficit in the Arab World

15

Cairo: Wednesday, July 23, 1952

The coup was almost bloodless. In Cairo, there was so little opposition the city fell like "a ripe mango."[1] The strategic garrison town of al-Arish in the Sinai fell the following day. As did Alexandria on the Mediterranean coast.

The port city was Egypt's summer capital. A home away from home for the great and the good as they sought refuge from the suffocating heat of Cairo where, in July, temperatures can easily hit 50 degrees Celsius. Among the exodus to the coast in the summer of 1952 was King Farouq. He had taken up residence at his Ras al-Tin palace. Farouq was the grandson of the man who built the Suez Canal—Khedive Ismail (r. 1863–79)—and the great-great-grandson of modern Egypt's founding father, Muhammad Ali (r. 1805–48).

By 1952, the dynasty's glory days were long gone. Farouq had been on the throne since 1936, and in many ways he symbolized everything that was wrong with Egypt. Wealthy, corrupt, and increasingly unpopular, the king had a roving eye and a dubious reputation. Allegations about his private life were rife. At high society events, pretty young women would often be shepherded out of the room by male relatives as soon as the king appeared.[2]

Reputation was not Farouq's only problem. He was dangerously out of touch with his own people. He lived in a world of prestige and privilege and his inner circle enjoyed a luxurious lifestyle of conspicuous consumption far beyond the dreams of the average Egyptian.

This was a country with a massive wealth gap. Too much money was in the hands of too few. In 1952, a mere six percent of the population owned a massive 65 percent of Egypt's agricultural land.[3] Social mobility was virtually nonexistent. Where you were born was where you were going to stay.

Politically, the king lived a life fraught with contradictions. Over Egyptians, he wielded absolute authority. He could (and frequently did) negate the outcome of elections by invoking his right to dissolve parliament. Yet his real freedom of action was very limited. Farouq was under the thumb of the British and he bitterly resented it. In theory, the Anglo-Egyptian Treaty of 1936 freed Egypt from London's control. In practice, Britain's ongoing military presence in Egypt allowed London to run events from behind the scenes.

Farouq hoped that a good showing by Egypt's military in the war in Palestine in 1948 would raise his standing and help him reclaim his lost popularity. The reverse turned out to be the case. Individual soldiers fought with bravery and commitment but felt let down by poor leadership, bad planning, and chronic lack of supplies. Returning home in defeat, veterans were scathing in their criticism of the king, his government, and his military top brass.

The humiliation of the war sealed King Farouq's fate. Not long afterward, a group of nine young army officers, all of whom had served in the 1948 war, formed a clandestine movement of Free Officers. Their aim was revolution. Egypt needed change and they planned to deliver it.

In October 1951, in a bid to shore up his own crumbling popularity, Prime Minister Nahhas Pasha of the Wafd Party revoked the Anglo-Egyptian Treaty. Parliament ratified the decision on the sixteenth of the month.[4] This treaty provided the cover for Britain's military deployment and veiled the gap between what Britain said about its role in Egypt and what Britain actually did in the country. Without it, Britain's presence in Egypt was not only unwelcome but illegal. Britain reacted by declaring a state of emergency.

From then on, events developed a momentum of their own. On January 25, 1952, British forces attacked an Egyptian police station in Ismailiyya, the city on the Suez Canal named after Khedive Ismail. Dozens of Egyptian policemen were killed. Dozens more were injured. The following day, all hell broke loose in Cairo. Any symbol of Britain (or the West), no matter how innocuous, was attacked. Among the businesses destroyed was the stationery store owned by Edward Said's father. The day came to be known as Black Saturday. At the end of it, over 30 people were dead and over seven hundred businesses lay in ruins. The scale of the destruction and the widespread discontent behind it laid bare the cracks in the old order. The uneasy alliance between the British, the king, and the political old guard was unraveling.

For Farouq, it would come to an end on his very own Black Saturday six months later. On Saturday, July 26, tanks encircled his palace in Alexandria. Fearing the worst, he accepted his fate and abdicated in favor of his son Ahmad Fuad, who was only six months old. He set sail that evening for exile in Italy with his wife, his son, and two hundred pieces of luggage. History was repeating itself: the deposed king traveled on the same boat his grandfather Ismail had used when he went into exile in 1879.[5] Farouq was lucky to escape with his life. Many of the Free Officers wanted to execute him. Only the intervention of their leader, Colonel Gamal Abdel Nasser, stopped them.[6]

Nasser was Farouq's opposite. A man of the people, Nasser had made his own way in life and was a rare example of successful social mobility. He was born in Alexandria on January 15, 1918, but his roots were a world away from the cosmopolitan city on the coast. His father was a Saidi, from a village in Upper Egypt near Asyut, and his grandfather was a fellah. These origins would later endear him to millions of Egyptians. In Nasser, they would see themselves.

Nasser's father worked as a clerk in the post office. It was a job that required him to relocate every few years and, as a result, Nasser spent his childhood in a variety of places: the big cities of Alexandria and Cairo and the remote villages of Upper Egypt and the Delta. For a time in his early childhood, he went to live with an uncle in the Khan al-Khalili quarter of Old Cairo so he could go to school there. During this period, Nasser's mother died unexpectedly. He was only eight years old at the time. The loss was exacerbated by his father's swift remarriage, something Nasser was said to have been less than happy about. As an adult, Nasser was known for his near-paranoid inability to trust people and a sense of detachment that bordered on insularity. Whether those tendencies can be traced back to experiencing such loss so early in his childhood, we will probably never know.[7]

By 1933, Nasser was back in Cairo. The 1930s were politically turbulent and, like many young men, Nasser got caught up in the heady atmosphere of the times. He was interested in the ideas of several political parties but was satisfied by none of them. In his view, the established parties did not understand the problems of ordinary people and were not doing enough to free Egypt from foreign rule.

In November 1935, Nasser got involved in more direct action. He attended a rally against British rule and ended up being shot and wounded. His participation in the protest got him kicked out of school.[8]

Another young man from the country who also made the move to the city and got caught up in the atmosphere of these times was Nasser's nemesis Sayyid Qutb.[9] But where Qutb chose a career in education and literature (and ultimately political Islam), Nasser chose the military. Paradoxically, it was thanks to the British that he was able to make that choice. In 1936, following the signing of the Anglo-Egyptian Treaty,

Egypt's Military Academy opened up its officer corps training programs beyond the narrow circles of the elite. The British encouraged this move. Now that Egypt was a legally recognized strategic partner of the British, London wanted that partner to pull its weight.[10] The democratization of Egypt's army at Britain's behest was not without a certain irony, as Britain's own military was one of the most highly stratified, rigidly structured, and class-conscious in the world.

Nasser applied to the Military Academy in 1936, was rejected, applied again in 1937, and this time was accepted. After his training, he was posted to Upper Egypt where he met and became friends with Anwar Sadat, the man who would succeed him as president in 1970. In the heart of Upper Egypt, with little to do in their spare time, young officers like Nasser and Sadat whiled away their leisure hours talking politics, outlining what was wrong with Egypt and how it could be fixed.

By 1948, Nasser had risen to the rank of major. During the war that year, he was credited with instigating a counter-attack against the Israelis in Falluja near Beersheba in the Negev desert, which enabled his men, pinned down and facing defeat, to hold out. He was shot in the chest, the bullet only narrowly missing his heart.[11]

Back in Cairo after the war, Nasser was one of the nine men who met secretly in 1949 to form the movement that would bring down the monarchy: the Committee of the Free Officers' Movement. In 1950, he was elected the committee's chairman.

For the next few years, the Free Officers worked in the shadows. They were not alone in wanting change. Such was the widespread dissatisfaction with Egypt's ruling class in the late 1940s and early 1950s that many groups were working toward the same goal. The Free Officers were aware of these groups and sought their support. The Muslim Brotherhood (the *Ikhwan al-Muslimin*) had built up an impressive following since it was founded in 1928 by a primary school teacher named Hasan al-Banna. The Brothers wanted a more just society and believed the way to achieve it was through Islamic principles. Communist and left-wing parties also enjoyed popular support, although not to the same degree as the Brotherhood. Like the Free Officers, left-wing groups believed Egypt needed radical social as well as political change.

Yet when the Free Officers eventually acted, they acted alone. What prompted them to launch their coup in July 1952 was fear of exposure. In spite of their efforts at secrecy, the king had become aware of the conspiracies against him. Ultimately, that knowledge did him no good. Because in losing the support of the young officer class in the army, the king effectively lost control of the whole army—the one indigenous institution in Egypt he could not rule without.

When the tanks encircled King Farouq's palace and the Free Officers sent him packing, they shrewdly claimed they had not acted in the interests of the army but in the interests of the people. In doing so, they sought popular legitimacy for their coup. They got it. Not only had they deposed an unloved king and his equally unloved government, but they had also struck a blow for Egyptian national pride, still reeling after the disaster of 1948, by giving the British a bloody nose.

The coup's popular legitimacy was further enhanced by the man appointed by the Free Officers to lead the country in the new era: General Muhammad Neguib. The Free Officers were young—Nasser was one of the oldest and he was only 34, whereas Neguib was in his fifties. The young officers were concerned their age and inexperience could be used against them by their opponents in the old order, whereas Neguib's age and rank radiated reassurance and gave the impression that Egypt was in safe hands. Furthermore, he was one of the few senior soldiers in the Egyptian army to emerge from the disastrous war of 1948 with any credibility.

While Neguib was the public face of the revolution, the leader of the Free Officers, and thus the real leader of Egypt, was Nasser. His background and his childhood spent in rural villages and the poorer parts of Cairo now stood him in very good stead. He knew how to appeal to the man on the street. One of the first reforms the new regime introduced was a reduction of the amount of land any one person could hold. The plan was a forerunner of the massive land distribution schemes Nasser later introduced and a direct attack on the *über*-rich landowning class. It was hugely popular among the dispossessed poor: the people Nasser saw as his natural powerbase.

There were, however, signs that populism was not going to mean power-sharing. Less than a month after the coup, a group of workers in a cotton mill near Alexandria took control of the business. The Free Officers feared the workers' actions might inspire copy-cat protests. Widespread industrial unrest would be a double loss for the new regime. Not only would it raise questions about the coup's populist credentials, it would be a huge boost for the Communist and left-wing groups. The Free Officers sent the troops in. The striking workers were arrested. Two were later hanged.[12]

The crackdown was a sign of things to come. By January 1953 all political parties had been dissolved. Belonging to the Muslim Brotherhood or the Communist Party became a criminal offence. The highest-ranking members in these groups were rounded up and jailed. On January 23, 1953, exactly six months after the coup, the National Liberation Party was set up. State-approved and state-sponsored, its purpose was to act as the link between power and the people. And it was to be the only link. From now on, *all* political activity in this vast country of millions of people had to be funneled through this one organization.

The one-party state had arrived.

Thanks to the Free Officers, Egypt was independent. But it was not free.

16

The Kings, the Colonels, and the Political Time Warp: The Return of the Middle Ages

1

It was not just Egypt. And it was not just Nasser.

Independence without freedom would become a theme of the postcolonial Middle East. In fact, it would become *the* dominant political theme of the twentieth century and create many of the tensions currently ripping the region apart. It did not matter whether the country in question was an artificially created state cobbled together by the Great Powers after the First World War (Iraq, Jordan, Syria). It did not matter whether the country in question had a coherent national identity stretching back millennia (Egypt) or whether it was a newly formed entity designed to meet the ambitions of a ruling family (the Gulf kingdoms). Nor did it matter whether the head of state was a king or a colonel or whether independence had come about through war or peace. Regardless of *how* the independent state came into being or who led it, the outcome was the same across the region. All the Arab states in the postcolonial Middle East, with the exception of Lebanon, had one thing in common.

They did not become democratic.

The question is: why?

2

For centuries, the two main power blocs in the Arab Islamic world were the monarchy and the military.[1]

The principle of hereditary succession was introduced to the caliphate in the seventh century when the Umayyad caliph Muawiya (r. 661–80) appointed his son Yazid to succeed him. There was more to this decision than a father's pride in his son. Muawiya sought to alter the entire political framework underpinning the caliphate by keeping power in his family. That family would then dominate the day-to-day business of power. They would occupy the most important jobs, enjoy the most lucrative perks, and keep their circle closed to outsiders. In effect, they would become the medieval equivalent of the one-party state and the forerunner of the authoritarian Arab ruling families of today.

Muawiya's decision was not universally welcomed and led to civil war. The caliph's critics believed that any new ruler should be chosen through a process of *shura* (consultation) within the community. Muslim reformers nowadays cite shura as an early form of consensus-building and proof that Islam is not incompatible with democracy.

Muawiya's critics accused him of turning the caliphate into a *mulk* (monarchy), which he had no right to do. The Prophet Muhammad had not done it. Nor had the four *Rashidun* (Rightly Guided) Caliphs who governed after Muhammad. Implicit in the description of these caliphs as "Rightly Guided" is the suggestion that Muawiya and the rulers who came after him veered from the correct way of doing things. The Prophet was, and still is, the ultimate role model whose actions (or *Sunna*) are the example every good Muslim seeks to follow. Yet Muawiya, who led the community Muhammad founded, ignored the Prophet's example.

In doing so, he also ignored the Quran. There is no shortage of kings in the Muslim Holy Book, but Quranic kingship is a very different concept from the hereditary power that came to be practiced across the Arab world. In the Quran, kingship belongs to God. Repeatedly, the Quran states that sovereignty belongs to God and to no one else.[2] Because God is the ultimate arbiter of power, He alone has the right to appoint kings on earth. The few who received this honor are familiar figures from the Bible: Abraham (4: 54), Joseph (12: 101), Saul (2: 247), Solomon (38: 35), and David (38: 20). All are honored because of their obedience to God. In all but Saul's case, they are also prophets.[3]

Kingship in the Quran is, therefore, a sign of God's favor. It is a God-given privilege. It is not a human's right. Muawiya and the dynastic rulers who came after him, including those who rule today, could try to pass their rule off as an Islamic version of a monarchy, but they would struggle to find Quranic legitimacy for doing so.

Yet in spite of the opposition to Muawiya in particular and to monarchy in general, Muawiya's Umayyad family ruled for nearly a century. In 692, his relative Abd al-Malik won the eight-year war waged against the family. The reason for this success was simple: the army. It was fiercely loyal and knew where its interests lay. The monarchy might be a closed circle, accessible to an elite with a common gene pool, but the military was egalitarian and offered a career path to anyone loyal to the caliph. The two groups reinforced each other and, in doing so, shared the spoils of power between them. The military kept the monarchy in power and the monarchy kept the military in pay. Together, they became the two pillars of the state.

With his victory in the civil war, Abd al-Malik, therefore, did more than consolidate his family's power. He consolidated the very idea of family power. From then on, dynasty would become such an enduring element of the political language of the Arab Middle East that it would survive the exile of the Ottoman dynasty in 1924 to reemerge in the monarchies and sheikhdoms of the Gulf, Morocco, and Jordan.

Abd al-Malik's victory ushered in another fundamental change to the power structure of the caliphate. And it, too, endures to this day. The army was *his* army. It was loyal to him and to his family, not to the state. In the early days of the caliphate, especially during the conquests in the 630s and 640s, the Muslim military was a people's army. Its primary loyalty was to Islam. After the first civil war in 656–61, that started to change. The community split and, as a result, the army split too. Men in arms fought for a faction rather than a cause. This change had profound consequences for the future of the military. The first civil war brought the Umayyads to power. The second kept them there. In both cases, it was not the popularity of the dynasty's ideas that led to their triumph. It was their military's strength. As a result, the fate of the monarchy and the military became so intertwined that neither could survive without the other. This identification of the military with a particular political faction led to the politicization of the military. With the army now so overtly partisan, anyone seeking to overthrow the Umayyads would need an army of their own. That, in turn, led to the militarization of politics.

The idea of dynasty as a way to exercise power became so entrenched in the Islamic world that when Umayyad authority fell apart, it was another dynasty who replaced them: the Abbasids (r. 750–1258). The secret of their success was the same combination of monarchy and military that had formerly worked so well for the Umayyads.

But early in the ninth century, disaster struck the Abbasid family. When the caliph Harun al-Rashid died in 809, sibling rivalry got the better of his successor sons, al-Amin (r. 809–13) and al-Mamun (r. 813–33), and they went to war against each other. It ended in victory for al-Mamun, but it came at considerable cost. (This was the same al-Mamun who inserted his name into the foundation stone of the Dome of the Rock.) The war shattered the unity of the ruling family and left the army divided against itself.

Watching from the wings was al-Mamun's brother, al-Mutasim, who was next in line to be caliph. Assessing the damage done by the war, al-Mutasim came to a very clear conclusion. It was impossible to be caliph without a loyal army and the only way to ensure the loyalty of the army was to pay for it. Very quietly, al-Mutasim began recruiting his own private army. By the time he came to power in 833, he had four thousand men under his command.[4]

This private army made up of slave soldiers and foreigners (mostly Turks) was nothing short of a revolution. It was not loyal to the caliphate, to the ruling family, or to Islam. Many of the recruits were Muslim in name only. Many did not even speak Arabic. This army was loyal *only* to the caliph. Power was now completely personal and completely unfettered. The caliph's authority was absolute. To maintain this state of affairs, all he had to do was maintain the army's pay.

Al-Mutasim did more than that. He made the military his core constituency. No longer did members of the ruling family occupy the key offices of state and enjoy the perks that went with them, the military did. This was a soldier-state in the making. But the critical question was what would happen when this caliph, or one of his successors, could not keep the army in the manner to which they were becoming accustomed?

The answer came not long after al-Mutasim's death. When his son and heir al-Wathiq (r. 842–7) died without appointing a successor, the army took matters into their own hands. They played kingmaker and installed their own choice as caliph, a son of their mentor al-Mutasim whose name was al-Mutawakkil (r. 847–61).[5]

Unfortunately for the military, things did not work out as planned. The new caliph tried to rule independently of their influence—he had a number of them fired, others killed, others stripped of their assets—so they stepped into the political process again and staged a coup. A group of senior officers killed the caliph as he sat drinking with his friends. The officers appointed one of his sons as his replacement.[6]

The murder of al-Mutawakkil in 861 was the first military coup in Islam. It was the start of a trend that persists to this day. When Colonel Nasser ousted King Farouq in 1952 and General el-Sisi ousted the Muslim Brotherhood's democratically elected president Muhammad Morsi in 2013, they were following the trail of military intervention in politics first blazed back in the ninth century.

After the coup in 861, politics became increasingly messy. Caliph followed caliph at breakneck speed. At times, the caliphate seemed like little more than a plaything in the hands of the army. Unable to rule directly because of their foreign origins but unwilling to lose their influence and the resources to pay their men, the army made and unmade caliphs at will, depending on who they thought would best protect their interests.

The political consequences of this turmoil would last far into the future. The monarchy-military political unit that had underpinned the caliphate for so long was in ruins. The two power blocs that had previously worked together to uphold the state were in direct competition for control of that state. There were now two ways to power: to be born into it or to fight for it.

Ironically, even those who fought for it became dynasties at the first available opportunity. With the ruling family in disarray, the army in crisis, and the state's finances in the red, the provinces staked their claim for greater autonomy. A number of far-flung provinces had been independent for some time. Spain since 756, Morocco since 788, Tunisia since 800. Now was the turn of areas closer to the center of power. In 868, the army sent a man named Ahmad ibn Tulun to govern Egypt. Once he settled into the job of running one of the wealthiest regions in the empire, he decided to keep it. He continued to pledge allegiance to the caliph but ruled Egypt as his personal fief.[7]

These quasi-independent rulers started off as governors (usually with very strong military connections), usurped power for themselves, then followed the caliph's example and monopolized power for their families. The Idrisids in Morocco. The Aghlabids in Tunisia. The Tulunids in Egypt. The same process was simultaneously occurring in the east of the caliphate where a series of families with strong military connections—the Tahirids, the Saffarids—ruled in the caliph's name.[8]

The pull of dynasty was so strong that even when these dynasties fell, they were replaced by different dynasties. The names changed but not the method of rule. No one followed the Prophet Muhammad's example and left the community free to choose their own leader. No one followed the example of the Rightly Guided Caliphs and left it to a consultative council to decide a new leader. Dynasty had become so established as the language of power that everyone adopted it.

The only alternative powerbase was the military, ruling as a soldier-state, and even they were not immune to the magnetic pull of hereditary power. From 1171, Egypt was ruled by the Ayyubid family. They employed an army of Mamluks: slaves bought abroad as children, brought up in the royal household, and trained to be the sultan's loyal soldiers. It was the same model al-Mutasim had used in the ninth century to build up his private army. And it produced the same results.

In 1250 the Mamluks seized power and installed one of their own as sultan. Theoretically, the Mamluks could not establish a dynasty because their sons were born free and did not qualify as Mamluks. But that did not stop them. In 1260, Baybars became sultan and within two years he appointed his son Baraka as his heir. Another son, Salamish, was soon appointed as the heir-in-waiting.[9] And Baybars was by no means the greatest dynast of the Mamluk era. That accolade went to Sultan al-Nasir Muhammad. Sultan on three occasions himself (1293–4, 1298–1308, 1309–40), nine of al-Nasir's sons, and three of his grandsons went on to succeed him.[10]

The Mamluk soldier-state-cum-dynasty in Syria and Egypt lasted until 1516 and 1517, respectively. And when the Mamluks lost power, they, like the Ayyubids before them (1171–1250) and the Fatimids before them (969–1171), lost it to another dynasty: the Ottomans of Istanbul. Ottoman authority in Turkey stretched as far back as the thirteenth century. The conqueror of Egypt and Syria, Selim I (r. 1512–20), was from the family's ninth generation. The Ottomans held power until the twenty-second generation when the last of the line, Abdulmajid II, was sent into exile in 1924.

From the beginning of Muawiya's caliphate in 661 to Abdulmajid's exile in 1924, the caliphate was in the hands of one family after another. These were not royal families. They were *ruling* families. They held all the power and made all the decisions. The public were their subjects not their fellow citizens. Dynasty, however, was not unique to the Islamic world. It was such a durable form of government it was once the order of the day across much of the world. The French King Louis XIV (r. 1643–1715) was so powerful he once famously declared "I am the state" (*L'état, c'est moi*). But Europe moved on from Sun Kings and the Divine Right of Kings. The Enlightenment, the French Revolution, the Industrial Revolution—all of these changed the relationship between king and country, Church and State, industry and workers, power and the people.

In this rapidly changing climate, European states had to embark on a process of reinventing how power was exercised. It was not easy. It was not painless. And it did not happen overnight. At times, it was laboriously slow. In France, for example, women did not get the vote until after the Second World War.[11] But, eventually, a new political dispensation began to take shape in which the people had a voice. The public arena was opened up to a plurality of views that, over time, led to the creation of a culture of democracy and the checks and balances on power such a culture involves.

No such transformation happened in the Middle East. In the nineteenth century when many parts of Europe were grappling to come to terms with the demands of the modern world, much of the Middle East was under European occupation. In terms of political development, the timing could not have been worse. Imperialism had the effect of arresting political development in the Arab world; of freezing the region in the past with outdated political structures wholly unsuited to the modern world.

Even worse, imperialism and the contradiction inherent in it—we are free but we will not extend that freedom to you—cast a long and dangerous shadow over the region. For some, it tainted everything connected with Western politics and led not only to a rejection of democracy but a rejection of anything to do with the West.

The Arab world, therefore, entered the modern era with its medieval power structures intact. When the caliphate ended in 1924, the monarchy and the military were still the two main power blocs in the Arab Islamic world. And neither of them showed any intention of wanting to lose that power.

3

The Second World War sounded the death knell of European imperialism in the Middle East. The cost of Allied victory was enormous. Britain was broke and France was broken. With so much rebuilding to be done at home, Britain and France could no longer afford their empires. But that did not mean they were willing to let go completely. Both wanted to retain influence in the region. Both saw it as a way to avoid being eclipsed on the global stage by the rising superpowers of the United States and the Soviet Union. That desire to hold on played into the hands of the Middle East's monarchy-military power blocs and defined how independence was achieved and how power was exercised after it.

Imperialism divided the Arab Middle East and North Africa in two.

One group was made up of the colonies. Algeria, Egypt, Tunisia, and Morocco fell into this category. Allied victory in the First World War added Iraq, Jordan, Lebanon, Palestine, and Syria. Allied victory in the Second added Libya. (Libya was occupied during the war. Britain controlled the provinces of Cyrenaica and Tripolitania in the east and center; France the province of Fazzan in the west.) In some of these countries, European power was exercised indirectly through puppet rulers who signed treaties rubber-stamping the European presence. In others, power was exercised directly and amounted to occupation in all but name. In all cases, the net effect was the same: foreign powers were in control.

The other group was made up of the client states. The Gulf kingdoms fell into this category. The Gulf was not subdued by arms but by diplomacy. With the aim of protecting the sea route to India, Britain made a series of treaty arrangements with ruling families in the Gulf during the nineteenth century. In return for not attacking British ships, these families received trade concessions and British military protection. Central Arabia was the exception. Not unified as the Kingdom of Saudi Arabia until 1932, it remained free of direct imperial interference. The Saudis did, however, accept British financial and military support in the Anglo-Saudi Treaty of 1915 in return for not attacking any British ally in the region.

Such support from Britain left the Gulf's ruling families free to concentrate on consolidating their own power over local rivals. This arrangement was a new twist on the centuries-old monarchy-military alliance, with Britain as the military part of the alliance. Consequently, Britain developed very close diplomatic relations with the region's ruling families and, whether by default or design, developed a vested interest in keeping them in power.[12]

In the client states, foreign powers were not directly in control the way they were in the colonies. Thanks to the terms of the treaties they made with local rulers, they did not need to be. The trade-off between the two parties meant both got what they wanted. For example, from 1868 to 1883 the sultan in Muscat faced a series of tribal uprisings against his rule. He turned to Britain for help and British forces fought his battles for him and kept him in power.[13] For the British, interventions like these were a highly cost-effective way of running their overseas empire. In terms of men, money, and material, it was much cheaper than occupying a country the size of Egypt.

These two experiences of European imperialism—colonization or clientage—would shape the Middle East long after Britain and France had left. And it continues to do so. This was because most of the colonies had to fight for independence. And to fight for it, they needed an army. That automatically privileged the role of the military postindependence. A classic example was Egypt. Straight after the military coup in 1952, the military held onto power and Egypt became a military state. Algeria was another country that had to fight its way to freedom. And the political results were the same as Egypt's.

The Algerian War of Independence (1954–62) was so costly in terms of lives lost—over a quarter of a million Algerians and over twenty thousand French—that it became a byword for colonial struggle. For France, letting go of Algeria was never going to be straightforward because the country had become completely enmeshed in French life. Huge numbers of French settlers saw the country as home and had no interest in leaving. They elected representatives to the Chamber of Deputies and their cause enjoyed considerable support among the French military. Even if they had wanted to, the French could not cut and run from Algeria. This raised the stakes and the war became so brutal and so all-pervasive that it tore Algeria apart.

The independence movement was made up of people from all walks of life, but after the war, it was clear who the winners were. The generals took over. Algeria's first president was Ahmad Ben Bella, a veteran of the struggle for independence. In June 1965, he was ousted in a military coup and General Houari Boumedienne took over. Within two years, Algeria was a military state.[14] In Algeria, as in Egypt, independence did not mean freedom.

For France, the political consequences of the war were also considerable. The Fourth Republic collapsed.

There were no such wars for the client states in the Middle East. These states negotiated their independence. The Gulf countries were not created secretly in Whitehall or at postwar conferences where lines were hastily drawn on a map for the convenience of the Great Powers. The state boundaries in the Gulf were drawn up between long-standing allies—the British and the ruling family in question—neither of whom had an interest in seeing any fundamental change. The British wanted to keep their influence. The ruling families wanted to keep their power. The status quo was, therefore, written into the process of state formation. This gave the ruling families, whose power predated the state, an unprecedented opportunity to create countries in their own image. Under such conditions, power was not delegated to any independent institutions. It remained the prerogative of the ruler and his family.

Oman became independent in 1955. Kuwait in 1961. Bahrain and Qatar in 1971. Six of the seven Trucial States (Abu Dhabai, Ajman, Dubai, Fujayrah, Sharja, and Umm Qaywayn) united in 1971 to form the United Arab Emirates. The seventh, Ras al-Khaymah, joined in 1972.

These are young countries with old patterns of power. The Bu Saids in Oman, the Sabahs in Kuwait, the Khalifas in Bahrain, the Thanis in Qatar, the Maktoums and the Nahayans in the United Arab Emirates— these families have held power for centuries. The countries they created in the later part of the twentieth century solidified that power. In the twentieth-century Gulf, the spirit of Louis XIV was alive and well. These families *are* the state.

Elsewhere in the Middle East and North Africa, seismic political shifts occurred after independence, but the basic patterns of power did not change. The binary of the monarchy or the military remained the norm. There was no attempt to introduce an alternative system.

Iraq and Jordan did not fit the standard description of a colony or a client state. Technically, they were colonies: the land was occupied by the

British during the First World War then carved up to suit British inter-ests. Yet their kings, as British appointees, were clients.

Transjordan was rebranded the Hashemite Kingdom of Jordan in 1946 when the country became independent and the amir, Abdullah, took on the title king. As usually happened when a client state became indepen-dent, the transition was peaceful and the king remained a firm friend of the British. As does his great-grandson, the current ruler, King Abdullah II, in power since 1999.

In Iraq, the British-appointed king, Faysal, provided the cover for British rule. Iraq was the first Arab country to become independent when the Anglo-Iraqi Treaty of 1930 was ratified in 1932. But Iraq was inde-pendent in name only and the Iraqis grew tired of Britain wielding power behind the scenes. As usually happened when a client was overthrown by his own people, this transition was far from peaceful. The military staged a coup on July 14, 1958, and killed the king, Faysal II (r. 1939–58). The officers behind the coup called themselves the "Free Officers" after the Free Officers in Egypt. And as was the case in Egypt, once these sol-diers seized power, they kept it and Iraq became a military state. The first president was the leader of the Free Officers, Brigadier General Abd al-Karim Qasim. In February 1963, he was ousted in another military coup—this one backed by, of all people, the CIA; and another soldier, Colonel Abd al-Salam Arif, became president. The colonel's vice presi-dent was a general.[15]

Libya was another kingdom where a military coup took place. In 1949, the United Nations passed a resolution calling for the country's indepen-dence. Two years later, the British withdrew and Idris al-Sanusi became king. Idris's family had founded the Sanusi Sufi order in 1837, and this order led the struggle against Libya's foreign occupiers—first the Italians in 1911, then the British and French in the 1940s. After independence, Idris claimed the crown as his reward.

During his lengthy reign, he came to be seen by many of Libya's younger generation as financially corrupt and too dependent on foreign powers. In 1969, a group of soldiers led by Muammar Gaddafi staged a coup and took power. Inspired by Nasser's Free Officers, they consid-ered themselves Libya's equivalent movement. In emulation of Nasser, Qaddafi assumed the rank of colonel even though he was a captain.[16] Like Nasser, once Gaddafi was in power, he had no intention of giving it up. Strictly speaking, Libya did not become a military state. No military junta was in charge. Calling himself the "Brother Leader," Gaddafi ruled alone in the style of a medieval monarch rather than a soldier-president who has to keep the army on side. But Gaddafi was no benign father figure. He monopolized coercive force in his own hands and used it excessively against his own people. Under his despotic, chaotic, and often insane rule, Libya became one of the most repressed places on the planet.

Like Libya, Morocco and Tunisia were North African countries that had experienced European occupation. And like Libya, Morocco and Tunisia became independent with monarchs at the helm. Morocco stayed that way. Tunisia did not.

Morocco became independent in March 1956. At the time, France was bogged down fighting the war in Algeria and another war in Indo-China. The prospect of having to fight on another front in North Africa brought the French to the negotiating table. An important figure in the independence movement was Morocco's sultan, Muhammad V, who claimed descent from the Prophet Muhammad and whose family had been in power since the sixteenth century. He led the country into independence and kept power after it. A year later, he declared himself king. Like the sultans and sheikhs of the Gulf, he was no constitutional monarch. Absolute power was his.[17]

Tunisia also became independent in March 1956. The same dynamic that led the French to negotiate with the Moroccans also led them to negotiate with the Tunisians. The key figure in the Tunisian drive for independence was Habib Bourguiba of the Neo-*Destour* (Constitution) Party and, in a pattern that is now all too familiar, he took power after independence and kept it. In 1957, the hereditary ruler of Tunisia (the *bey*) whose family had been in power since 1705 was deposed and Bourguiba became president. Two years later, a new constitution gave him absolute power. Tunisia did not become a military state along the lines of Egypt—the Tunisian military was relatively small—but it did not become free. Bourguiba used the full coercive powers of the state to monopolize power and establish authoritarian rule.[18]

In the heart of the Middle East, the country that once ruled the Arab world took a different path to independence. Syria became independent almost by accident. Britain and France reoccupied it in 1941 and it was not long before old imperial rivalries resurfaced. Both wanted Syria in their sphere of influence after the war. To avoid either one gaining overall control, they agreed to grant Syria independence after the war, thinking it would never actually happen. Damascus called their bluff and declared independence in 1946.

Thanks to French efforts to build up Syria's military during the Mandate, the army was one of the strongest institutions in newly independent Syria. And it soon made its presence felt in politics. In 1949 alone, there were three military coups. It was the shape of things to come. When the brief union with Nasser's Egypt (the United Arab Republic) ended after three years in 1961, the military's involvement in politics scaled new heights. In the 1960s there were almost too many coups to count.[19] The end result of all those coups was the presidency of air force general Hafiz al-Asad in 1971 and the complete military takeover of the state.

4

The exception to the military-monarchy monopoly of power was Lebanon. It, alone, did not become a military republic or an absolute monarchy. Instead Lebanon's religious diversity, cosmopolitanism, and long-established commercial community took the country in a different direction.

The constitution of 1926, put together during the French Mandate, legislated for power-sharing between the country's three main groups. The Lebanese Republic would have a Christian president, a Sunni prime minister, and a Shi'i speaker of parliament. These offices were allocated on the basis of the population figures at the time. They took no account of likely future population growth or the fact that one community, the Shi'is, had a much higher birth rate than another, the Christians.

Lebanon became independent in 1945. The transition was peaceful largely thanks to the efforts of the country's two main political groupings. Two years earlier, the French-leaning National Bloc and the Syrian-leaning Constitutional Bloc formed a National Pact.[20] This kind of consensus-building meant Lebanon became independent without the kind of bloodshed or repression seen elsewhere in the Arab world. Coalition governments became the norm. The young republic used its new-found independence and openness to become a regional leader in many businesses including banking and publishing.

That openness did not last. In 1958, a coup tried to turn Lebanon into a Nasser-style republic. It took the intervention of the US military to maintain the status quo. But the genie was out of the bottle. The 1958 foreign intervention would not be the last. The story of Lebanon for the rest of the twentieth century was of a country whose internal complications were played upon by outside powers determined to use the instability resulting from those complications to achieve their own geopolitical agendas in the wider region, regardless of the cost to Lebanon and the Lebanese people. Syria, Iran, Israel, the Palestine Liberation Organization (PLO), and the United States—all, at one time or another, became embroiled in Lebanon. Lebanon in the 1970s and 1980s was like many of the current wars in the Middle East: a political struggle that turned into a civil war that turned into a sectarian war that turned into a proxy war.

As for the Lebanese themselves, they split along religious lines. Religion and identity became the same thing. While the 1926 Constitution, with its inbuilt division of power, spared Lebanon from the autocratic rule that blighted the rest of the Arab Middle East, it could not save the country from civil war. From 1975 to 1990, a horrendous sectarian struggle, made even worse by the involvement of outside powers, ripped Lebanon apart. Even today, long after the war has ended, many of the tensions that sparked the war in the first place remain unresolved and simmer beneath the surface.

*   *   *

From the Atlantic Ocean to the Persian Gulf, there was a common denominator in the politics of the Arab world in the twentieth century.

Independence was no brave new dawn. It was a return to the Middle Ages. Rather than taking the Middle East in a new political direction, independence institutionalized the role of the monarchy and the military. Authoritarian rule, whether by a king or a colonel, remained the standard expression of power.

The incredible tenacity of this trend speaks volumes about the nature of power in the Arab Middle East and who has access to it. In the twentieth century, power was still the privilege of a select few: a ruling family backed by a loyal army or an army loyal to itself. Politics was still militarized and the military was still politicized.

The Arab world was stuck in a time warp.

17

I Am the State: Power, Politics, and the Cult of Personality

1

As soon as the kings and the colonels took power, their main priority was to keep it. To do this, they developed narratives to legitimize their authority and to bridge the gap between the rulers and ruled.

For the kings, the narrative was tradition. For the colonels, it was revolution. These narratives were then backed up by a mixture of hard and soft power. The hard power was coercion. The soft power was patronage (in the oil-rich Gulf kingdoms) and populism (in the less wealthy military states).[1] In spite of the different narratives and different approaches, the goal for both camps was the same: complete control of the state, complete control of the levers of power, complete control of the political arena.[2]

The monarchies were well placed to achieve their aim. Most of them had exercised power long before the state existed. Some of them had been in power as far back as the eighteenth century: the Bu Said family in Oman since 1741, the Sabah family in Kuwait since 1752, the Khalifa family in Bahrain since 1783. This long-term relationship with power gave them the opportunity to build a state system that shut out all rivals. And because these families had been around for so long, they already had substantial networks of supporters in place. Tribal leaders, religious scholars, the commercial community—all had their niche in society and all knew how to access patronage.

That patronage became even more important after oil and gas were discovered in huge quantities across the Arabian peninsula. Oil was discovered in Bahrain in 1932, the same year the Kingdom of Saudi Arabia was founded. The oil deposits along the kingdom's east coast made it one of the richest countries in the world. It is still the world's biggest producer and its ability to act as a swing producer gives it a uniquely dominant position in the global energy market, as is often evident at OPEC meetings on production levels.

Gulf rulers have used that immense oil wealth to create generous cradle-to-grave welfare systems that have enabled their citizens to expect the security of life-long state employment, access to first-class health care, and the financial support to study at some of the world's elite universities. Such levels of state funding are almost unimaginable to cash-strapped students in the West or to anyone who has to pay for medical treatment. The Gulf economies have also benefited from low, or in some cases, zero taxation. (This system, however, makes no provision for what will happen if the oil price plummets and the money runs out.)

This generosity has a political point. It is designed to generate goodwill for the ruling family and create a climate where people benefit so much, they come to the conclusion it is best not to rock the boat. The political calculation made by the ruling families is equally straightforward. Since they were responsible for creating this disproportionately generous system of state benefits, only they can be trusted to protect it.

The ruling families also promise to protect the external security of their states. Here, the long-standing diplomatic and military relationships between the Gulf ruling families and the United Kingdom served them well postindependence. Long after the British Empire had faded into memory and there was no strategic need to protect the route to India, the UK continued to conduct military exercises in the Gulf and maintain close military ties with its former clients in the region. This ongoing relationship brought the Gulf into the American-led Western defense alliance. During the Cold War, that alliance provided a sense of external security which the Gulf states, with long porous borders and relatively small armies, could not have provided for themselves.

The Cold War alliance of the West and the Gulf was mutually beneficial. In geostrategic terms, the West wanted to secure the supply of oil, the lifeblood of Western economies, from possible Soviet attack. That meant protecting the oil fields and the shipping routes, hence the need for military bases in the region. American presidents and British prime ministers had an economic aim too: they wanted to protect the privileged position of US and UK oil companies so that if any new oil fields were discovered, they would be first in line to reap the rewards.

For the Gulf ruling families, the alliance with the West was so beneficial, it became a virtuous circle. By placing themselves under the Western defense umbrella, they also reinforced their position at home. Without ever saying it openly, Washington and London had no wish to lose such reliable allies. The Gulf rulers opened their territory to Western military bases, opened their air space to Western air forces, and opened their exchequers to buy Western-made weapons. During the Cold War, Western leaders often talked of the lack of freedom for the people of the Communist Bloc. They talked much less of the lack of freedom for the people of the Gulf. They were too concerned with maintaining regional stability.

Stability became the mantra of the rulers and the watchword of their allies. In a number of ways, it played well with the conservative nature of society in these countries. Much of that conservatism came from religion. In the Gulf, a very conservative interpretation of Islam was harnessed by state authorities to cement the status quo. The religious establishment was privileged over other groups, especially in the Kingdom of Saudi Arabia, and society was effectively split in two: political power belonged to the princes and the public space to the preachers. In Saudi Arabia, it was a particularly effective trade-off for the ruling family. By giving the religious scholars so much say over social issues, the ruling family tied them into the power structure and ensured religious endorsement for their rule.

There was another significant upside to having the religious establishment so firmly on side. Once the ruler had identified himself so strongly with the faith, it became incredibly difficult, if not impossible, to criticize him because criticizing him became the equivalent of criticizing the faith.

This religious underpinning of power performed yet another key function: it helped deflect criticism from abroad. Western leaders publicly bought the line that the conservative kings of the Gulf ruled in accordance with their religion. That made their Western allies reluctant to interfere (or, more cynically, it gave them cover *not* to interfere) when human rights groups in the West complained about abuses of power in any of these countries. Western politicians, mostly of Christian heritage, did not want to appear as if they were attacking Islam. A more cynical interpretation would be that they did not want to upset an alliance so profitable to their geopolitical interests and to their defense and oil industries.

In Jordan and Morocco, religion played a critical role in promoting regal legitimacy. Both families claim descent from the Prophet Muhammad. That connection allows them to tap into the respect Muslims have for their Prophet and use it as a way of bridging the gap between rulers and ruled. The Jordanian monarchs belong to the Prophet's clan of Hashem (Hashem was the Prophet's great-grandfather) and this relationship is demonstrated in the country's name: the Hashemite Kingdom of Jordan. The constant reminders of the connection to the Prophet are meant to make it harder to criticize the king. This king, like his Moroccan counterpart, is not just any king; he is a descendant of Muhammad. Implicit in this is the suggestion that any criticism of the king is, by default, a criticism of the Prophet's family.

Relationships like these have the effect of making power very personal. And this was intentional. The personalization of power was a major part of the political landscape of the Arab world after independence. Identifying the head of state *as* the state was so effective that everyone did it: kings and colonels alike. It gave a ruler unlimited economic, political, and coercive power. It blurred the lines between the public and the private and made the state finances the ruler's to dispose of as he pleased. It created the circumstances where all opposition—political parties, trade unions, student groups—was stifled and parliaments, if they existed at all, existed as an echo chamber for the ruler's decisions.

And, perhaps most crucially of all, it meant the development of a cult of personality that turned the public space into a cross between a fascist rally and a version of *1984*. Big Brother was *everywhere*. You could be checking into a hotel in Morocco or strolling along a street in downtown Amman: oversized pictures of the nation's ruler gazing down upon his people would always be somewhere in view. Sometimes, there would even be *two* rulers in the posters. In Bahrain, after the regime's brutal crackdown against the peaceful protestors at Pearl Roundabout in March 2011, billboard-size posters popped up all over the capital featuring the Bahraini king with his Saudi counterpart. The Saudis had provided military support for the crackdown. And just in case Bahrainis missed the message the regime was sending them, the posters were emblazoned with words specifically addressed to the Saudi king from his Bahraini opposite number: Shukran Jazilan, Thank you.

In general, the idea behind these ubiquitous posters was to show the ruler as the father of the nation, looking paternally upon his people, but the reality is much more cynical. The psychological impact of seeing the head of state wherever you go is immensely powerful. It is a form of propaganda that is designed to seep into you without you even noticing and to modify your behavior without you even realizing.

Politically, the consequences of the cult of personality are even more powerful. The personalization of power has kept Arab countries, monarchy and military state alike, in a state of chronic institutional underdevelopment and removed any possibility of oversight or accountability of those in charge. Instead of building independent institutions through which power could be exercised, public services delivered and the economy developed, power has remained vested in the ruler and his inner circle. Across the Middle East, there is a therefore an enormous black hole at the heart of power. This institutional gap means that in the event of any change to the status quo, any new order will literally have to start from zero and build from the bottom up—a truly daunting task.

In the Gulf kingdoms, the personalization of power means the ruling family occupy nearly all the main offices of state. In this, they have taken on the role of the ruling party in a one-party state. With one main difference: this is a very exclusive political club—one you can only enter through birth or marriage. Key ministries like the interior, defense, foreign affairs are given to the ruler's brothers or sons or uncles. The same goes for key diplomatic postings, especially to Washington. The succession is restricted to the family and, in most cases, it is the ruler acting alone who makes the decision or who has the final say. There is little or no consultation or consensus-building involved.

It is a state of affairs remarkably similar to the caliphate under the Umayyads or the Abbasids in the 600s and 700s when caliphs held all the power, gave all the plum jobs to relatives and used their military to defeat opponents. And, as was the case in the medieval era, the options for getting rid of a ruler were limited to an external revolution that brought down the whole state or a plot from within the family.

In the monarchies of the modern Middle East, palace coups (sometimes rebranded as "medical coups") have become the method of choice to remove an incompetent or a problematic king. In all cases, after the coup, power has remained in the family. Jordan's King Talal (r. 1951–2) was quickly and quietly removed to make way for his son Hussein (r. 1952–99). Saudi Arabia's King Saud (r. 1953–64) was ushered off the stage to make way for his brother Faisal (r. 1964–75). (Faisal was shot dead in 1975. This, too, was an internal act—the work of an "unstable" relative with a grudge against the king, according to the official version of events. The unofficial version of events is a conspiracy theorist's dream in which the CIA tops the list of likely assassins—their goal to punish Faisal for the oil embargo in 1973 and to make sure no such embargo ever happened again. But no evidence is ever cited.) In 1970, Oman's Sultan Said (r. 1932–70) was pushed from power by the Oman's long-time backers, the British, acting in conjunction with the sultan's son Qabus. A dangerously despotic dictator with a reputation for brutality, Said was considered a liability and had to go.[3]

This monopolization of power by a small elite has led to a trickledown culture of corruption that has leaked into all aspects of public life where *who* you know has become much more important than what you know. In Arabic, this is known as *wasta* which comes from the word meaning "the middle." That, in itself, is an acknowledgment that to plot a course through the Byzantine bureaucracy in these countries, you cannot do it alone. You need a middleman.

Furthermore, the concentration of power in the hands of such a small elite has raised the stakes for anyone opposed to the regime. And not only because these regimes are merciless toward political opponents. Since there is no separation of power, since the ruler *is* the state, then bringing down the ruler could involve bringing down the state. That, together with the lack of independent institutions in place to support the state, means any regime collapse could spell chaos.

The ruling families of the Arab world have long played on a fear of chaos to maintain the status quo. In a region beset by colonial wars, proxy wars, civil wars, and terrorism, this better-the-devil-you-know policy has been deployed to great effect, especially since the Arab Spring, to encourage people not to risk change. The policy is not new. It has been around since the seventh century. The caliph Muawiya was the first to use it. He came to power through a civil war and knew he did not have the whole-hearted support of the community. His answer was to play on the fear of communal strife (*fitna*) to bolster his position. History casts a long shadow in the Middle East. His modern counterparts are doing exactly the same.

2

The military states took a different route to legitimize their authority. Where the monarchies emphasized tradition and religion, the military republics emphasized revolution and the nation.

From the military's point of view, it was a tactic that made perfect political sense. The nation helped foster a sense of communal identity. While the conservative monarchies looked to Islam to provide this, the military republics could not. Many of them had large Christian communities who had to feel part of the new order. In some of the military states, promoting the national identity helped promote the idea of the nation itself. A country like Egypt, with seven millennia of history behind it, already had a well-developed sense of national identity. New countries like Iraq and Syria did not. The leaders of these states had to create a sense of belonging. Patriotism provided the opportunity.

There was another reason the military looked to the nation rather than the faith as a means of legitimacy. The military saw themselves as modern, progressive, even radical, and believed a secular state best represented that outlook.

When it came to the revolution, in many countries across the Arab world, it was the army who brought the old order down. The army therefore believed they were the only group in society strong enough to protect the revolution from any return of the old guard.

This particular idea played well with many ordinary people who were glad to see the back of a political order that had done nothing for them and was widely seen as corrupt and incompetent. In contrast to the old order, the leaders of the postrevolutionary Arab republics were men who looked and talked like the ordinary man in the street. They did not come from elite families. They had not been educated abroad. They had come up the hard way. Nasser was a classic example. Before the revolution, it would have been unthinkable for the leader of Egypt to be a man whose grandfather was a fellah and whose father was a clerk. When Nasser took to the stage to deliver a speech at a mass rally, he managed to pull off the politically impossible: to be ordinary and extraordinary at the same time. The crowds loved him for it. In him, they saw a different Egypt—an Egypt in which someone spoke for them.

Academics and analysts often treat politics and the study of power as a purely rational exercise. But in reality, politics can be a hugely emotional experience, especially for people who have been locked out of the process for a long time. Nasser was able to tap into that. He was also able to manipulate it. When he became president in November 1954, he used that groundswell of popular support to personalize his power and create a political system that ruthlessly crushed any opposition. Like the monarchs in the Middle East, Nasser established such a strong cult of personality that he, like them, became the state. To challenge him was to betray the revolution. To criticize him was to side with the imperialists. Loyalty to the nation and loyalty to Nasser became one and the same.

Nasser was constantly on the lookout—almost to the point of paranoia—for Western plots against him. The CIA-led coup in Iran in 1953 which overthrew the popular prime minister, Muhammad Mosaddeq, and brought back the not-so-popular Shah was what Nasser feared could happen in Egypt. When British, French, and Israeli forces attacked Suez in October 1956 after Nasser nationalized the canal, Nasser saw it as an imperialist plot to unseat him.

Instead, it strengthened his grip on power. His nationalization plan was popular with Egyptians and he used the Suez War to reinforce the idea that only he, and the army who supported him, could protect Egypt from outside interference. Even though militarily, Suez was a defeat for Egypt; politically, it was a triumph for Nasser. After Suez, the assets of anyone British, French or Jewish were seized and the threat of Western intervention became a useful tool in suppressing or silencing internal dissent. Everyone needed to unite against the outside threat.

According to Egyptian novelist Samia Serageldin, part of Nasser's genius was his ability to find scapegoats for his, and the regime's, failings. In Israel and the Western powers, he found them.[4] External opponents in the West were blamed for Egypt's underdevelopment. Colonialism had held the country back, exploited its resources, and integrated it into the global economy on unfavorable terms. Regional enemies like the Arab monarchies were branded as reactionary and as stooges of the West. In a deliberate move, Nasser turned Egypt away from the West and toward the Soviet Union for the technical, military, and financial aid needed to develop the country's infrastructure.

But after so many decades of foreign rule in Egypt, Nasser was reluctant to rely too heavily on any one power. Internationally, he steered a more neutral course and along with India's Nehru and Yugoslavia's Tito, Nasser became a leading light in the Non-Aligned Movement of postcolonial countries. The Bandung Conference in 1955 gave him, and Egypt, a high-profile place on the international stage. It played well at home. So too did his calls for Arab unity.

At home, Nasser entrenched his power through a carefully calibrated system of populism and pressure. High-profile infrastructure projects like the Aswan Dam showed Egypt was casting off the shadow of colonialism and advancing toward modernization. In populist terms, Nasser's fiery anti-imperialist rhetoric (especially against Israel) resonated with all sections of society. As a veteran of the 1948 war, he spoke with an authority on the plight of the Palestinians that King Farouq never had. It was not just Egyptians who admired him for this. His radio broadcasts were listened to across the Arab world. People would eagerly anticipate what the Voice of the Arabs had to tell them, including people in the conservative countries of the Gulf where the kings and sheikhs were opposed to practically everything Nasser and his regime stood for.

Important though their country's newly elevated international position was to Egyptians; what really sealed the deal between the president and many of his people was the massive land redistribution project he introduced. Under the sequestration orders issued by the regime, the massive estates of wealthy landowners were confiscated and given in smaller lots to the people who farmed them. In one fell swoop, Nasser destroyed the economic power of the old political class, eliminating them as a possible threat, while simultaneously cementing his place as the people's president. For the first time in their lives, many fellaheen owned land.

Other changes that made a radical difference in people's daily lives included the provision of health care and free education, subsidized consumer goods, and the guarantee of a government job. Over time, this would lead to a bloated bureaucracy and chronic underemployment. But in the early years of the new regime, these changes were truly revolutionary and had such a positive transformative impact on so many lives that plenty of people did not look too closely at the sort of state Nasser was actually building.

This was an authoritarian one-party state with no room for alternative views. The country was run by the Revolutionary Command Council, made up of Free Officers, and whoever controlled it controlled Egypt. Increasingly, that person was Nasser. And increasingly, he maneuvered behind the scenes to concentrate power in his hands and to eliminate any form of potential opposition; both from within the RCC and from without. On June 18, 1953, the monarchy was abolished and Egypt became a republic with General Neguib as the first president. Revolutionary tribunals were established to try figures from the old regime, thereby destroying the old party of power, the Wafd, and the credibility of the judiciary in one move. Censorship became law. Internal opponents, like the Muslim Brotherhood or the Communists, were criminalized as a security threat to the regime and the revolution. Nasser banned the Muslim Brotherhood in February 1954.

State repression against the Brotherhood reached a whole new level after one of their members, Mahmud Abdel Latif, tried to assassinate Nasser at a rally in his hometown of Alexandria on October 26, 1954. (He said afterwards he had been forced into it.) Nasser's gutsy performance— proclaiming defiantly to the crowds, "If I die, you are all Gamal Abdel Nassers," as the bullets whizzed past him and struck a light bulb above his head—inspired two hundred thousand people to take to the streets to welcome him on his return to Cairo.[5]

The Brotherhood now felt the wrath of a hostile state. Many were rounded up and sentenced in what were little more than show trials. Their Supreme Leader, Hassan al-Hudaybi, was sentenced to life imprisonment and two members of the Supreme Council were hanged.[6] It would get worse. During the 1960s, the repression of the Muslim Brotherhood by Nasser's regime reached quite shocking proportions and thousands of their members were sent to what were essentially gulags.

On November 14, 1954, barely a fortnight after the assassination attempt on Nasser, the 36-year-old colonel achieved his ultimate ambition. On the flimsy and highly improbable pretext of conspiring with the Muslim Brotherhood, General Neguib was removed from the presidency and Nasser took over. His popularity with his fellow officers and much of the masses made him virtually untouchable. Power in Egypt was now so highly personalized; there was no legitimate means left to question it. Parliamentary elections were dropped. Presidential elections merely confirmed the status quo. In the first such election, held in June 1956, Nasser polled 99.9 percent of the vote.[7]

The revolution had turned Egypt into a military state with a leader who had powers akin to a pharaoh. This complete merging of the military and the political had repercussions at home and abroad. Military power soon extended far beyond politics. The army monopolized large sections of the economy to finance their budget. This type of command economy and the subsequent lack of any independent regulation skewed the internal market and, over time, reduced Egypt's commercial competitiveness. It also closed large parts of the economy to newcomers. Here, too, who you knew was more important than what you knew. Here, too, to get ahead you had to be part of the system.

Another side-effect of the military takeover played out within the military itself. In societies where the military is an independent institution which *serves* the state, its primary function is to defend that state. In Egypt, that was not the case. The primary function of Egypt's military was to maintain its control of the state. Every other military priority, including the issue of what to do about Palestine, came after that. In the state Nasser built, Egypt was a country that had effectively been occupied by its own army.[8] And because the person who made the political decisions was also the person making all the military decisions, Egypt's army lacked any independent oversight—a serious flaw that threatened its battlefield effectiveness.

What happened in Egypt mattered because Egypt was, and still is, no ordinary country in the Arab Middle East: it is a bellwether for the region. Where Egypt leads, others follow. Under Nasser, Egypt's political model was replicated across the region. Syria, for one, was so inspired by Nasser and his ideas of Arab unity that, for a time, the country joined with Egypt to form the United Arab Republic (1958–61). The union ultimately failed when Damascus discovered it was expected to be the junior partner in the alliance.

Even after the divorce, Syria stayed true to the basic ideas of Nasser's Egypt: a military-run state, a regime monopoly of coercive power, a command economy, a welfare system designed to provide access to services previously supplied by religious endowments or private patronage, and a bureaucracy that aimed to absorb as many university graduates and school leavers as possible. Syria, like Egypt, also steered a foreign policy course away from the West and turned to the Soviet Union for military assistance. In return, Moscow achieved its long-held dream of access to a warm-water port on the Mediterranean in Tartus. Other military states pursued similar social policies to Nasser. For the oil-rich ones such as Algeria, Iraq, and Libya, funding public services was a much easier feat than it was for a country like Egypt. Not only did Egypt lack natural resources, it had a rapidly growing urban population; all of whom needed jobs.

The Arab world's military states also adopted Egypt's model of one-party politics where all political activity was funneled through one state-sanctioned organization. In Syria and Iraq, it was the Baath (Renaissance) Party. In Algeria, it was the *Front de Libération Nationale* (FLN). In Tunisia, it was the Neo-Destour Party. In Libya, there was no such organization because Gaddafi insisted he was not actually in charge. He was the Brother Leader not the president.

Like Egypt, the leaders of the military states (the Brother Leader included) adopted a cult of personality that cast the head of state as the protector of the revolution and the embodiment of the nation. This cult was reflected in the billboard-size posters of the leader in various paternal poses that appeared in every public place. It was also reflected in his ability to win almost 100 percent of the vote in presidential elections. (Usually, he was the only candidate.) No other leader, however, managed to scale the heights of Nasser's popularity. In spite of the repressive nature of his regime, Nasser, right to the very end of his time in power, enjoyed almost god-like adoration from sections of the Egyptian population.

That popularity was one of the reasons he struck fear into the hearts of the monarchs of the Middle East. They feared Nasser in the same way, and for the same reason, they fear the democratic mandates won by the Muslim Brotherhood in elections held since the Arab Spring: it undermined their legitimacy and threatened their power.

And their fears were not ungrounded. In Saudi Arabia in 1969, a group of "Free Officers" (including the king's personal pilot) were caught plotting to overthrow King Faisal and turn the Kingdom of Saudi Arabia into a Nasserist-style republic.[9] The Kingdom of Morocco narrowly avoided a similar fate in 1972 when General Oufkir was executed for his part in a coup attempt against King Hassan II. Not content with punishing the general, the king took his revenge out on the general's family. His widow and six children (one of whom was only a few years old) were held without charge in an underground jail in the desert for nearly 20 years. Their ordeal only ended when they managed to dig their way out and escape. The general's eldest daughter, Malika, recounted the family's nightmare in *La Prisonnière* which became an international bestseller.[10]

In the 1950s and 1960s, the Arab world divided into two camps: both were authoritarian but one was radical, revolutionary, and anti-Western; the other was conservative, religious, and pro-Western. When the Eisenhower Doctrine of January 8, 1957, recognized Communism as the main threat to the Middle East and offered financial assistance to anyone fighting it, Nasser saw it as a threat because of his links to the Soviet Union.[11] The monarchies, with their long-established links to the West, were only too happy to sign up to the Doctrine.

The stage was set for the two camps to clash. The battleground for this proxy war was Yemen.

3

In the 1960s, Yemen was a microcosm of the power struggles across the Middle East. Here, as was the case just about everywhere else, the monarchy and the military battled it out for overall control.

Here, too, the imperialist legacy lingered. Yemen in the 1960s was a country with a complicated history—complicated because the north and the south had very different historical experiences.

The north of Yemen is rugged, mountainous, and geographically inaccessible. For that reason, it became home to a Shi'i family, the Zaydis, who ruled for an almost unbelievable amount of time—*eleven centuries*—from 893 to 1962.[12] Their leader did not take the title caliph or king. Instead, he was an Imam: technically the term for a prayer leader but in Shi'ism, a term for political leader too. The Zaydis had first come to the region during the Abbasid era when it was common for Shi'i rebels to flee as far as possible from the central authority in Baghdad. After a failed rebellion, they would run for their lives and literally keep running until they ran out of land. That is why there are clusters of Shi'is in coastal regions across the Arab world: Hasa on the east coast of Arabia, Bahrain in the Persian Gulf, northern Yemen on the Red Sea coast, and Lebanon on the Mediterranean. It was the same story on the southern shores of the Mediterranean. The Fatimids, who ruled Egypt for two centuries, were Shi'i, and they launched their invasion of Egypt from their base in Tunisia.

In contrast to the north, Yemen's more accessible south, with its arable land, its long coastline and its strategically well-positioned port of Aden, caught the eye of empires and, as a result, underwent a more chequered history. Under the Rasulid dynasty (r. 1229–1454), it became Sunni. Then, in the sixteenth century the Ottomans arrived. During this period, Yemen turned into a something akin to a political revolving door. The Zaydis came back. Then the Ottomans did. Then, in 1839, the British arrived in the south and, as so often happened when the British turned up somewhere in the Middle East, they did not leave. Nearly a century later, in 1937, the south became a crown colony of the British Empire.[13]

An uneasy division of power prevailed for the first half of the twentieth century. The Zaydis reclaimed the country following the end of the Ottoman Empire in 1924. But the British, ruling in alliance with local sultans, remained the real power in the south.

In the second half of the twentieth century, everything changed. Thanks to geography, Yemen's destiny had long been entwined with Egypt's. The Bab al-Mandab strait on Yemen's south-western coast is the entry point for shipping routes into the Red Sea from Asia and is one of global shipping's chokepoints—so-called because whoever controls it has the ability to strangle global shipping and cause a global economic crisis. In 2015, an estimated 40 percent of global trade passes through the picturesquely named Gate of Lamentation. Back in 1956, Britain and France waged a war over control of the Suez Canal but it does not actually matter who controls the canal because if the Bab al-Mandab is not open, nothing is going through from Asia to Europe or from Europe to Asia.

In the 1950s, thanks to Nasser's vision of Arab unity, Yemen's destiny once again became entwined with Egypt's when Yemen joined the short-lived United Arab Republic of Egypt and Syria as a federal partner.[14] When the Union collapsed, the by-now-predictable happened. A group of soldiers, tribes, and anyone else opposed to the Imam staged a coup and brought the one thousand and 69 years of Zaydi rule to an end. North Yemen became the Yemen Arab Republic and aligned itself ideologically with Nasser's Egypt.[15] Nasser sent his army to help the republic bed down. The YAR was radical, republican, and secular. In other words, it was the complete opposite of its neighbor to the north: the religious, conservative Kingdom of Saudi Arabia.

And the kingdom did not like it one bit. Having one of Nasser's satellites on its doorstep was too close for comfort. What happened next has become all too familiar in the region. In one of those strange alliances of mutual convenience which seem to occur so often in the Middle East (especially right now) and which have nothing to do with shared ideology and everything to do with shared interests, Sunni Saudi Arabia sided with the Shi'i Zaydis in order to strike at Nasser.

For the next five years, war waged between the new rulers of north Yemen and the old ones that was really a proxy war between President Nasser's Egypt and King Faisal's Saudi Arabia for control of the Middle East. The two sides fought to a standstill then withdrew in 1967. Neither won but both, arguably, lost. In 1967, some of Egypt's elite troops were still deployed in Yemen which meant they were not available to fight in the Six-Day War. Whether they would have made any difference, we will never know. But, arguably, it was not the wisest military decision for Egypt to go into battle against a well-trained, well-armed people fighting for survival with the country's best troops stationed somewhere else.

As for Faisal, even though the disaster of 1967 was Nasser's to bear, events of that year were hardly to his credit. His kingdom was Islam's birthplace, home to Mecca and Medina, two of the religion's Holy Cities, and it was under his watch that Islam's third Holy City, Jerusalem, was lost to Islam. In a bid to bolster their own power at the expense of the other, this colonel and this king helped create a set of circumstances that set the Palestinian cause even further back than the Catastrophe of 1948.

Ultimately, Nasser's brand of revolutionary one-party republicanism made more progress in the south of Yemen. In 1962, popular protest against British rule turned violent with the National Liberation Front (NLF) at the forefront. In 1967, the same year that the war in the north ended, the British withdrew from Aden. Events then unfurled in the same way they had across much of the Arab world: the NLF took control of the newly named People's Republic of South Yemen (PRSY) and became the party of power. Two years later, the PRSY changed names again. Now ideologically anti-Western and aligned with the Soviet Union, its new name was the People's Democratic Republic of Yemen (PDRY). The "democratic" in the title was somewhat ironic: the PDRY was a one-party state backed up by a strong military.[16]

The events of 1967 clearly showed how prominent the role of the military was in the politics of the Arab world. War was used by kings and colonels alike as an instrument to achieve a political goal. But events of this year also showed up one of the most glaring contradictions in the region's power structure.

In the postindependence *Arab* Middle East, the military regimes placed the army at the center of the state. Nothing in these countries was more important than the military. Yet, the most highly militarized state in the *entire* Middle East, where every adult (male and female) is legally required to serve at least three years in the armed forces and must carry out a period of military service every year after that until middle age, did not become a military state. It became a democracy.

What made the State of Israel different?

4

This is a highly contentious issue. Not only because it feeds into the wider Israeli-Palestinian debate but also because Israel's democratic credentials are often cited by Israeli politicians as a reason why the West should take sides in this struggle and support Israel rather than the authoritarian Arab regimes.[17] The issue of democracy has therefore become every bit as partisan as every other issue in this debate.

But what makes the issue of Israel's democracy so contentious is that it is true. Israel, whatever else its critics may throw at it, *is* a democracy. Questions may be raised about the nature of that democracy—Arabs in

Israel will tell you that they face discrimination in many aspects of life and that Arab neighborhoods are deliberately underresourced—but the fact remains that Israeli citizens freely elect their governments and freely criticize them for their shortcomings. They also freely vote them out.

The debate over Israel's democracy is further complicated by the issue of Palestinians who are Israeli citizens. This is because in Israel, they have access to the kind of open electoral system that does not presently exist in large parts of the Arab world. For Arabs, it can be emotionally uncomfortable to know they have voting rights in the State of Israel that many of their fellow Arabs do not have in their own countries. The difference between how Israeli governments treat their Arab citizens and how Arab regimes treat theirs is then cited by supporters of Israel as further proof of the country's democratic credentials and as another reason why the West should side with Israel.

This viewpoint is then complicated further by the fact that the political power of Arabs in Israel is growing. They are the descendants of the people who lived in the area before 1948 and they now make up over 20 percent of Israel's population. In the elections on March 17, 2015, they began to flex their political muscle. Standing as a joint list, the Arab parties maximized their vote which meant the Zionist parties, from the left and the right, had to factor them into the political equation for the first time. Given the fragmented nature of Israeli politics and the near-certainty of coalition governments—Prime Minister Netanyahu's Likud Party won the March 2015 election with less than a quarter of the Knesset's 120 seats—if the Arab parties continue to cooperate like this, they could end up having the final say in who forms a future government. Even if they do not join a governing coalition, they could block one set of parties from taking power.

But what really makes the whole issue of Israel's democracy and the lack of it in Arab states *so* controversial is what is often implied but rarely said. In the corridors of power in the West, the question of why Israel is a democracy when so many Arab countries are not taps into a deep-seated (but incorrect) cultural assumption that goes back to days of empire: that Arabs are not wired for democracy. And for "Arabs," what is really meant is Islam. That assumption enabled Britain, the home of parliamentary democracy, and France, the home of revolutionary freedom, to subdue large parts of the Arab world and to do it with a comfortable sense of entitlement and moral superiority. And the suspicion that Islam is somehow incompatible with democracy has lingered. The actions of groups like ISIL have done nothing to dispel this point of view. If anything, they have reinforced it and made more people accept it as true.

Judaism, on the other hand, is viewed differently in the West. It is one of the paradoxes of Western history that Judaism as a faith was respected long before the Jews who practiced it were. Western civilization rests on the twin pillars of the Greek and Hebrew heritage. The Mosaic Law code is integrated into legal systems across the Western world. The Houses of Parliament in London have a prominent visual reminder of this in one of the most important rooms in parliament's buildings. The Grand Committee of the House of Lords, which oversees most of the legislation from the Lords, meets in the Moses Room. There, an entire wall is covered with a giant mural of Moses bringing the tablets of law down from the mountain to the Israelites.

With the West taking its inspiration from Judaism in the law, the assumption followed that since the West is compatible with democracy, Judaism is too. The same assumption has not been made with Islam. As a result, Islam, the religion, gets blamed for political problems it neither created nor sanctioned. Postindependence, power in the Arab world was seized by soldiers and sheikhs. Yet, as we have seen, this is a state of affairs not endorsed by the Quran or the Prophet. The Quran does not sanction hereditary power as a means of rule. Muhammad did not nominate a successor. Instead, he left the Muslim community free to decide their own future. And when he was in charge of that community, he did not govern through an army. He governed through consensus. Islam is therefore not theologically inclined toward the patterns of power that have prevailed across the Arab Middle East after independence—even if, in some cases, it has been deliberately manipulated to justify them.

Why Israel became a democracy after independence and the Arab states did not has nothing to do with religion. The answer is really quite simple. It was a choice. In Israel, the people in a position of power after independence chose to make their country a democracy. In the Arab world, the people in a position of power made a different choice.

The Israelis then built up the institutions necessary to support their state and developed the democratic processes to sustain them. This led to an entirely different relationship between the citizen and the state than the relationship that occurred in the Arab world. This, in turn, affected all aspects of life in Israel, creating a culture of openness that, over time, laid the groundwork for research and development to take off in a way that did not happen elsewhere in the Middle East. The knock-on effect on the Israeli economy has been considerable. The modern Israeli tech sector, a global leader in its field, is an example of that openness.

However, the most marked example of the different relationship between the citizen and the state in Israel than that in the Arab states is the military. Because the Israel Defense Force (IDF) is essentially a conscript army, it belongs to the *people* of Israel, rather than the state, in a way that professional armies do not. It also means that whoever is running the state cannot take advantage of the army to achieve a political agenda against the wishes of the people. All of that critically alters the balance of power between the state, the people and the army, in favor of the people. In Israel, the *people* are the army and the state works for them.

That is not the case in the Arab military republics. There, the army is the state and the state works for the army. The people are left out of the equation. It is not the case in the kingdoms either. There, too, the military's role is to maintain the status quo. And as the Arab Spring has shown, that can mean deploying troops over the border to help a fellow king quash popular protest and stay in power against the wishes of his people.

The key question, then, is why did Chaim Weizmann, the first president of Israel, and David Ben-Gurion, the first prime minister, along with those around them, take the decision to democratize when the Arab kings and colonels did not?

The majority of the first generation of Israeli politicians came from Russia. (Future prime minister Golda Meir, born in the United States, was an exception.) Many of them were involved in antitsarist politics and the experience of growing up under an authoritarian regime profoundly shaped their political thinking. Having escaped such despotism, they had no wish to revisit it in their Promised Land. What, instead, they brought with them to the Middle East was the political affiliations they had back in Russia. Before Israel even existed, the Jewish settlers in Palestine were already espousing multiparty politics.

Jewish history also played a role. Not only the experience of the Holocaust but the fact that Jews had so long been on the other side of power. In Europe, they were obliged to campaign for a citizenship that was granted without question to others born in the same country. Even in the Islamic world where Jews enjoyed legal protection from persecution, they were still not full citizens. None of this—not the persecution or the second-class status—was an experience any of them wanted to go through again. The whole point of having their own country was to make their own rules. That ambition to leave the past behind and to live freely, along with the inbuilt suspicion of authority that had developed over so many centuries as outsiders, pointed Israel toward an open political system.[18]

The prestate organizations of the *Yishuv* gave them the means to start building the independent institutions of the State. These bodies already had elective leadership structures in place and that pattern was carried through into the state-building period.[19]

This is not to say that the State of Israel became an egalitarian Utopia. Aside from the ever-present security situation and the issues associated with it, Israel is socially divided between Ashkenazi and Sephardi, with the Ashkenazim dominating the top jobs in politics and the professions. It is something of an irony that Britain has had a Sephardi prime minister whereas Israel still has not. In the early years of the state, newly arrived Sephardim from Morocco or Iraq were settled in kibbutzim near the border with Lebanon or in the middle of the Negev desert—places where Ashkenazim did not always want to go.

And politics was not just dominated by the Ashkenazim. It was dominated by one party: Labor. It was not until 1977 that politics opened out and the Likud Party first formed a government and Menachem Begin became prime minister. Part of his success was due to his ability to reach out to Sephardi voters. It is a trend his fellow Likudnik, Binyamin Netanyahu, has continued and with the same degree of success.

If these are the reasons Israel went down the democratic path, why, then, did leaders like Egypt's Colonel Nasser and Jordan's King Hussein do the opposite?

It came down to how they achieved power. Bestselling Egyptian novelist Alaa al-Aswany neatly encapsulates the problem of power in the Arab world when he says that it is the way a ruler comes to power that will determine how he exercises it.[20]

The Arab rulers, kings and colonels alike, did not come to power through an election so they did not stay in power that way. They took power by shutting the people out of the equation and, ultimately, they ended up keeping it that way.

18

The Problem of Absolute Power: From Stability to Stagnation

1

Absolute power leaves no aspect of life untouched. In authoritarian societies, power becomes the end and the means to the end. The result is that everything in the public arena is manipulated toward maintaining the status quo. This leads to a form of political stability that is so stultifying, it might be more appropriate to call it stagnation.

The statistics say it all. A typical example is the Hashemite Kingdom of Jordan. From 1946, the year Jordan became a kingdom, to the present, only four men have ruled the country: King Abdullah (ruled until 1951), King Talal (r. 1951–2), King Hussein, (r. 1952–99), and King Abdullah II (r. 1999–).

To put this in context, when King Hussein succeeded his father in 1952, Harry S. Truman was President of the United States. By the time Abdullah II succeeded Hussein in 1999, a further nine men had served as president (three of whom, Dwight S. Eisenhower, Ronald Reagan, and Bill Clinton, were two-term presidents).[1]

Morocco has had even less political churn than Jordan. Since independence in 1956, the country has had only three rulers: King Muhammad V (ruled until 1961), King Hassan II (r. 1961–99), and King Muhammad VI (r. 1999–). The average reign of a Moroccan king is almost five times the length of an American presidency.

The monarchy with the lowest churn of all is Oman where the average reign of a sultan is equivalent to *ten* American presidential terms. The present sultan, Qabus, has been in power since 1970. He succeeded his father, Said, who ruled for 38 years (1932–70).

Longevity in power (or presidents-for-life) is also a feature of politics in the republics. Egypt's Nasser was president for 16 years (1954–70), Tunisia's Ben Ali for 23 (1987–2010), and Syria's Asad for 29 (1971–2000). Libya's Brother Leader Gaddafi topped this list with his quite staggering 42 years in power (1969–2011).

At the start of the twenty-first century, a whole new twist on power took place in the Arab world when presidents began acting like kings. It started in Syria where, centuries earlier, the hereditary principle was first introduced to Islamic politics. The Syrian political model shared many characteristics with other republican regimes across the Arab world and, in this instance, where Syria led, others would soon follow.

As he neared the end of his life, President Hafiz al-Asad took steps to ensure that his son Bashar succeeded him. Bashar was not originally intended for this role. As the second son, he was allowed to pursue the career of his choice (he was an ophthalmologist) and it was his older brother Basil who went into the military as preparation for the presidency. In a military republic like Syria, time in a uniform was an essential stepping stone on the way to power. When Basil was killed in a car accident in January 1994, Bashar was recalled from his studies in London and fast-tracked through the military ranks. It was never publicly stated that he was the successor son but when posters began to appear all over Syria of the father and the son together, Syrians would have understood the message.

Article 83 of the Syrian constitution stated that any candidate for president had to be at least 40 years old. In June 2000, just before Hafiz died, that age was reduced to 34 which, conveniently, happened to be Bashar's age. The amendment to the constitution not only facilitated the passage of power from father to son, but also meant that the father's final act as president (and the one that shaped the son's presidency) was an unadulterated act of power. The power of the Asad family, and the clique-elite of soldiers, family members, in-laws and members of the Alawi sect who backed them, was projected far into the future. With Bashar at the helm, their influence, wealth, and power were secured.

Syria, once one of the most radical states in the Middle East, had become a *jamlaka*. Not a republic (*jumhuriyya*) or a kingdom (*mamlaka*), a whole new word had to be invented to describe a republic that acted like royalty and a president who ruled like a king.[2] In this new system, the people were—yet again—shut out of power and the gap between the ruler and the ruled remained as wide as ever.

All of which raises the question of what happened to Hafiz al-Asad, a military-president in Nasser's mold who took power in a coup, during his three decades as president that he ended up becoming as royal as the royals?

It is a cliché to say that absolute power corrupts absolutely but clichés have a certain truth. During Hafiz al-Asad's three decades in power, he was ruthless in crushing any opposition to his rule. As was the case with the ruling class across the Arab Middle East, Asad tolerated no dissent. Once the initial period of postindependence excitement passed in the military republics and hard political and economic realities kicked in, the early populism that was used to legitimize power gave way to increasing repression. Regimes became less interested in legitimizing power than in exercising it. People regularly disappeared in the night. Political opponents were detained without trial for years. Torture was routine. In Syria, even Hafiz al-Asad's own brother Rifat was not spared his wrath when the president thought Rifat had conspired against him when he was incapacitated by a heart attack in 1983. Rifat was lucky to escape with his life but spent years in exile.

Rifat's fate, however, pales in comparison to the horror that happened in Hama the year before. The city's famous waterwheel was said to have run red with blood after Asad's crackdown against the Muslim Brotherhood in 1982. To this day, no one knows how many people were killed by Asad's army of Alawi militias. (Rifat had played a key role in this crackdown. He was on the ground directing the militias on his brother's behalf.) The figure most often cited is twenty thousand, but the exact figure may be more. After the crackdown, even belonging to the Muslim Brotherhood became a capital offence.

In these circumstances, where there is no check or balance on a president's power, no one to challenge or criticize him, no limit to his length of time in office, power develops an almost drug-like dynamic of its own. To keep the current system in place and protect the privileges that go with it becomes the only goal. And those privileges are considerable. Because of the president's monopoly on coercive power and his ability to eliminate or silence dissent, every part of national life is under his control. The entire economy is at his disposal. In Syria, that wealth has been used to enrich family members (Hafiz's in-laws the Makhlufs are said to have a fortune running into the billions) and to reward supporters (retired cabinet members and army generals are often pensioned off with lucrative defense contracts).[3]

The use of public money in this way has a distorting influence on the economy and institutionalizes corruption. It privileges defense spending above all other areas—in Syria, for example, nearly half the budget is earmarked for defense[4]—and leaves other sectors of the economy suffering from chronic underinvestment. It also has huge social implications. Just as the gap between people and power has widened since independence in the Arab world, so too has the gap between rich and poor. The rich have consistently become richer because the ruling elite have used their political power to, effectively, asset-strip their own country.

The longer this system lasts, the more reluctant the beneficiaries are to lose it. Partly for the obvious reasons of self-interest but partly, too, from fear: a new political dispensation will, in all likelihood, call the old regime to account. In these circumstances, the confiscation of assets would be the least of their worries. This is where the idea of a scorched earth policy kicks in. In the event of a rebellion or uprising, the old guard calculate that it is better to dig in, defend their ground and take the risk of hanging together rather than conceding defeat and hanging separately. In order to avoid this scenario ever happening, it becomes a political necessity to keep power in the hands of the old guard. And as the Umayyad caliph Muawiya discovered in the seventh century, the best way to maintain the status quo and project the privileges of the present into the future is to create a ruling family with a loyal militia to protect it.

2

As far as ruling families are concerned, there is no shortage of them in the Middle East. For the nearest example, all Hafiz al-Asad had to do was look to his Jordanian neighbor where the passage of power from father to son had taken place with effortless ease in 1999. (And this smooth transition happened in spite of the potential disharmony within the family after King Hussein sacked his brother Hassan, the long-serving Crown Prince, at the last minute to make way for his son Abdullah.)

In his book *The Rise and Fall of Arab Presidents for Life*, Harvard Professor Roger Owen talks of a phenomenon in the Arab world which he calls the "demonstration effect."[5] Because Arab heads of state meet on such a regular basis at summit conferences of organizations like the League of Arab States (and, to a lesser extent, the Gulf Cooperation Council) and issue joint communiqués stating a common position on many issues, a certain "clubbiness" has developed amongst them, regardless of whether their countries are conservative kingdoms or a military republics.[6] The challenges these leaders face are common enough to warrant a common approach. Hence "the demonstration effect": i.e. what works for the ruler of one country might very well work for the ruler of another.

In these circumstances, political models of republicanism or royalty, and political ideologies of religion or revolution, are less relevant than results. And it becomes possible for a republican president to appropriate the structural stability of a monarchical system to achieve his own ambitions.

There was another reason why, at the start of the twenty-first century, Hafiz al-Asad and other presidents in the region—Gaddafi in Libya, Mubarak in Egypt, Saddam Hussein in Iraq, Ali Abdullah Saleh in Yemen—were looking to turn their republics into quasi-monarchies. In the ideological battle that waged between the military republics and the conservative kingdoms postindependence—a battle typified by events in Yemen in the 1960s—the kingdoms won.

The Six-Day War was a disaster for Nasser. As a veteran of the 1948 war, Palestine was an issue close to his heart. The manner of the defeat in 1967 was not just a political humiliation to him; it affected him very deeply on a personal level too. In military terms, the war could not have been worse for the Arab armies. Not only did the Israeli military successfully repel invasion on three fronts, they took huge swathes of territory from Egypt (the Sinai peninsula), Jordan (the West Bank including Jerusalem), and Syria (the Golan Heights). Right to the end, Egyptians were kept in the dark about the extent of Arab losses because state-controlled media gave misleading reports about how the war was proceeding.

The defeat would have been difficult for any Arab leader to bear. For Nasser and the ideology he espoused, it signaled the beginning of the end. The Cairo crowds would not accept his resignation. To do so, in their eyes, would have meant yet another victory for Israel. But after 1967, Nasser was never the same. His health suffered and his political credibility was irreparably damaged. The war had revealed the limits of his political vision. His was a military state that could not win wars. Since 1948, the Palestinians had been desperately hoping for rescue from the uncertainty of their situation. And many of them hoped Nasser, as the leader of the Arab world, could provide it. Psychologically, as well as territorially, Palestinians had been living in limbo for nearly two decades: almost as if what had happened to them could not have been real. After 1967, there was no denying that Israel was a reality. And there was no denying that the Arab states, led by Nasser, had not been able to do anything about it.

This realization led to a number of political realignments and much soul searching across the Arab world. This was the moment the balance of power tipped toward the oil-rich ruling families in the Gulf. This was when Palestinians started looking to the Palestine Liberation Organization (PLO) to represent their interests. Many people in the Arab world also looked in a new direction for an answer. For both solace and a political alternative, large numbers now turned to Islam.

Nasser died in 1970 and was succeeded by his long-time associate and fellow soldier Anwar Sadat. From the moment Sadat took office, his goal was to reclaim Sinai and to restore Arab honor. To that end, all Arab assets were marshaled. On the battleground, it did not ultimately make much difference. Egypt's initial success in crossing the Suez Canal during the war in 1973 was soon wiped out by an Israeli counter-attack which left Egypt's Third Army trapped on the east of the canal.[7]

But this war is remembered just as much, if not more, for events which occurred away from the battlefield. Prior to the war, Sadat built alliances that cut across the monarchy-military divide in the Arab world with the result that the 1973 war saw the oil card played for the first (and only) time. The oil embargo by the Gulf states against Western countries who supported Israel was brief but effective. It pushed the price of oil through the roof, introduced price instability into the market, and set Saudi Arabia on the way to becoming the wealthiest country in the world.

After the war, Sadat made a separate peace deal with Israel which enabled him to achieve his goal of reclaiming Sinai. Israel also achieved a number of strategic objectives after the war. Sadat's controversial visit to Israel on November 8, 1977, and the US-brokered Camp David Accords in 1978 that led to the Egypt-Israel Peace Treaty in March 1979 secured recognition for Israel from an Arab neighbor and led to the establishment of diplomatic relations between the two countries. For Israel, it meant the country's southern border was secure because Egypt was legally bound to stay out of any future Arab conflict with Israel.

While Sadat and Israel gained what they wanted from the diplomacy after the war and the oil-rich kingdoms gained from the spike in oil prices after the embargo, it is hard to see what the Palestinians gained from October 1973. The West Bank, the Gaza Strip, and the Golan Heights were still occupied. The refugees from 1948 were still refugees. The essential problem was still unresolved.

In this way, 1973 was something of a watershed. Palestine was an issue that united Arabs across the world. Before 1967, they looked to the leaders of the Arab world to do something about it. For many of those leaders, most notably Nasser, Palestine was a critical part of their political agenda. Events of 1967 changed that agenda. And events of 1973 confirmed that change. The war of 1967 was fought to reclaim Palestine. The war of 1973 had much narrower goals. For Arab leaders, Palestine had gone from a cause to a slogan. They were happy to use it as a legitimizing device for their own power—opposing Israel and supporting the Palestinians was something everyone could agree on, rulers and ruled alike—but after 1973, there was no sustained effort to address the problem in a way that would put pressure on Israel or Israel's Western backers to resolve it.

Every so often, there would be vast injections of cash from oil-rich states to Palestinian organizations and proposals like the Arab Peace Initiative suggested by Saudi Arabia's King Abdullah, under which Arab states would recognize Israel in return for Israeli withdrawal from the

Occupied Territories. But there was no concerted effort to deploy the diplomatic and commercial assets of the Arab world to help Palestinians achieve their own state. The Gulf Arab states controlled the supply of the commodity upon which the Western economy depended yet they never played the oil card again. Instead, every Arab state concentrated on looking after their own interests and those states with economic and commercial links with the West had no intention of risking those investments for the Palestinians.

The reason Arab leaders were able to behave this way is the same reason they were able to exercise power so absolutely: the enormous gap between power and the people meant the powerful did not have to take the wishes of their people into consideration. If the leaders of the Arab world had to renew their right to rule every four years at the ballot box, they almost certainly would have done something to help the Palestinians because their people would have demanded it.

From the 1970s onwards, Palestine became useful for Arab leaders as a tool to rally the masses and to deflect internal criticism of their own failings. But Palestine was not their priority. The presidents of the military republics were more concerned with cementing their own authority following the fall of their hero Nasser.

As for the conservative kingdoms, they were about to find themselves facing a new and much more dangerous threat: one that they still have not found a way to deal with. In 1979, a new battle began: the battle over who speaks for Islam.

Part V

The Sacred Versus the Secular: Who Speaks for Islam?

19

Mecca: Tuesday, November 20, 1979

It was the first day of a new year. In fact, it was the first day of a new century. In the Islamic calendar, November 20, 1979, corresponded to the first day of the month of Muharram, 1400. And for a few hundred men and women gathered in the Holiest Mosque in the Holiest City of Islam, this day was to be the start of a new era. They were going to bring down the Saudi ruling family and establish a new Islamic order.

The Kingdom of Saudi Arabia was established in 1932 but the Saudi family's rule went back much further than that. In 1744, Muhammad ibn Saud was amir of a small oasis named Diriyya in the center of Arabia. He was not one of the most important tribal sheikhs in the region but that year, he made an alliance with a reformist preacher that would change history and set his family on the path to power and wealth. The preacher's name was Muhammad ibn Abd al-Wahhab and his teachings called for a return to an Islam purified of any innovations (*bida*) added to the religion since the Prophet's death.

This stripped-down, austere, iconoclastic brand of Islam banned a motley array of activities. Pastimes as diverse as visiting the graves of saints, smoking, tambourine-playing (or music of any kind), to wearing silk: in short, everything that Muhammad ibn Abd al-Wahhab believed had not been part of the Prophet's life. His narrow interpretation of the faith is a long way from the cosmopolitan, engaging, and free-thinking Islam that gave birth to one of the greatest civilizations the world has ever known.

A reflection of the harsh desert environment where it is was born; this version of Islam became known as Wahhabism. As well as banning anything it considered an innovation, Wahhabism espoused a particular dislike of Sufism and Shi'ism and called for *jihad* against non-Muslims and militant action against any Muslims who did not follow Wahhabi teachings.[1] In other words, Muhammad ibn Abd al-Wahhab used his preaching to give himself—and whoever backed him—the exclusive right to speak for Islam. This same sense of exclusivity, together with the call for jihad against non-believers and the right to act against any Muslims who disagreed with them, would later be claimed by extremist groups such as al-Qaida and ISIL whose narrow view of Islam was greatly influenced by Wahhabi teachings.

Many tribal leaders in Arabia disapproved of these teachings but, in 1744, Muhammad ibn Saud recognized that an alliance with the preacher would give him a religious legitimacy he otherwise lacked. Together, they would conquer with the sword in one hand and the Quran in the other. Muhammad ibn Saud gave the Wahhabi preacher shelter in his oasis and so began the Saudi-Wahhabi alliance that is now into its third century. In a new twist on the monarchy-military alliances of old, the Saudi family would rule, their tribal allies would support that rule, and Muhammad ibn Abd al-Wahhab would sanctify it. In return, the Wahhabi preacher was given complete freedom over the religious agenda in any of territories the Saudis conquered. The relationship between the two families was then sealed by marriage. King Faisal's side of the family (which includes the former long-serving Foreign Minister Saud al-Faisal) is both Saudi and Wahhabi.

The alliance worked well for both parties. The puritan simplicity of the Wahhabi message and its uncompromising insistence on tawhid (unity of God) resonated with some of the nomadic tribes and settled communities in the isolated areas of central Arabia. It found less support in the cities of the Hijaz where life was lived at a different pace.

By the early nineteenth century, the Saudi family and their supporters had gained so much territory that they were in control of the Holy Cities in the west and were challenging Ottoman control of Basra in modern-day Iraq. It took an invasion force from Egypt led by Muhammad Ali's son to halt the Saudi advance and end the threat to Ottoman sovereignty in the heart of Islam. The day of the Saudi surrender in 1818 was a date that would, two centuries on, become famous the world over: September 11. The defeated Saudi amir, Abdullah, was sent to Istanbul where he was beheaded.

But the Saudis were nothing if not resilient. The rest of the family lived to fight another day and, as the nineteenth century progressed, they were, once again, in charge of large parts of Arabia. When that period of rule was brought to an end in 1891 by the rival Rashidi family, the Saudis were still not finished. In 1902, Abd al-Aziz (better known as Ibn Saud) returned from exile in Kuwait, reclaimed the Saudi stronghold of Riyadh, and began to build the third Saudi state: the one that would culminate in the kingdom established in 1932 and is named after his family.

It was this family and this state which the rebels in Mecca aimed to destroy. The rebel movement was led by a charismatic preacher named Juhayman ibn Muhammad al-Utaybi and his brother-in-law Muhammad ibn Abdullah al-Qahtani. Religion and rebellion were in Juhayman's blood. His grandfather was a member of the *Ikhwan*, or Brotherhood, who were once the backbone of the army of Ibn Saud, the founder of the third Saudi state and the country's first king. The Ikhwan were warriors who could strike the fear of God into their opponents. People often ran at the sound of their approach rather than risk the consequences of staying to face them. It was thanks to their ferocity and unwavering loyalty that Ibn Saud was able to see off his rivals, concentrate power in his hands and begin the process of state creation.

But, in the late 1920s, the Ikhwan's loyalty wavered. They did not like the state Ibn Saud was creating and they objected openly to some of his policies. They did not approve of his treaty with the British. They did not think kingship was Islamic. And they strongly disapproved of Ibn Saud's indulgent lifestyle and multiple marriages.[2]

They rebelled. Ultimately, to no avail. Ibn Saud understood only too well that a ruler was nothing without a loyal army and he brought in fighters from the Najd province, the Saudi heartland in central Arabia, to stop the rebellion. Juhayman's grandfather was killed fighting against Ibn Saud's forces in the Battle of Sabila in 1929.[3] Juhayman was born ten years later in the Qasim province in what had once been an Ikhwan settlement. He grew up hearing stories of the Ikhwan's glory days and of the doomed rebellion that put an end to the movement. As an adult, he joined the National Guard where he reached the rank of corporal. But he seemed to feel something was missing in his life and in his early thirties, after over a decade in the National Guard, he made an abrupt career change and enrolled at the Islamic University in the Holy City of Medina in 1972.[4]

The Islamic University was more than a theological college. Part of the university's remit was to train the religious establishment of the future. The division of power between religion and politics worked out between the Saudis and the Wahhabis in the middle of the eighteenth century still held firm. The Saudi family controlled the political arena. The religious preachers controlled the social space. It was the preachers who interpreted the religious law (the *sharia*) and the religious police who enforced it. By ceding so much of the public arena to the religious establishment, the Saudis ensured their support for the status quo.

The atmosphere at the university was heavily influenced by the political thinking of Egypt's Muslim Brothers. During the 1960s when Nasser's crackdown against the Muslim Brothers went into overdrive, King Faisal offered sanctuary to many Brothers fleeing Egypt. He saw it as a way to use Islam to undermine Nasser. He even went as far as to object to the death sentence given to Sayyid Qutb in August 1966 and called for Nasser to show clemency.[5] The university was set up to rival Cairo's famous seat of religious learning, the Azhar.[6] (One of those given refuge in the kingdom was Sayyid Qutb's brother Muhammad. He taught at universities in the kingdom where one of his students was a young Osama bin Laden.)[7]

King Faisal's policy proved to be something of a double-edged sword. During Juhayman's time at the university, he took his studies very seriously. The Muslim Brothers believed that religion and politics were one and the same and, with that in mind, Juhayman looked at the Saudi state and came to the same conclusion that his grandfather's generation of Ikhwan had come to 50 years earlier: that the Saudi state had not quite turned out the way its most loyal supporters had hoped it would. At the highest levels of power, there appeared to be a gap between Islam as it was preached and Islam as it was practiced.

Juhayman did not keep his views to himself and, as a result, he was expelled from the university in 1974.[8] For the next few years, he wandered in the wilderness, preaching and publishing religious texts which gained him a reputation for piety among like-minded men and women. His writings on religion also attracted the attention of the Saudi security forces. He was arrested and detained for a brief period in 1978 but ultimately released without charge.[9]

His message continued to resonate, however. Saudi Arabia at this time was a country full of contradictions and those contradictions were creating a deep sense of social angst in some quarters. Thanks to the oil embargo, the kingdom was fabulously wealthy. But it was a change that happened almost overnight in a place that was chronically underdeveloped and culturally behind the times. Women of any age needed a male guardian. The economy was suddenly awash with petrodollars and development took place at breakneck speed. That development was uneven and many in the kingdom did not feel they benefited from it.

Estimates suggest that oil revenues rose from US $1.2 billion in 1970 to US $22.5 billion in 1974. By the end of the 1970s that figure had quadrupled.[10] The state lacked the mechanisms or the infrastructure to absorb all that money. The 1970s therefore saw an influx of Western companies and workers into the kingdom who, attracted by generous tax-free incomes and the sort of salaries they could never expect to earn at home, came to fill the skills gaps in the labor market. To descendants of the Ikhwan like Juhayman, the arrival of so many Westerners was proof the Saudis were too closely allied with, and too reliant on, infidel foreigners.

The presence of Westerners on sacred Islamic soil also tapped into the thorny issue of whether non-Muslims should be allowed to live in the

Islamic Holy Land. Some religious authorities cite the *hadith* (saying) of the Prophet—"There can be no two religions in Arabia"—as proof Arabia should be for Muslims only.[11] Other authorities limit this prescription to the Holy Cities of Mecca and Medina. For anyone already inclined to question the regime's religious credentials, the arrival of the Western work force added to their belief that the Saudis had travelled a long way from their Wahhabi origins.

The 1970s also saw a rise in conspicuous consumption among the ruling class. Grand palace complexes were built at home and members of the ruling family were often spotted living the high life abroad.[12] To Juhayman and those like him, this gap between how the Saudi family ruled in public and how they lived in private was proof of their moral and financial corruption. In their eyes, the family had lost their right to rule.

In the early hours of November 20, 1979, Juhayman al-Utaybi launched his rebellion against the Saudi regime by taking over the Grand Mosque in Mecca. The annual pilgrimage had just ended and the Mosque was still full of pilgrims who had yet to return home. A mosque might not seem the most obvious place to start a revolution—the French started theirs by storming a prison; the Russians by storming a parliament—but Juhayman knew his history. Throughout the Islamic era, Mecca had often been the scene of rebellions against the ruling elite. The Holy City is the direction of prayer and the destination of pilgrimage. The pilgrimage is the fifth and final pillar of the faith and it is the responsibility of whoever controls Mecca to make sure that obligation can be fulfilled. From a rebel's point of view, it is the perfect place to attack a ruler's religious legitimacy and undermine his political credibility.

Furthermore, the pilgrimage is great cover for a conspiracy because it is almost impossible to police. Juhayman and his followers took advantage of the freedom of movement it offered and gathered in Mecca under the guise of pious pilgrims. No one in power suspected a thing.

The rebellion presented the Saudis with a dilemma. To end it, they would have to send troops into the Grand Mosque. But the Quran prohibits fighting in the Haram al-Sharif. How, then, were they to end an armed rebellion and avoid fighting in the sacred enclosure?

The religious establishment came to their rescue. Fighting was indeed banned in the precincts of the Grand Mosque but Quran 2: 191 states: "Do not fight them at the Sacred Mosque until they fight you there. If they fight you, kill them. Such is the reward of unbelievers."[13] As the Saudis had not started the violence, the religious establishment deemed any action on their part to be in line with this verse.

In the battle for public opinion, the Saudi rulers were helped by the unlikeliest of sources: the rebels themselves. There was much public disquiet about the decision to use the Grand Mosque as a platform for revolution. Even among people who agreed with the rebels' analysis that the Saudis were corrupt. Graffiti scrawled in the toilets of Riyadh University months after the revolt summed up this feeling: "Juhayman, our martyr, why didn't you storm the palaces?"[14] King Khaled himself apparently acknowledged this point of view. He reportedly told foreign visitors weeks after the siege that Juhayman might have had more luck with the public if he had attacked his palace instead of the Mosque.[15]

Then there was the controversial issue of the *Mahdi*. As soon as Juhayman launched the rebellion, he declared his brother-in-law Muhammad al-Qahtani to be the Mahdi, the one who guides. In Islamic religious thought, the Mahdi is a Messianic figure who will usher in an era of divinely guided justice. But the Mahdi is a figure more common in Shi'i thinking. Saudi Arabia, by contrast, is predominantly Sunni. The rebel leader's decision to promote his brother-in-law as a Shi'i-style redeemer did not go down well with the Saudi public.

The rebels held out for two weeks. By December 3, it was all over. The Saudis, assisted by a commando unit from the French *Groupe d'Intervention de la Gendarmerie Nationale* (GIGN) brought the crisis to an end. According to some reports, they flooded the Grand Mosque's underground passages with water and dropped electricity charges into them. One newspaper report described the rebels as "floating out like kippers."[16] Rebels, pilgrims, and members of the security forces were among the dead. The Mahdi was killed and Juhayman soon would be. He and 62 of the rebels were publicly beheaded in January 1980.[17]

The Saudi ruling family were consummate political survivors and they had survived yet again. But the rebellion rattled them. On a very public level, it revealed all was not well in the kingdom. Saudi Arabia had become a contradiction: a rapidly modernizing country with a medieval power structure and the cracks were beginning to show. The endorsement the ruling family received from the religious establishment was no longer enough to bridge the gap between power and the people. If anything, the reverse was happening: pious young Saudis were turning away from the official line and rediscovering Islam on their own terms. The Saudis might still claim to speak for Islam but, after 1979, it was clear that not everyone in the kingdom agreed with them.

This was not the only challenge the Saudi family faced. Someone else in the Islamic world was trying to claim the exclusive right to speak for Islam. As the siege unfolded in Mecca, another siege in another Muslim city was gripping the world's attention. On November 4, Iranian students stormed the US embassy in Tehran. Ayatollah Khomeini's Islamic Revolution was underway.

20

1979: The View from Tehran

1

Iran has long occupied a unique place in the region.

The country has a history of going its own way. It was one of the few places conquered by the Arab armies in the seventh century that kept its sense of national identity after the conquest in 640. Unlike the countries of what we now call the Arab world, Iran was conquered by Islam but not by Arabic. Mindful of their illustrious past as one of the greatest powers on the planet, Iranians held fast to their national language Persian and, as a result, Iran never became part of the Arab world. Nor did it become a part of the Middle East (it is too far away).

Iran's tendency to take a different path from the rest of the region extended into religion. Under the Safavid dynasty (r. 1501–1722), Iran became the first part of the Muslim world to become a Shi'i state. And it was not simply a case of a Shi'i elite ruling over Sunni masses, as happened under the Fatimids in Egypt. In Iran, Shi'ism struck roots across society. Ruler and ruled alike adopted it.

In 1979, Iran again set off in a different direction from the rest of the region. While power in the Arab world was split between the military and the monarchies, Iran opted for something entirely different. In April 1979, in a decision that had been approved by 98.2 percent of the voting public in a referendum the previous month, Iran became an Islamic Republic.[1]

Tehran was on its way to becoming a theocracy.

2

So, how and why did Iran take such a radically different course from the kingdoms and the military republics of the Arab world?

In theory, the structure of power in Iran before 1979 was not so different from the structure of power in the Arab countries. After the collapse of the centralized caliphate, Iran like the rest of the region experienced rule by one family after another. And as was the case in the rest of the region, these were families who wielded absolute power for very long periods of time, usually until another family with a better army came along and ousted them. The two centuries of Safavid family rule, for example, were ended by the Qajar family who, in turn, ruled for well over a century (1794 to 1925).

The twentieth-century way for a ruling family in the Middle East to lose power was through a military coup. Here too, Iran was no different from the rest of the region. Qajar rule was brought to an end in 1925 by a colonel in the Cossack Brigade. In February 1921, Colonel Reza Khan staged a coup and began the process of concentrating power in his own hands. The Qajar Shah, Ahmad, remained in office but not in power. Four years later, Reza Khan had accumulated enough power to oust him, make himself Shah, and launch the Pahlavi dynasty that would last until the revolution in 1978.

Imperialism was a factor in much of the Arab world and Iran, too, was affected by it. The country was never fully occupied by an outside power but, like its Arab neighbors, Iran did not escape colonial meddling in its affairs. It was not just the country's potential oil reserves that attracted the interest of the Great Powers. It was geography. Iran lay on the land route to India. Britain's imperial obsession had long been to secure every possible route to India and London wanted to control Tehran (or to control whoever controlled Tehran). In Iran, Britain's main rival was Russia and Russia's imperial obsession was its long-standing need to access warm water. Landlocked on its long southern border, Russia's strategy was to push west into the Mediterranean and south towards the Indian Ocean.

Much of the rivalry between Britain and Russia in Iran was economic: the two even indulged in a battle of the banks; each one setting up a rival bank to try and consolidate their grip on Iran's economy at the expense of the other.[2]

An incident in 1890 showed how imperialism worked in Iran and how the Iranian people responded to it. Significantly, it also revealed an alternative power bloc to the monarchy and the military. In 1890, Shah Nasir al-Din (r. 1848–96) gave a British businessman a 50-year monopoly on the Iranian tobacco industry. The terms of the deal included production and retail of the crop as well as rights over its import and export. It was a license to print money. The businessman sold the concession to Britain's Imperial Tobacco Company.[3]

Iran's merchant community, based in the bazaars, were in uproar over the concession. It cut them out of the market. It threatened their livelihoods. It handed the profits of this lucrative trade to foreigners. For help, the *bazaaris* turned to the religious establishment. The religious scholars (*ulama*) responded by using their influence to ban the use of tobacco. The leading Shi'i cleric, Mirza Hussein Shirazi, went so far as to issue a *fatwa* against tobacco.[4]

In this battle between the king and the clerics, the clerics won. In the face of such widespread protest, Shah Nasir al-Din had to rescind the tobacco concession. Although many of the senior clerics lived outside Iran in the Holy Cities of southern Iraq, the tobacco protest showed they were more in touch with the concerns of ordinary people of Iran than the Shah was.

During the crisis, the clerics had proved themselves remarkably astute in marshalling the power of religion to help the businessmen in the bazaar. This would prove critical in the years ahead, especially during the Islamic Revolution. The bazaar was more than a place of business; it was all of society in microcosm. The alliance between the mosque and the market was, therefore, much more than an alliance between faith and finance. It was a building block for the clerics to take a more active political role in society. Added to this was the legitimacy they derived from being so far from official power. That distance from power, both geographically and politically, made them immune to the ups and downs of the Shah's fortunes and consolidated their credibility as an alternative powerbase. As outsiders, they questioned what the Shah did. They did not serve him.

In this respect, they were very different from their Sunni counterparts who had long been co-opted into the political establishment. Saudi Arabia is a prime example. During the Mosque siege in 1979, the ruling family turned to the religious establishment for help in countering the rebels' claims that the Saudis had forfeited their right to rule. As fully paid-up servants of the state, the religious scholars backed the Saudis as legitimate rulers and approved their course of action to reclaim the Grand Mosque, even though it led to non-Muslim French troops entering Mecca which was a breach of Muslim practice.

The co-option of the Sunni religious establishment was not unique to Saudi Arabia. It was standard practice across the Arab world and had been for a long time. In essence, it boiled down to the nature of power in an Islamic state. The community which the Prophet Muhammad established was based on religion. His authority to lead that community was unique: his prophecy.[5] After he died, the men who led the community had to find a different way to bridge the gap between power and the people. The four Rightly Guided Caliphs (r. 632–61) were men who had known the Prophet personally and who were, for the most part, able to connect with the rest of the community through their credentials as early converts to the faith.

That situation changed when Muawiya became caliph in 661 after a civil war. He chose to fill the gap between people and power with the stability of his monarchy and the soldiers of his military. It was a political model others were willing to follow. In this context, religion was harnessed to shore up the ruler's religious credentials: caliphs led the pilgrimage and appointed their successor sons to do the same; they led jihad; they built mosques and madrasas, and had Friday prayers said in their name. In general, they created the environment where Islam could be freely practiced and the five pillars of the faith could be fulfilled.

What they did *not* do was issue religious rulings. That responsibility fell increasingly to the growing class of religious scholars: men who collected and codified the sayings of the Prophet into a body of law and whose knowledge of that law qualified them to issue rulings based on it. This gave them enormous social power as they, not the caliph, made the laws that shaped society and determined how people lived their day-to-day lives. In this context, it was the religious scholars, not the caliph, who spoke for Islam.

This state of affairs was challenged when al-Mamun became caliph in 813. He, like Muawiya, took power after a civil war. Perhaps because he wanted to step out of the shadow of fratricide hanging over him, al-Mamun decided to assert his religious credentials. To do this, he took up a very obscure doctrine on the nature of the Quran and made it official policy.[6] This doctrine was called Mutazilism and it claimed that the Quran was created and did not exist coeternally with God. All of this might sound overly theological and not in any way relevant to the high politics of the state but al-Mamun knew what he was doing. He knew this issue went right to the heart of his authority as caliph and he knew he could use it to wrest power back from the religious scholars.

That is because in Islam, power belongs to God. The Quran is the law. No one, not even the caliph, is above it. And because the law already exists, the caliph has no ability to legislate. He can only interpret it. But at this time, it was not the caliph who was interpreting the law, it was the religious scholars. Mutazilism offered the caliph a way to change this and tilt the balance of power back in his favor. Because if, as Mutazilism suggested, the Quran was not coeternal with God, then the caliph had a lot more room for maneuver when it came to legislation.

When al-Mamun made the doctrine official policy, he set up a trial, a *mihna*, of religious scholars to see who would agree with it. This was no open free-flowing debate. The scholars had the choice of agreeing with the caliph and keeping their jobs (and their lives) or disagreeing and facing the consequences of his wrath.

The doctrine was not popular with the public and the religious scholars were caught between their beliefs and the power of the state. The mihna rapidly turned into an inquisition and a political witch hunt. Torture was used to break scholars who would not bend to the caliph's will. Most famously, the scholar Ahmad ibn Hanbal refused to abandon his beliefs and endured an array of medieval torture techniques and to no avail. He still refused to break. The public loved him for it.

In the long run, the mihna did not work. Al-Mamun's immediate successors continued the policy (he made it a condition of succession) but in the late 840s, the caliph al-Mutawakkil recognized reality and abandoned it. In this battle between the caliph and the clerics, the clerics won. What happened afterwards set the tone for the relationship between the scholars and the Sunni state.

Politics and religion went their separate ways in Islam. It did not result in society splitting between the sacred and the secular, as happened in Europe after the Reformation, where religion retreated into the private realm. Islam remained a public religion. Nor did the scholars become an alternative source of power outside the political establishment. Instead, a balance of power was worked out between the two power blocs that saw the caliphs control the political arena and the scholars the social one. (This is the same division of power the Saudis and the Wahhabis agreed on when they joined forces in the middle of the eighteenth century.) Rather than oppose each other, the two blocs reinforced each other: caliphs needed religious endorsement for their rule; the scholars gave it. Scholars needed funds to pay for their training and teaching; the caliphs gave that.

In the Islamic world, where faith and identity are one and the same, the religious establishment was always likely to enjoy a substantial amount of power. But in Sunni society, they chose not to use it politically. They stayed within their own sphere of influence and left politics to others.[7]

For the Shi'i clerics, there was no such co-option. Because, before the Safavid dynasty, there was no Shi'i state. The nature of the Shi'i faith is another reason why Shi'i religious scholars tended to stand apart from the state. Their religious doctrine has a somewhat contradictory attitude to power. On the one hand, Shi'i doctrine could be idealistic and radical to the point of encouraging rebellion at all costs against an unjust ruler. On the other, it could be resigned and cynical and call for an "arm's length" approach to anything associated with power.

These wildly different attitudes stem from the Shi'i belief that political authority belongs to the Prophet's family. In the absence of the Hidden

Imam, who is the missing member of the family who will one day establish justice on earth, many Shi'i clerics have deliberately chosen to keep their distance from the moral compromises associated with power. As a result, much of the Shi'i religious establishment developed in isolation from the political establishment. There are, however, exceptions and a number of clerics in Iran during the rule of the Safavids, Qajars, and Pahlavis worked for the state and received government salaries. But many others stayed as far as possible from power. The latter included the Azali branch of Shi'ism whose members were downright hostile to the rule of the Shahs. [8]

In wider society, Shi'i clerics performed the same functions as their Sunni counterparts—shaping the social space, delivering judgments, interpreting laws—but many of them, especially the Azalis, did so unencumbered by the trappings of power. That gave them credibility in the eyes of ordinary people.[9] It also meant that in the event of popular protests against the ruling elite, the clerics could not be called upon by those in power to prop up their rule. On the contrary, the Shi'i clerics were more likely to side with the people.

The power of the clerics was evident during the Constitutional Revolution of 1905–6 when they formed one of the largest blocs in the assembly responsible for drafting the constitution. The constitution was an attempt to curtail the power of the Shah and establish a constitutional monarchy based on Belgium's. In what would become a familiar pattern after the Arab Spring, those with the most to lose from the new order—that is, the old order and the foreign powers that profited from it—did their utmost to bring it down.

Shah Muhammad Ali deployed the Cossack Brigade against parliament in 1907 and 1908.[10] Then, in 1909, he mounted a full-scale counterrevolution. Even though his efforts failed and he had to abdicate in favor of his young son Ahmad, parliament's future was still in peril.[11] Britain and Russia were ready to intervene, especially as oil was discovered in Iran in 1908. Russia invaded from the north, Britain from the south, and in the midst of the mayhem and factional infighting in Tehran, parliament could not agree on a prime minister and was dissolved on December 20, 1911.[12]

The Qajar Shahs remained in power until 1925 but their authority was heavily curtailed by the British and the Russians and, after the First World War, by the British alone.

When Colonel Reza Khan seized power and appointed himself Shah in 1925, he knew where his power base was and, equally importantly, where it was not. Reza Pahlavi Shah, as he was now known, built up the army and neutralized the power of the clerics. As part of that process, he created a secular state and placed education and sharia law—two areas where the clerics ruled supreme—under state control, thus depriving the clerics of much of their social power and employment opportunities. The changes that resulted from the new laws were very public, and intentionally so: Western dress was made compulsory and, in 1936, the veil was banned. Iran *looked* like a different country even if, beneath the Westernized surface, it was still the same.

Reza Pahlavi veered towards the West in more than matters of dress. The Bolshevik Revolution in 1917 took Russia out of the Iranian equation and left Britain's role in the country unchallenged. The 1919 Anglo-Iranian Treaty made Iran a virtual colony of Britain and gave London unfettered access to the country's oil. The Shah tried to negotiate a better deal with Britain through the Oil Agreement in 1933 but even under this new deal Britain retained a controlling (and tax-free) interest in the industry until 1993.[13]

The West's role in Iran continued during the Second World War. In 1941, Britain and the Soviet Union forced Reza Pahlavi to step aside in favor of his 23-year-old son Muhammad Reza. Iranian oil was needed for the Allied war effort and London and Moscow calculated that the inexperienced son would be easier to manage than the father.

After the war, Western influence intensified. The Shah needed American military support to fend off a possible Soviet attack and the relationship between Washington and Tehran was mutually beneficial: Washington wanted to secure Iran's oil for the Western economy. When the populist Prime Minister Muhammad Mosaddeq passed a law in 1953 nationalizing the Anglo-Iranian Oil Company, thereby nullifying the sweetheart deals which benefited Western interests at Iran's expense, the British and Americans staged a coup and deposed him.

From then on, the Shah's power was absolute and he was not afraid to use it. He ruled with increasing autocracy. His secret police force, the SAVAK (rumored to be trained by the Israelis), became notorious. His reliance—or, some would say, his dependence—on the West set him at odds with the merchants and the mosques and strengthened their alliance. Both blocs resented the growing Western influence. The preferential deals granted to foreign companies hurt the bazaaris financially and the compulsory Westernization of public life worried the religious establishment.

When popular protests broke out against the Shah in 1977, Iran was in a similar position to many Arab states on the eve of the Arab Spring: the country was run by a long-serving autocratic ruler allied to the West who enforced his power through a repressive police state and who was surrounded by a clique-elite getting richer as everyone else got poorer. And, as also happened during the Arab Spring, popular discontent with the regime was so widespread; the protestors came from all walks of life.

The protests in Iran, however, were different from those in the Arab Spring in one critical way: Iran's protests found a leader and that leader was supported by a powerful infrastructure and an extensive network of long-standing alliances. From exile in Iraq then in Paris, Ayatollah Khomeini became the rallying point of the protests and the international face of the revolution. As a leading Shi'i cleric with a history of opposition to the Pahlavi regime and a frugal lifestyle that was the ultimate contrast to the glamour and wealth of the ruling class, Khomeini was perfectly placed to denounce the Shah. In the long run, he was able to do much more than that. With the religious establishment backing the protests and calling for the Shah's downfall, Khomeini placed Iran's religious infrastructure at the disposal of the protestors. Mosques became sanctuaries. Sermons became rallying cries. Funerals of the men and women shot by the security forces became public demonstrations against the Shah.[14]

Even more importantly, Khomeini held the disparate protest groups together by tapping into the common reference points of Iranian Shi'ism they all shared.[15] To groups as wide-ranging as middle-class mothers, poor peasants, striking workers, left-wing intellectuals, cosmopolitan students, urban merchants: Khomeini, the Shi'i ayatollah, set himself up as a symbol of what they all had in common. By reminding them of their shared Iranian and Shi'i identity, he managed to convey the impression that opposing the Shah was not only a religious duty; it was the inevitable will of God. That combined sense of national purpose and religious obligation helped to sway the army's loyalty towards the protestors and facilitate the fall of the Shah. When the Shah went into exile on January 16, 1979, it was therefore Khomeini, rather than a colonel or a king, who stepped forward to establish what he called the government of God. He returned from exile in Paris on February 1, 1979, and began to build the Islamic Republic.

3

He did it with remarkable speed.

The following month, a referendum was held on whether Iran should be an Islamic Republic. The answer was a resounding yes. Turnout was said to be high. According to official reports, nearly 90 percent of the electorate voted and 98.2 percent of them were in favor of the Islamic Republic.[16]

In December, another referendum was held. This time, the issue before the public was the country's new Islamic constitution. Again, voters turned out in large numbers and, again, the result was decisive: 99.5 percent voted yes.[17] More elections followed in 1980: for the presidency in January and for parliament in March through to May.

Within fifteen months of his return from exile, Khomeini had overseen the creation of an entirely new political system: one that turned the clerics' ability to interpret Islamic law into legislative power. In doing so, he overturned nearly 1,400 years of political practice across the Islamic world. In Iran, there would be no separation between the rulers and the religious establishment. In Iran, the religious establishment had become the state. Khomeini's willingness to consult the public at every step of the way gave people confidence in the new republic and in the man at its helm. In addition, the fact that Khomeini publicly stated he did not want a member of the religious establishment to run for the presidency reassured many that the scholars would not concentrate power in their own hands.[18]

Khomeini, in other words, was not doing a "Nasser": he was not manipulating the revolution to take the presidency for himself. But under the constitution he helped draft, he did not need to. Khomeini, as Supreme Leader, was the real ruler of the country—all the powers usually associated with a president belonged to him—and he was not elected by the public. Nor was there was any mechanism for the public to get rid of him. In a situation where the (elected) president could be overruled by the (unelected) Supreme Leader, the Islamic Republic had the potential to turn into a political monoculture. In Iran's case, it was not a culture monopolized by sultans or soldiers but by scholars. And that put them in the powerful position of claiming the exclusive right to speak for Islam. They could, if they so chose, give the impression that opposing them was akin to opposing God.

Not everyone agreed with what was happening in the new Iran. But what, arguably, cemented the Islamic Revolution, silenced its opponents, and entrenched the rule of the ayatollahs was the Iran-Iraq War. With the nation under invasion, Iranians rallied round the flag.

On September 22, 1980, Saddam Hussein sent the Iraqi army into Iran. What motivated him to invade his neighbor had more to do with what was going on in the Arab world than events in Iran. There was a leadership vacuum in the Arab Middle East. Egypt, the region's former leader, was in the wilderness after Sadat's peace deal with Israel. The Arab League suspended the country's membership in 1979. Under the Abbasids, Iraq had led the Arab world for five centuries and Saddam Hussein seized this moment to reclaim that leadership role. A soldier-president in the Nasserist mold, Saddam had developed a very public cult of personality. Victory over his Persian neighbor and the restoration of Baghdad as the capital of the Middle East would send that cult into overdrive. Or so he hoped.

Wars in the Middle East are rarely about what they appear to be about. They have a depressing habit of developing a momentum of their own which makes them a magnet for other tensions in the region and, in a very short period of time, the war that started is no longer the only one being fought. This is one of the reasons Middle Eastern wars often last so long: the Iran-Iraq War lasted eight years (1980–88); the war in Lebanon fifteen (1975–90). With so many competing agendas at work, finding a formula to end these wars is not a straightforward process of resolving the issues between the original protagonists. It involves untangling a complicated web of conflicting domestic, regional and international interests. And more often than not, the underlying issues are not resolved with the end of the war. As soon as the next conflict starts, they flare up again. The Iran-Iraq War is an example of this.

What started out as a war of ambition on the part of Saddam Hussein ended up as a proxy war between Saudi Arabia and Iran over who speaks for Islam. The ruling family of conservative Saudi Arabia based their legitimacy on religion. They were the Custodians of the Two Holy Mosques. But republican, revolutionary Iran claimed sovereignty belonged only to God—not to a man, and certainly not to a king.

By making these claims, the Islamic Republic threw down the gauntlet to the rulers of Saudi Arabia. If Khomeini's revolution succeeded and spread across the region, the Saudi rulers risked losing more than the building block of their state; they risked facing the same fate as the Shah.

But this was not stated openly. Instead, the Iran-Iraq War was presented as a Sunni-Shi'i sectarian struggle and not as an undeclared battle over the use of Islam as a political weapon. The Sunni-Shi'i angle was contentious because it had the potential to stir up intercommunal tensions. It was also hugely misleading. The Saudis did not have a problem with the Shah who was every bit as Shi'i as the ayatollahs and they had fought a war in Yemen in the 1960s to support the Shi'i Zaydis. The common denominator in both cases was that the Shah and the Zaydis were monarchists.

The Saudi problem with the Islamic Republic was not its Shi'i faith but its Islamic ideology. The Saudis therefore financed Saddam Hussein's war against the Islamic Republic for the same reason they fought Nasser in Yemen in the 1960s and the same reason they would later take on the Muslim Brotherhood after the Arab Spring: they oppose any political system that might appeal to their people and undermine their vice-like grip on power. The war also gave them the opportunity to rein in the power of Saddam Hussein. The secular soldier-president was cut from a different political cloth from the Saudis. As long as he was exhausting his forces in the fight against Islamic Iran, he would not be in any position to lead the Arab world.

For the Saudis, placing the war with Iran within the context of a Sunni-Shi'i struggle helped them to redefine the political narrative at home. Domestically, the ruling family were facing opposition on more than one front. In 1979, Shi'is in the eastern province of Hasa openly marked the Shi'i festival of mourning for the Prophet's grandson al-Husayn who was killed by the Umayyad army in the seventh century. This festival, *Ashura*, is one of the most important in the Shi'i calendar. It was banned by the Saudis nearly three decades before the kingdom was even created. Worried by events in Iran, the ruling family were particularly wary of any public display of Shi'i solidarity at this time and sent the National Guard in to break up the crowds.[19]

In 1980, protests in the east escalated. On the first anniversary of Ayatollah Khomeini's return from exile, large demonstrations and strikes were held in Shi'i areas. Eastern Saudi Arabia is the center of oil production and the strikes threatened the supply of the commodity that fuels the kingdom's economy. The National Guard were sent in to break up the protestors and this time they did it violently.[20]

The Shi'i protests in Saudi Arabia stemmed from domestic issues: in the ultraorthodox Sunni kingdom, Shi'is were second-class citizens, often publicly called by the derogatory term *Rafidi* which means rebel or renegade or, at its worst, apostate; the implication being that Shi'is are not true Muslims. In spite of this and in spite of the fact that the demonstrations were a popular protest against autocratic power, the Saudi rulers chose to cast the rebellion in 1980 as an Iranian-sponsored uprising. Blaming Iran for what were, in essence, expressions of people power became a key part of Saudi geopolitical strategy. From this time on, the Saudis would see the hand of Iran wherever it suited them. And they would see Shi'is as a fifth column. In 2011, for example, they claimed the popular protests against the King of Bahrain were the work of Iran—even when they very obviously were not.

Within the context of the territorial war between Iraq and Iran in 1980 and the pseudosectarian war between Sunni Saudi Arabia and Shi'i Iran, another war was raging: a superpower-sponsored satellite struggle worthy of the nineteenth century's Great Game. In this war, the West sought control of the region's resources and waterways to keep Moscow out. Iran and Iraq are two of the world's biggest oil producers. They border the Persian Gulf and have access to the Strait of Hormuz. Iran under the Shah had been firmly in the West's camp. Iran under the ayatollahs was not. Neither was Saddam Hussein. Like his Baath presidential counterpart Hafiz al-Asad in Syria, Saddam looked to Moscow for superpower assistance.

For Washington, the combined threat of a Soviet satellite in Baghdad and an anti-American regime in Tehran meant the Gulf War could not be ignored. Washington judged Saddam Hussein to be the lesser of two evils and supplied him with weapons and satellite imagery revealing Iran's troop movements. It was a cynical calculation—Saddam Hussein had an atrocious human rights record against all his opponents especially the Kurds, the Marsh Arabs and the Shi'is in the south—but this was before *Glasnost*. The Cold War still raged and cynical calculations based on *Realpolitik* were a common feature of foreign policy.

The Iran-Iraq War ended in 1988 because both sides were exhausted. Often compared to the futile trench warfare of the First World War, this war saw both sides fight to a standstill, lose enormous numbers of casualties, destroy their economies and gain nothing. Khomeini likened accepting the UN-sponsored ceasefire deal to swallowing poison.

Even though the Cold War ended soon afterwards and that should have removed the East-West power struggle from the Middle East, the underlying issues of the Iran-Iraq War were not resolved. There was so much unfinished business, the war did not really end. Iraq's massive economic debts led to the invasion of Kuwait in 1990 which prompted the US-led Operation Desert Storm to liberate Kuwait the following year. The unfinished business of that war led the United States and the United Kingdom back to Iraq in 2003 to dismantle an arsenal of Weapons of Mass Destruction that did not exist. The turmoil caused by that war and its chaotic aftermath contributed to the sectarian tension and instability that enabled ISIL to take over large parts of the country in 2014.

The wars-within-wars have also continued. The pseudo-Sunni-Shi'i sectarian war rages on, currently wreaking havoc in Iraq, Syria, and Yemen and killing no one knows how many people.

And the battle over who speaks for Islam has intensified with new, non-state actors challenging the old order for the use of religion as a political weapon. Of these non-state actors, one side of the equation would challenge the status quo by going to the violent extreme. The other side of the equation would prove to be even more of a threat to the old order by doing what the kings and colonels, the soldiers and sheikhs had never done: winning free and fair elections.

21

1979: Holy War and Unholy Alliances

1

The year 1979 was an eventful year in the Islamic world.

The year began with the political earthquake in Iran which saw the exile of the Shah swiftly followed by the triumphant return of Ayatollah Khomeini. By year's end, the Islamic Revolution was in full swing. In a sign of how much had changed, Iran turned its back on old alliances. No longer a friend of the United States, Islamic Iran occupied the American embassy in Tehran reportedly to prevent its use for a repeat of the 1953 US-led coup which reinstated the Shah.

In the last months of 1979, the ruling family of Saudi Arabia had their own near-miss with revolution when the Grand Mosque of Mecca was taken over by religious militants disillusioned by the way their country was run. By the time the siege ended in early December, the established order in the Middle East and their Western allies might have been forgiven for breathing a collective sigh of relief and thinking the worst was over.

Then came Christmas and on December 25, 1979, Soviet tanks crossed into Afghanistan. Kabul's Bagram air base was already under Soviet control. For months, Moscow had been worried about their client in Kabul, President Hafizullah Amin. He was deploying increasingly harsh methods against his own people and was rumored to be making overtures to the United States.[1]

Soviet Russia wanted control of Afghanistan for the same reasons tsarist Russia had coveted the country. It was a vital link in the chain to the warm waters of the south. In 1979, Moscow went for regime change, sent the troops in, and killed President Amin. The new president, Babrak Karmal, was considered more likely to do what President Brezhnev in Moscow told him. The Soviet army now effectively occupied the country.

Over the next decade, ten of thousands of Soviet soldiers would see service in one of the most inhospitable, difficult terrains for an invading army in the world. Alexander the Great had not been able to get past the Hindu Kush. The Arab armies in the seventh and eighth centuries did not do much better. Even the mighty British Empire was routed in the country that has become known as the graveyard of empires. The British army suffered the worst defeat in its history in Afghanistan in 1842. Of the thousands of British soldiers deployed in the Afghan offensive, only *one* survived to tell the tale.[2]

The British author-historian-journalist Jan Morris visited Afghanistan in 1960. During her visit, she discussed events of 1842 with locals and asked what would happen if a foreign army were to invade Afghanistan today. The answer one old man gave her was prophetic: "'The same,' he hissed between the last of his teeth."[3]

For the United States, the Soviet invasion of Afghanistan presented an opportunity to encourage imperial overreach. The Soviet Union, while not exactly in trouble, was not as secure as it looked. As protests in Czechoslovakia, Hungary, and Poland showed, large numbers of people across the Communist Bloc were unhappy with Moscow's control of their affairs. Some of this discontent was economic: the Communist command economy was not delivering for ordinary people. Some of the most famous images of this time are of Russians queuing daily for bread and other basic foodstuffs. For Soviet economic planners, the issue was complicated by the arms race. Given the need to keep up with defense spending in the US, Moscow diverted disproportionate sums to its own defense budget. Even though the Soviet Gross National Product (GNP) was half the size of America's, Moscow spent the same amount of money on defense.[4]

The idea of imperial overreach had a long history. Britain and France used it to great effect during the Crimean War in the 1850s when they sided with the Ottoman Empire against tsarist Russia. Britain and France had no wish to see either side emerge victorious from that war. Their strategy was to have Istanbul and St. Petersburg fight to a standstill and exhaust themselves militarily and financially in the process, thereby making both less of a threat to Anglo-French ambitions elsewhere in the region. (This was the same strategy the West adopted in the Iran-Iraq War. Washington did not particularly want Saddam Hussein to win but needed the ayatollahs to lose.)

The proxy war the West waged in Afghanistan against the Soviet Union saw an unlikely group of parties come together to achieve the common goal of saving Muslim Afghanistan from the Communist infidel. The Americans could not fight openly for fear of escalating the Cold War, so they sent CIA operatives in to equip and train the locals. The Pakistanis assisted with logistics and intelligence. The Saudis opened their cheque books and, most importantly of all, they allowed the kingdom's religious establishment to declare the war against the Soviet occupier a jihad. Turning the proxy war into a holy war changed the nature of the struggle. Communism had not gained the traction in Muslim countries that it had in other parts of the postcolonial world because it challenged the belief in God. A war of liberation against an infidel occupier was a narrative that made sense to a lot of young men across the Arab world.

For the Saudi ruling family, the strategy was nothing short of genius. It gave them the chance to reassert their religious legitimacy in the aftermath of the siege in the Grand Mosque. Society across the Arab world had moved towards a more overt, politicized Islam after the Arab defeat in the Six-Day War. By taking a leading role in supporting the jihad in Afghanistan, the ruling family were able to marshal this militancy for their own purposes. It meant they could export potential troublemakers from the kingdom, stop any Soviet advance in the region, and strengthen Riyadh's growing alliance with Washington.

Since the oil embargo in 1973, Riyadh's relationship with the United States had deepened. Riyadh relied on American expertise to keep the oil flowing and on American defense to keep the kingdom safe from territorial threats like Saddam Hussein's Iraq and ideological ones like Ayatollah Khomeini's Iran. However, the relationship between Riyadh and Washington was about a lot more than weapons and oil. It was blossoming into other areas. Increasing numbers of Saudi students attended school in the United States. Increasing numbers of Saudi companies did business with American companies. And increasing amounts of Saudi Arabia's enormous oil wealth was recycled in the banks, high-end property, and stock markets of the West. In a short period of time, Saudi Arabia had become the unofficial leader of the Arab world and one of America's most reliable allies in the region.[5]

But regardless of how close and cordial elite-to-elite relations were between Riyadh and Washington, the fact remained that they were strange bedfellows who had next to nothing in common ideologically. The United States was the leader of the Free World with a constitution and a political system that divided power between the executive, the congress, and the senate. Saudi Arabia was an absolute monarchy with a medieval power structure closed to everyone but the ruling family. This was no meeting of the minds. It was an alliance of shared interests rather than shared beliefs.

In terms of foreign policy, there was nothing unusual in this. Unlikely political alliances were not new, especially in times of war. The Second World War, for example, is often described as a war for freedom against fascism. Yet one of the main players on the Allied side was the Soviet Union which, under Stalin, was no workers' paradise. In spite of this, Moscow arguably played *the* greatest role fighting fascism. It was thanks to Russian resistance in the Battle of Stalingrad that the course of the war turned against Germany and Soviet casualties, at around 25 million, were higher than anyone else's.

What made the Riyadh–Washington alliance *so* unlikely was Washington's broader policy in the Middle East. No matter how reliable Riyadh was as an ally to Washington, the Saudis always came second in America's regional priorities to Israel. This resulted in a number of inconsistencies in Riyadh's adoption of—and support for—jihad as a means to achieve America's objectives in Afghanistan.

Uncomfortable questions such as why there was a jihad to liberate Afghanistan but no comparable effort to liberate Jerusalem. Or why the Kingdom of Saudi Arabia and the conservative countries of the Gulf were so closely allied with the United States when Washington was Israel's patron and protector.

As long as the war in Afghanistan lasted, these questions would stay beneath the surface. But as soon as the war ended, they risked coming out into the open and demanding answers the Saudi establishment could not give.

2

The war in Afghanistan ended in the spring of 1988. It was Mikhail Gorbachev who brought the war to an end. After nearly a decade of fighting for no obvious gain, he ordered the Russian troops home. The last of the Soviet soldiers left Afghanistan in February 1989.

Washington had every reason to be jubilant. The strategy of imperial overreach—of making the cost of empire greater than its rewards—had worked magnificently. The war had exacerbated already existing economic, political, and social tensions within the Soviet system and it was not long before the whole system collapsed. Afghanistan had proved to be the graveyard of yet another empire.

In the long run, the war would have serious repercussions for the West, too. When the Taliban took over Afghanistan in 1996, the country became a magnet for jihadis fully committed to the cause of global jihad.

One of the consequences of the war was that it provided an opportunity for thousands of young men across the Arab world to come together and fight in a common cause. They did so legitimately with the full backing of many of the regimes across the region. In the course of the war, the jihadis learnt as much about weapons as they would have done had they joined the regular army. They also learned guerrilla fighting and covert operations—essential skills for any insurgent army wanting to bring down a regime they opposed. And perhaps most importantly of all, young men from places as far apart as Algeria and Arabia met with other young men who shared their belief in a different way of doing things. The jihad in Afghanistan took these isolated individuals and made them into a community. It is no coincidence that Osama bin Laden (whose job in the jihad was logistical) called his organization "*al-Qaida*" which means base or foundation. He was building a network of people who shared a similar outlook. From the outset, al-Qaida was an organization with the potential to operate beyond borders, to be a transnational movement that would fight an ideological war rather than a territorial one.

All of this posed no problem for the Americans or their Arab allies when the jihadis were working with the establishment to fight a common enemy. But even before the war in Afghanistan ended, there were signs this might not always be the case. On October 6, 1981, a group called Organization for Holy War (*Jamaat al-Jihad*) killed the Egyptian president, Anwar Sadat, as he reviewed a military parade commemorating the war against Israel in 1973. The young leader of the group (himself a member of the military) famously shouted: "I am Khalid al-Islambouli, I have killed pharaoh, and I do not fear death."

In Egypt, militant Islam had been growing under the radar for years. The enormous gap between power and the people was fertile grounds for extremist groups to take root. In a country where merely expressing an opinion was enough to warrant a lengthy prison sentence, some militants adopted an all-or-nothing strategy. In the absence of any public space to express views that differed from those of the regime, these groups resorted to violence. Most of them were not mass movements but small cells of people totally committed to their goal.

In organizational terms, they posed no serious long-term challenge to an authoritarian state like Egypt. Ideologically, it was a different matter. Many of these groups embraced the idea that modern Muslim society was living in a state of ignorance, or *Jahiliyya*. Jahiliyya was a loaded term because it referred to the Age of Ignorance that existed in Arabia before Islam. Militants deliberately used the word to convey their belief that the current rulers of the Arab world were not true Muslims. As a result, they were free to excommunicate them. Through the process of excommunication (*takfir*), militants countered the legitimacy of the ruling elite and the religious scholars who backed them with their own claim to speak for Islam. In doing so, they also claimed the right to decide who was—and who was not—a true Muslim.

In Egypt in the 1970s and 1980s, militant groups had little opportunity to implement the idea or to demonstrate how it would work in practice. But the consequences of the idea have been far-reaching because ISIL laid claim to it and they now claim the right to speak exclusively for Islam and to decide who is, and who is not, a true Muslim. Their fight, therefore, is not only against people who are not Muslim but against Muslims who do not share their interpretation of Islam.

3

The unfinished business of the war in Afghanistan dovetailed with the unfinished business of the Iran-Iraq War in the summer of 1990 and set in motion several of the wars currently raging across the region.

On August 2, 1990, Saddam Hussein's army invaded Kuwait. The Iraqi economy had completely collapsed during the war with Iran and needed high oil revenues to fund reconstruction. But oil prices were artificially low because of overproduction. Saddam identified Kuwait as one of the overproducers, invaded, and declared Kuwait the nineteenth province of Iraq.[6] Neighboring Saudi Arabia nervously looked on, worried it might be about to become the twentieth.

At this point, Osama bin Laden offered his services to the Saudi rulers. Bin Laden was a national hero. Up until now, he was also part of the establishment. He came from one of the kingdom's wealthiest families but gave it all up to go and fight the jihad in Afghanistan. By choosing to turn his back on a life of luxury, he earned the respect of many people across the kingdom. In the summer of 1990, with the Iraqi army on the kingdom's northern border, Bin Laden offered to raise an army of one hundred thousand Afghan veterans to defend the country. The Saudi family declined the offer and turned instead to Washington. Five days after Iraq invaded Kuwait, the first deployment of US troops arrived in the kingdom. The decision to call them in was the king's.[7] The long-standing contradictions in the relationship between Saudi Arabia and the US now began to come out into the open.

For the United States, the motivation for fighting the war was to liberate Kuwait from the dictatorship of Saddam. There was a certain irony here. Kuwait itself was not a free country. It was ruled by the Sabah family and had been since the mid-1700s. Like the other ruling families in the region, the Sabahs were no constitutional monarchy. Their word was law. The leader of the Free World therefore found itself in the unlikely position of fighting to liberate the people of a country who were not actually free. This sort of contradiction might have made sense under the

Eisenhower Doctrine during the Cold War but the Cold War was over. America had won. In this new post-Cold War context where the United States was the world's only remaining superpower, the US-led operation in the Gulf started to look more about securing the status quo and the financial advantages that went along with it than with promoting any sort of freedom agenda.

It was also dangerous for the United States to risk involvement in the internal politics of the Arab world. Previous American deployments in the region, for example those in Lebanon in the 1950s and 1980s, had not ended well. The West, in general, lacked credibility with the people of the region because of its imperialist past. The United States had no such colonial history in the Middle East but it suffered from being seen as Israel's first line of defense and was not viewed as a disinterested party. Added to this was the complication that alliances in the Arab world are constantly shifting. During the Iran-Iraq War, Saddam Hussein was on the same side as the Gulf leaders. Two years later, he had invaded one of them and was threatening to invade another. But the real danger to the United States of fighting a war in the Muslim world is that wars in this region have a tendency to suck in outside players in a way that makes it extremely difficult for them to leave. The Soviet Union had discovered that to their cost in Afghanistan.

For the Saudis, the motivation for inviting the Americans to deploy on their soil was equally fraught with contradictions and dangers. King Fahd (r. 1982–2005) had recently taken on the title Custodian of the Two Holy Mosques (*Khadim al-Haramayn al-Sharifayn*) as a way of demonstrating his religious legitimacy as the protector of the pilgrimage and the birthplace of Islam. But when he needed to defend Islam's Holy Places, he had to rely on non-Muslims to do it for him. For the likes of Bin Laden, this was a very public national humiliation. It showed to the whole world that Saudi Arabia could not defend itself and that the billions of dollars spent on Western-made military equipment in recent years had been a waste of money.

Even worse were the religious implications of the American deployment. It breached the Prophet's reported saying that there could be no two religions in the Arabian peninsula. According to the journalist and writer, Abdel Bari Atwan, who travelled to Afghanistan in 1996 to interview Bin Laden, Bin Laden's hatred of the Saudi ruling family and the United States started here. That hatred first found expression in sermons in mosques. It later turned violent. [8]

On August 7, 1998—the eighth anniversary of the American deployment to Saudi Arabia—truck bombs exploded outside the US embassies in Kenya and Tanzania. Hundreds of people were killed. Bin Laden later claimed that the Americans had not taken the message he was sending them seriously because the bombs had not exploded on American soil and the majority of the fatalities had not been American. Al-Qaida then attacked the *USS Cole* off the coast of Yemen in 2000 and the fatalities on that occasion were American sailors.

It was the next major al-Qaida attack on civilians that brought Bin Laden to the world's attention. The attacks of September 11, 2001, on the United States killed nearly three thousand people, left America in a state of shock, and set a new benchmark of horror in terrorist tactics. Like the date of the attacks in Kenya and Tanzania, the date of these attacks was not random. September 11 was the anniversary of the end of the first Saudi state. On that day in 1818, the forefathers of the current king surrendered their last stronghold in central Arabia to the Egyptian army led by the ruler of Egypt's son.

Whether Bin Laden was sending a message to the Saudi elite that their kingdom was about to suffer a similar fate, we will probably never know, just as we will probably never know if the aim of the attacks on September 11, 2001, was to drive a wedge between the Saudi ruling family and their American allies. What we do know is that in going to the extreme and assuming the right to speak for Islam, Bin Laden laid the foundation for the jihadi groups operating across the Middle East right now and that each new incarnation of the jihadi message is becoming even more extreme than the one before.

There is, however, an alternative to the all-or-nothing extremism of the jihadi groups and the Arab Spring would reveal it.

22

The Arab Spring and the Democratic Alternative

1

On Friday, December 17, 2010, a young man from a small town in southern Tunisia went to work as usual. By the end of the day, he had set in motion the chain of events that would lead to the Arab Spring.

What happened to 26-year-old Muhammad Bouazizi on that December day is now seen as a touchstone moment—similar to the shooting of Archduke Ferdinand and his wife Sophie nearly a century earlier—that sets the dominoes tumbling and causes the established order to collapse almost overnight. On the face of it, Muhammad Bouazizi was an unlikely revolutionary. He was the sole breadwinner in his family (his father died when he was a teenager) and he supported his mother and six siblings from the money he made selling fruits and vegetables from a cart. He could not afford a permit and was often harassed by local officials looking for a bribe so he could continue trading. On December 17, local officials confiscated his goods and tried to take his scales. The scales were not his so he refused to hand them over. At that point, a female police officer slapped him—a painfully public humiliation for a young Arab man to endure. He went to the police station and to the governor's office to plead for the return of his goods. No one helped him. In despair, he stood outside the governor's office, drenched himself in gasoline and set himself on fire. He died in the Ben Arous Hospital in the Tunisian capital on January, 4, 2011.

Ten days later, Tunisia's long-serving president, Zine El Abidine Ben Ali, in power since 1987, was forced out of office by massive public protests and went into exile in Saudi Arabia. Less than a month later, Egypt's long-serving president, Hosni Mubarak, in power since 1981, was also forced out of office by public protests. The story was repeated across the region. Libya's long-serving Brother Leader, in power since 1969, was in similar trouble. As was Syria's President Bashar al-Asad, whose family had been in power since 1971. Even the kingdoms were not immune: King Hamad of Bahrain faced unprecedented public protests calling for the downfall of his regime.

What made these protests different from protests of the past was their sheer scale. The Arab Spring was not ideologically driven. It was not even political in the traditional sense. The protests were as much about dignity as democracy. They were popular in the truest sense of the word. People across the Arab world looked at Muhammad Bouazizi and saw themselves. They identified with his daily struggle to provide for his family in increasingly difficult economic times. They, too, knew what it was to deal with an indifferent state. And they, too, despaired that anything was going to change any time soon. People across the Arab world lost their fear when they had nothing left to lose.

The Arab Spring took place against a catastrophic economic climate and a political backdrop rife with contradictions. The elite remained firmly in place and continued to enjoy the privileges of power at a time when the majority of their people were struggling financially. The price of wheat rocketed in 2010 making the cost of a staple foodstuff like a loaf of bread almost prohibitively expensive for many. The global credit crunch negatively affected tourism—a key component of North African economies—because tourists across Europe were tightening their belts.

Young men were particularly affected by the economic difficulties. In a society where religion governs social mores, men are expected to put the money together for a dowry before they marry. But with the economy directed by those at the top for those at the top, it was not easy for young men without connections to advance into the economic independence of adulthood. The result is deep frustration and a sense of emasculation. In *The New Middle East*, Professor Fawaz Gerges draws attention to the high rate of sexual impotency in Egypt. He notes it is a "phenomenon that has escaped attention" but is an indication of what is really going on at a social, economic, and political level in the country.[1]

Yet the economic crisis had no political repercussions because people in the Arab world had no access to power. If you look at a photograph taken at an Arab League Heads of Government Summit in 2000 and compare it to one taken in 2010, you would see almost all the same players in place. Saddam Hussein would be a notable exception. What helped hold this system so firmly in place was the increasing tendency of the presidents-for-life to appoint one of their sons to succeed them, as happened in Syria in 2000.

What made this stability look all the more anachronistic was the drive for democracy in the region: the US-led war on Iraq in 2003 led President George W. Bush to promote what he called a "Freedom Agenda" in the Middle East. When the Weapons of Mass Destruction for which the war was fought were not found, the rationale for the huge American war effort was reinvented to make it a struggle of freedom over tyranny. It was a noble aim on the president's part but it left him open to accusations of double standards while Washington willingly continued to ally with presidents-for-life and monarchs without mandates.

The American commitment to democracy in the Middle East was seriously called into question by the Hamas victory in Palestinians elections in 2006. In another failure of intelligence in the region, Washington had not expected the group to win in spite of much evidence on the ground pointing to such a victory. The Bush administration responded by ignoring the result. Together with the UN, the EU, and Russia, Washington placed sanctions on Hamas. Many Palestinians believe the sanctions and the subsequent Israeli siege of Gaza—which bans everything from certain types of chocolate to dual purpose industrial equipment entering the territory—is a form of collective punishment because they dared to vote for a party that puts Palestinian interests before those of Israel and the West.

How to deal with the established order in the Middle East, while simultaneously supporting democratic change, is a conundrum for Western leaders and it has been for some time. It goes back to the days of empire in the nineteenth century when the British ruler of Egypt, Lord Cromer, mused that Arabs should only be given the right to rule themselves when they could be trusted to do so in a manner that suited Western interests. In the twenty-first century, democratically elected presidents and prime ministers in the West claim to support the idea of democracy in the Middle East. But in practice, especially after 9/11, they have done the opposite. They have drawn ever closer to the Arab ruling class and ignored that ruling class's criminalization of peaceful political protest as terrorism.

President George W. Bush's priority after 9/11 was to keep America and Americans safe from further attacks. Intelligence sharing necessitated cooperation with leaders in the Arab world. And the darker side of the War on Terror—the rendering of prisoners for torture in locations that were off the grid—was facilitated by Arab leaders who had no qualms about torturing their own people. But it left the president's commitment to a "Freedom Agenda" looking like another example of Western hypocrisy.

The links between the West and the Arab elite grew even closer in the wake of the global recession when the cash-strapped countries of the

West were grateful for investment from the cash-rich oil economies of the Gulf. So much Arab money poured into London, the process became known as the "Gulf stream" and at least one British bank was recapitalized with Gulf money. Everything from football clubs and football stadiums to high-end department stores and iconic buildings to university Arabic departments and professorships were bought or funded by oil money.[2]

The uncomfortable truth is that Western leaders want stability in the region more than they want democracy. They want the oil to flow, the chokepoints of global trade to stay open, and Israel to be safe. They will support whoever can achieve that. It is one of the great unspoken truths of Western policy that the Western political establishment actually fears democracy in the Middle East. It fears the loss of control, the uncertainty, and the potential chaos. Most of all, it fears that the democratically expressed will of the people of the Middle East will run counter to Western interests in the region.

During the Cold War, the West supported the people of the Communist Bloc against the regimes. In the Middle East, the West has done the opposite. It has supported the regimes against their people. And they have done it in the name of securing the status quo.

Arab rulers have just as much interest in preserving that status quo. Where they once justified their rule in religious, national, paternalistic or anti-imperialist terms, the overriding discourse in recent years has been the need to secure "stability." They know that plays well in the West. And it suits them too. Stability means no change. No change means they stay in power.

To explain this state of affairs where the West says one thing and does another and where leaders in the Middle East brook no opposition to their rule, an idea emerged in the West called "Arab Exceptionalism": the belief that Arabs were different from everyone else; that they did not want democracy; that Islam was incompatible with it; that force was the only language Arabs understood.[3] The idea of the Arabs as an "exception" explained away the lack of democracy in the Middle East and allowed a complacent alliance to develop between the democratically elected leaders of the West and the dictators of the Middle East.

The massive protests of the Arab Spring ripped that idea to shreds. No longer could Arabs be depicted as docile sheep humbly submitting to the rule of a president or king. One of the great successes of the Arab Spring is that it humanized Arabs. For so long caricatured in the West as bearded jihadis waging violent war against infidels, Arabs suddenly appeared on television screens across the world as people with the same concerns as everyone else. Employment and education, housing and healthcare, dignity and democracy—these were the issues they spoke of, not establishing a Salafist version of the caliphate or waging eternal jihad. And just like everyone else, they, too, wanted the right to elect and unelect their own governments.

When Tunisians and Egyptians won that right for themselves, the elections had a clear winner: the Muslim Brotherhood, known as *Ennahda* in Tunisia and as the Party of Freedom and Justice in Egypt. This was what the old order and their friends in the West had so long dreaded: power in the hands of people who would not do their bidding.

2

In June 2012, the results of the first free and fair presidential elections in Egypt's seven-thousand-year history were announced. The second round run-off offered a choice between two very different Egypts: that of Muhammad Morsi, the candidate of the Muslim Brotherhood and Ahmad Shafiq, the candidate of the military. Morsi won by over a million votes. But to do so, he had to rely on the votes of large numbers of young secular liberals who were not his natural supporters. Having no desire to see Shafiq lead the military back to power, they lent Morsi their support.

For the Muslim Brotherhood, Morsi's victory was the culmination of almost a century of struggle and persecution. The organization was the brainchild of Hasan al-Banna (1904–49) who was in his early twenties when he set it up. After graduating from college in Cairo, the Ministry of Education sent al-Banna to work as a primary school teacher in Ismailiyya on the Suez Canal. During his time in the city, al-Banna saw first-hand what occupation really meant and it did not sit comfortably with him. The easy living of the Europeans who were employed by the canal company was a world away from the poverty and daily grind of ordinary Egyptians and the casual arrogance of the British army was a sharp contrast to the chronic state of Egypt's dependence.

Al-Banna was not part of the metropolitan, Westernized elite. He came from the country and grew up in a religious household where his father led prayers in the local mosque.[4] Al-Banna himself was heavily influenced by the writings of the Muslim reformist Rashid Rida (1865–1935). Rida's book *The Caliphate or the Supreme Imamate* (1923) outlined the framework for an Islamic state. Published not long after the Ottoman Empire ended, Rida's vision of an Islamic state resonated with those who understood their identity in Islamic terms and who felt no affinity for the new, secular nation-states of the Middle East.

Five years after the book's publication, al-Banna established the Muslim Brotherhood (al-Ikhwan al-Muslimin) which was dedicated to building an Islamic society from the bottom up. The movement chimed with a need in society and grew rapidly.[5] Its expanding base of members spread the message by preaching in mosques. More than that, al-Banna understood the problems of ordinary people—he came from the same background—so there was a very practical, self-help side to the Brotherhood. Like the waqfs, the system of religious endowments that functioned as a prestate welfare system, the Brotherhood provided social services for the poor, including health and education, which they otherwise could not have afforded.

The movement's message of brotherhood (there would later be a sisterhood for female members) and its widening support base eventually led it into the political arena and to a clash with the established order, a clash which, at times, became violent. Around 1940, the Brotherhood set up the "Secret Apparatus" (*al-Jihaz*) although it remains unclear how much al-Banna was involved in this decision.[6] The 1940s were politically turbulent in Egypt and the Brotherhood's Secret Apparatus was one of a number of groups involved in clandestine acts of sabotage against the king. (Ironically, of all the anti-regime forces at work in Egypt in the 1940s and early 1950s, it was the military—the defenders of king and country—who brought the king down.)

The Brotherhood would suffer for the Jihaz, then and now. It allowed the authorities to label the organization's members terrorists and to justify outlawing their peaceful political activity on the grounds of state security. Hasan al-Banna was killed by agents of the state on February 12, 1949, in a revenge attack for the assassination of Prime Minister Mahmoud Fahmi Nuqrashi by a Muslim Brother less than two months earlier.

The Brotherhood did not die with al-Banna. Even though it was banned until 1951, it remained sufficiently influential for Nasser's Free Officers to hold talks with its leadership. Nasser was aware of the Brotherhood's wide reach in society and of the dedication of its members. Volunteers from the Brotherhood fought with distinction in 1948 and helped the Egyptian army (including Nasser) when they were pinned down in Falluja near Beersheba.[7] Nasser came from the same background as many of their members so he recognized the movement's potential to become an alternative powerbase. Under Nasser, the Brotherhood were not just banned; they were persecuted.

The movement's most iconic figure during this period, the school teacher turned poet turned political philosopher whose fame has long outlived the obscurity of his execution in the dead of an August night nearly 50 years ago, was Sayyid Qutb.

Qutb, like al-Banna (and Nasser), came from the country. He was born in the village of Musha in Upper Egypt in 1906 and he, too, moved to

Cairo for his education. His journey to political Islam was a long and gradual one. Published poet, literary critic, religious exegesist, teacher, and civil servant (he spent two years in the United States studying educational techniques for Egypt's Ministry of Education), Qutb was a thoughtful, intelligent man of many talents who, if you read his life story, seems like a restless soul in search of something. In the Muslim Brotherhood, he found it. But in doing so, he lost his freedom and, ultimately, his life.

His writings after he joined the Brotherhood secured Sayyid Qutb's place as *the* philosopher of modern political Islam. His most famous work *Milestones* (1964), written while he was in prison, argued that Egypt under Nasser was like Arabia during the Jahiliyya, the Age of Ignorance before the Prophet brought Islam. Under these circumstances, the only reasonable course of action was to flee like the Prophet did when he left Mecca for Medina in 622.

Qutb's depiction of Nasser as a pharaoh and his indictment of Nasser's Egypt as unIslamic could lead to only one destination in the one-party state Nasser built. The mid-1960s were the high watermark of Nasser's power in Egypt and across the Arab world. Many people still saw him as their savior (the disaster of 1967 had yet to happen) and his authority was virtually unchecked. After a show trial in which Sayyid Qutb faced a range of charges from terrorism to possession of weapons to plotting a coup, he was sentenced to death on August 21, 1966, and hanged eight days later.

As happened with Hasan al-Banna, the Muslim Brotherhood did not die with Sayyid Qutb. If anything, his death and his dignity in the face of it fuelled his legend. If Nasser hoped Qutb's death would be the end of him, he was badly mistaken. Qutb's influence has grown since his death and his writings have projected that influence into the twenty-first century. You cannot understand what's really going on in the Middle East today without understanding Sayyid Qutb's philosophy of political Islam. What makes him so important is that he lived out his resistance to the state and, by doing so, showed what a one-party state does to its opponents.

For political Islamists who face persecution and prison for their beliefs, Sayyid Qutb is a very powerful role model. For those who do not share his Islamist worldview, he is an anathema. Furthermore, his theory of resistance has been claimed by moderates and militants alike. After 9/11, he was often referred to as the godfather of al-Qaida even though he was not himself a violent man and was not personally involved in acts of terror. This adoption of him by militants such as al-Qaida and ISIL has made him into a controversial figure. That controversy has often obscured much of his message and made it all too easy for authorities in the Arab world to cast the Muslim Brotherhood as closet terrorists because Qutb was a Brother.

For the established order in the Middle East, the real problem with Sayyid Qutb and the movement he belonged to is that they just will not go away.

In Egypt, Nasser's successor Anwar Sadat (r. 1970–81) went for a different approach from the persecution of the past. Sadat styled himself "The Believer President" and initially tried to co-opt the Brotherhood as part of his strategy to neutralize the Communists and Islamize his presidency. But it did not work. During his three decades in power, Hosni Mubarak (r. 1981–2010) went for mixture of persuasion and persecution. But that did not work either. Over the years, the Muslim Brotherhood has established a core base of support that seems satisfied to take the long view of history and to wait for events to move their way. And even though the movement's leadership has, at times, vacillated between outright resistance to power and a more pragmatic approach, that core base of support has remained solid.

To achieve this, the Muslim Brotherhood have been assisted by the closed nature of politics in the Arab world. Since multiparty politics are virtually nonexistent in the region, the mosque became a focal point for opposition. The leaders of the one-party republics and the no-party kingdoms of the Middle East could ban membership of political parties but they could not stop people going to the mosque. After 1967 and the renewed interest in Islam as a political force, the mosque became more than a place of prayer. It became the center of an alternative community where social services were coordinated, cassette tapes of banned preachers were circulated, and like-minded people felt free to share their views in a safe place.

This process was not limited to Egypt. The ideology of the Muslim Brotherhood recognized no borders and branches opened up across the region. From Turkey to Tunisia, Algeria to Syria, the Brotherhood spread. Its reach was wide but it enjoyed more success in the secular republics where religion has been forced to the margins of public life than in the conservative countries of the Gulf where religion features strongly in the public arena. Across the region, however, the different branches of the Muslim Brotherhood would suffer the same consequences of being on the wrong side of power. Just as Nasser recognized the movement's potential to be an alternative powerbase and took draconian steps to deal with the challenge it posed, other Arab leaders did the same.

In Syria, following a sustained campaign of Islamist opposition to his rule, President Hafiz al-Asad launched a full-on assault in 1982 on the city of Hama which he considered a Brotherhood stronghold, killed thousands of civilians in the process, then made membership of the Muslim Brotherhood a capital offence.

In Tunisia, after taking power following a "medical" coup in 1987, President Ben Ali allowed greater participation in parliamentary elections in 1989. But when Islamists polled strongly, the president banned the movement, labeled its members terrorists, and imprisoned thousands of them. Many others, including the movement's leader Rachid al-Ghannouchi, had to flee to Europe.[8] Al-Ghannouchi was not able to return to Tunisia until after the Arab Spring.

In Algeria, in 1991, a similar process occurred but with more catastrophic results. In the 1980s, Algeria's economy was going through a period of sustained decline and the military regime was forced to bow to public pressure for more open elections. The Islamic Salvation Front (FIS) polled well in the parliamentary elections of 1991 and looked set to form a majority government. In response, the military staged a coup and took complete control of the state. They received the backing of Western leaders, notably France's President Mitterand, who were concerned about regional security and the stability of oil supplies. FIS never got to exercise their electoral mandate. Algeria descended into a civil war that was so brutal, beheadings became a common occurrence. The war ended when the military reclaimed the state. Since then, they have played on people's fears of a return to chaos in order to cement their grip on power.

In the Occupied Territories of the West Bank and Gaza, the Palestinian Muslim Brotherhood is known as the Islamic Resistance Movement (*Harakat al-Muqawama al-Islamiyya* or Hamas for short). Like other branches of the movement, they, too, built up a solid core of support by spreading their message through the mosques, by taking care of people's social needs, and by having leaders who came from the same background as the majority of people. But the Palestinian movement is different from the Brotherhood elsewhere in the Arab world because it operates under Israeli military occupation. Hamas therefore defines itself, first and foremost, as a resistance movement and has an armed wing named after a Palestinian resistance fighter in the 1930s, Izz al-Din al-Qassam, who fought against the British occupation.

When Hamas won the elections to the Palestinian Legislative Council (PLC) in 2006, taking 72 out of the 132 seats, Washington, to Israel's relief, refused to recognize the results. The Americans and the Israelis consider Hamas a terrorist organization and refuse to deal with it. America's allies followed suit and disregarded the results of what were generally believed to have been completely free and fair elections.

You will have noticed a very obvious pattern here: any time Islamists win free and fair elections, the results of those elections are immediately ignored by the old order and their allies in the West.

Morsi's election victory in 2012 was supposed to change that. The popular protests of the Arab Spring were supposed to have swept away the old certainties of Arab Exceptionalism and the old contradictions of the West saying one thing and doing another in the Middle East. There was supposed to be a new Middle East where the gap between people and power was bridged, not by state-sponsored repression or by oil money, but by democratic elections.

The new Egypt was going to be like Turkey. After the end of the Ottoman Empire, the Turkish war hero, Atatürk, steered Turkey almost single-handedly to becoming a secular republic. Since 1923, the Turkish Republic plotted a course away from its imperial past towards a future as a fully fledged independent nation-state. For decades, the military repeatedly intervened in politics, staging coups and making and unmaking governments at will. Nevertheless, Turkey managed to develop the independent institutions necessary to ensure that when the Turkish people elected an Islamist party—the Justice and Development Party (AKP)—to power in 2002, the results of the election stood and the AKP's Recep Tayyip Erdogan became prime minister.

This is what the Muslim Brotherhood thought would happen in Egypt after the Arab Spring. In an interview with the British currents affairs program *Newsnight* on March 12, 2015, Amr Darrag, a former minister in Morsi's cabinet and now in exile in Turkey, said he, like many others in the movement, had been naïve. They had honestly believed that in the twenty-first century, it would be impossible for the Egyptian military to overthrow Egypt's democratically elected president while the West looked on and did absolutely nothing. But that is exactly what did happen. Morsi did not make it to the end of his first year in office.

In ousting him, the Egyptian military had an unlikely ally: large numbers of the Egyptian people.

3

So, what went wrong for President Muhammad Morsi?

Supporters of the Brotherhood will say he never had a chance. According to this view, the military "deep state" in Egypt never lost its grip on power in spite of the Brotherhood's victories in the parliamentary and presidential elections. All the key institutions of the state—the police, the military, the judiciary, the media, even the religious luminaries at al-Azhar—were appointees of the old regime and their loyalties still lay with Mubarak and the military. The generals were simply biding their time, paying lip service to democracy while waiting for the opportunity to step in and show Morsi the door.

To do this, they had the backing of the old order across the region. In the interests of securing stability (i.e. preserving their own power), the Kingdom of Saudi Arabia and the United Arab Emirates had already helped put down the uprising in Bahrain. They were ready to do the same in Egypt because if the democratic experiment in Egypt worked, people in the Gulf might very well want to try it too.

Opponents of this view will say President Morsi misinterpreted his mandate. He was elected by a combination of Brotherhood supporters and liberals who lent him their support to keep the military out of power. According to this view, the president once in power governed solely on behalf of the Brotherhood, assumed the right to speak for Islam, introduced a constitution that was too heavily weighted towards religion, and forgot he was president of all Egyptians.

The cracks began to show in the fall of 2012. Members of the National Salvation Front, an umbrella group of different parties, were alarmed by the president's decision on November 22, 2012, to issue a decree placing himself beyond the power of the courts. Morsi's aim was to protect the new democratic constitution from judicial interference. Almost all of the judiciary were appointed by Mubarak and Morsi believed they were working against him. He promised to revoke the decree after the referendum on the constitution. But Morsi's opponents feared the accumulation of so much power in one person's hands and they called the decree "Pharaoh's Law." Under public pressure, the decree was revoked.

But the incident suggested some of the secular groups who had voted for Morsi were experiencing "buyers' remorse." There was also a growing sense among some of the young revolutionaries that they had lost control of their revolution. They had been responsible for organizing the demonstrations on January 25, 2011, which set the uprising in motion, yet it was the Muslim Brotherhood who reaped the political rewards.

Discontent grew throughout 2013 and culminated in mass protests against Morsi at the end of June. The military seized the moment, forced Morsi out of office and arrested him. A wide range of Egyptians including members of the National Salvation Front, the youth movement *Tamarrod*, large numbers of Egypt's Coptic Christian community, women's groups, and Salafist parties (who are more Islamist than the Brotherhood) took to the streets on July 23, 2013—the anniversary of Nasser's coup in 1952—to show their approval of the military's actions.

Many Egyptians did not approve, however. And they do not understand why so many of their fellow citizens willingly helped the military back into power. Consequently, from the summer of 2013, Egypt has become a deeply divided country.

There are divisions, too, within the anti-Morsi camp: the protests which led to the coup were not a case of a simple binary choice between the military or the Muslim Brotherhood. Many protestors wanted Morsi out but wanted a wholly new system with more robust institutions to replace him.

The divisions in Egyptian society have deepened even further since the crackdown against the Muslim Brotherhood that started in the summer of 2013. And General Abdel Fattah el-Sisi's victory in the presidential elections of 2014, which were far from free and certainly not fair, has done nothing to address those divisions. If anything, he seems determined to make them worse, as if by dividing he really will conquer. (Sisi's opponent in the run-off round, Hamdeen Sabbahi, polled nearly ten million votes in the presidential elections of 2012 but saw his vote mysteriously drop to under one million in 2014, making him come third in a two-horse race: there were more spoiled votes than votes for him.)

There is a strange contradiction about the Egyptian military's overly aggressive role in politics and their seizure of power on the back of a tank: the military actually has supporters in Egypt. Ahmad Shafiq's vote in the elections of 2012 showed that. But the military leadership clearly do not believe they have sufficient support to risk going to the polls in a free and fair contest and, like the colonels of old, their concern is less with winning power than with exercising it and enjoying the privileges of it. Since the coup, they have therefore rolled back any democratic progress made since the Arab Spring and have reinstated the one-party military state that Nasser built.

All of which means there is no room in the new Egypt for dissent. The repression began with the Muslim Brotherhood but, in a chilling echo of Pastor Niemoller's famous words about the Nazis, it has not ended with them. Everyone from the leader of the April 6 Movement which helped start the revolution to journalists from al-Jazeera, teenage schoolgirls protesting on the sidewalk in Alexandria, and gay men minding their own business—all of these people and many, many more now find themselves on the wrong side of power. Under el-Sisi, Egypt is believed to have somewhere in the region of twenty thousand political prisoners. The gap between power and the people is as wide, if not wider, than ever.

4

The coup in Egypt reverberated around the region.

The old order was back in business. The crowned heads of the Gulf and the Arab presidents-for-life had never wanted to see democracy thrive in the region. If it did, they risked losing everything.

Allegations would later surface that the mass protests of June 2013 in Cairo were not quite the spontaneous demonstrations they appeared to be. The United Arab Emirates were said to have funded secular groups to oppose President Morsi, Saudi money was said to have financed anti-Morsi media companies, and the fuel shortages in June 2013 that precipitated the protests were rumored to have been deliberately planned to damage President Morsi.

It was not just Arab heads of state who were happy to see Morsi go and the military return to power. Media reports suggested Israel had lobbied the US Congress and EU member states not to cut aid to Cairo in the wake of the coup. In the interests of security, Israel preferred to see a president in Cairo who would maintain the status quo and honor the Camp David Accords. Israel also wanted to undermine Hamas. Morsi, as a Muslim Brother himself, had already shown himself much too supportive of his Palestinian colleagues for Israel's liking. During the 2012 Israeli offensive on Gaza, Morsi took a strong stance in support of the Palestinians. In the 2008 war, Mubarak had shut the border crossing at Rafah, set the security forces on anyone who protested against the decision, then left the Palestinians to fend for themselves. In 2012, Morsi sent his Prime Minister Hisham Qandil to Gaza while the territory was under attack to show the Palestinians they were not alone. (It says a lot about the Egyptian military's priorities that one of the first acts after the coup was to close the border with Gaza, again leaving the Palestinians to it. In 2015, Egypt became the first Arab state to label Hamas a terrorist organization.)

For the State of Israel, a country which takes pride in its democratic credentials, the decision to side with a dictator over a democrat was an issue of security. But will it prove to be a massive miscalculation? Israeli strategists have a depth of knowledge about the rest of the region that outflanks anything similar in the countries of their Western allies. That knowledge has deep roots. The study of Islam as an academic pursuit was pioneered in Europe by a Hungarian Jew, Ignaz Goldziher. In the early twentieth century, many of the leading scholars of Islam were Jewish. That pursuit of knowledge carried on after the State of Israel was created. Israeli security analysts study Arabic and Islam in a way that their Arab counterparts do not study Hebrew or Judaism. That gives Israel an information edge when it comes to analyzing and anticipating what their Arab neighbors might do next and preparing how to respond.

In this instance, however, it is not clear how effective Israel's decision will prove to be in the long run. There are already signs that it could turn out to be counterproductive. President Morsi did not revoke the Camp David Accords. He did not recall his ambassador from Tel Aviv. He did not expel the Israeli ambassador to Cairo. But since he was ousted, there has been a massive upsurge in jihadi violence in northern Sinai where groups affiliated to ISIL have been killing Egyptian soldiers by the score because they regard el-Sisi as illegitimate. But ISIL will not stop in Egypt: the Levant in their name includes historic Palestine. Northern Sinai is adjacent to Israel's long southern border and it is therefore ISIL's closest access point to Israel. Israel, in its bid to secure the status quo, may have indirectly helped create the circumstances where Sinai becomes a launch pad for attacks against its citizens.

Israel's Western allies also welcomed the return of the military to power in Egypt. This was a decision that, at best, was fraught with contradictions and, at worst, smacked of double standards. On Libya, the UK, the US, and France secured a UN Security Council Resolution (1973) to allow for the protection of civilians from Colonel Gaddafi's militias. The Western powers then stretched that resolution to its limits—according to the Russians, they broke four different clauses—so they could participate in the military campaign to bring down Gaddafi. The same three countries lobbied for a similar resolution against Bashar al-Asad but Russia, as a long-time ally of Syria and still smarting over the Libyan resolution, was not about to abstain again and allow another Western-sponsored resolution to pass. Moscow threatened to use its veto. The resolution never went through and the Syrians have been left to suffer the consequences of the world's inaction.

In these two cases, the UK, the US, and France had no long-term strategic relationship with either Asad or Gaddafi. Egypt was entirely different. The second biggest recipient of US aid and a strategic defense partner in the region, Cairo was firmly in the West's camp. General el-Sisi promised to keep it there. Washington had never been sure that President Morsi, with his Islamist agenda, would do the same. American military aid to Egypt was fully restored in 2015.

*   *   *

The Arab Spring showed that Muslims had had enough of being dictated to and wanted the right to speak for themselves. The large numbers of Christians in the Middle East also wanted the right to have their voices heard. The fall of Morsi, the war in Syria, and the unraveling security situation in the region have enabled the established order to reclaim the ground they lost during the Arab Spring and to entrench their counter-revolution. They, once again, claim the right to speak for Islam. Their Western allies, for reasons of self-interest, have supported them.

In the twenty-first-century Middle East, democracy still comes a very distant second to long-entrenched interests.

Untangling the Web: What Now?

The Middle East is currently going through one of the most turbulent periods in its history. States are collapsing before our eyes, and every time you switch on the news, it seems as if another suicide bomb has exploded in another city and another war has started in another country. Each day, the human suffering scales new heights. No one knows for sure how many people have been killed, injured, or displaced in the recent wars. The optimism of the Arab Spring now seems a very distant memory.

The causes of all these conflicts are not new. They go back to the First World War and the end of the Ottoman era when the Great Powers of Europe imposed their will on the Middle East with their lines on a map and their nation-states. That postwar settlement established a political order that left so many questions unanswered and so many issues unresolved. For decades, those questions and those issues were swept to one side as the kings and colonels who ruled the region pursued their own agendas and furthered their own interests. They kept the people firmly shut out of power. The political leaders of the West, who had so much to say about the democratic rights of people in the Communist Bloc, turned a blind eye when it came to the rights of people of the Middle East. Their concern to secure stability in the region trumped all other considerations.

The Arab Spring brought the Arab people back into the equation. When the iron grip of dictatorship loosened, the questions that had been sidelined for so long suddenly demanded answers. Questions about the legitimacy of the states created after the First World War and the nature of politics in those states.

The great hope of the Arab Spring was that the quest to find answers to these questions could be done peacefully through the democratic process. But the fact that a number of leaders intervened to thwart the will of the people (and did so with the backing of other Arab leaders while the West looked on) has set the democratic process back indefinitely. By their actions, these rulers have shown they will not tolerate any change in the region because it might threaten their own interests. That means if anything is going to change in the Middle East, *everything* will have to change. In the meantime, the gap between power and the people is being filled by violent jihadi groups like ISIL who have no interest at all in democracy and no interest in anyone who does not agree with their philosophy.

In essence, all the problems in the Middle East come down to that one core issue—the massive gap between power and the people. Until that is resolved, until the people of the Middle East feel they have a stake in the governance of the Middle East, until they are left alone to work out how to achieve it, what is going on now will continue. And the gap between power and the people will continue to be filled by the status quo of kings, generals, and sheikhs on the one hand and the likes of ISIL on the other. Except that each new incarnation of the extremist ideology will be more violent than the last.

Democracy has many disappointments, but its greatest strength is that if you have a president or a prime minister whose policies you do not support, you have the consolation that in four years' time, you will have the chance to vote them out. Until the people of the Middle East have that chance too, it is hard to see how any of the major challenges facing the region will be resolved.

Notes

1   Sarajevo: Sunday, June 28, 1914

1. Strachan, *First World War*, 3.
2. Ibid., 3; Gilbert, *First World War*, 17.
3. I am grateful to Professor Alan Jones for drawing the story of Colonel Redl to my attention.
4. Gilbert, op. cit., 14.
5. Finkel, *Osman's Dream*, 21.
6. Gilbert, op. cit., 16.
7. Ibid., 16–7; Strachan, op. cit., 9.

2   The British Empire and the Arab World: Ambition, Austerity, and a Class Apart

1. Hitti, *History of the Arabs*, 722–6.
2. Hopwood, *Egypt*, 12–3.
3. See Owen, *Middle East in the World Economy*, chapters 2, 3, 5, and 9, for Egypt's economy during this period.
4. Hitti, op. cit., 750.
5. Morris, *Heaven's Command*, 420.
6. Hitti, op. cit., 750.
7. Lapidus, *History of Islamic Societies*, 516–7.
8. McMillan, *Fathers and Sons*, 91–2.
9. Morris, *Pax Britannica*, 244–5.
10. Lapidus, op. cit., 516; Morris, ibid., 246.
11. Kedourie, *Politics in the Middle East*, 157.
12. Montague, *When Friday Comes*, 2–3, 8–9.
13. Hopwood, op. cit., 13.
14. See Said, *Out of Place*, and Said Makdisi, *Teta, Mother and Me*, for an inside view of the impact of European education on Arabs.
15. Morris, *Pax Britannica*, 245.
16. Ibid., 515.

3   The French Empire and the Arab World: From the Crusades to the Civilizing Mission

1. Lapidus, op. cit., 587.
2. Ibid., 587–8.
3. Maupassant, *Bel-Ami*, 28.
4. Lapidus, op. cit., 587. See also Norwich, *The Middle Sea*, 497.
5. Hitti, op. cit., 636.
6. Ibid., 643.
7. Ibid., 743.
8. Sebag Montefiore, *Jerusalem*, 312.
9. Ibid., 318; Norwich, op. cit., 429.
10. Quoted from Norwich, ibid., 498.
11. Lapidus, op. cit., 587.
12. Ibid., 589.
13. Ibid., 588–9.
14. Ibid., 588.
15. Ibid., 589–90.
16. Hitti, op. cit., 747–8. See also Said Makdisi, op. cit., 156, 176, and 186.
17. Owen, op. cit., chapters 6 and 10.
18. Hitti, op. cit., 734–6.

4   The Russian Empire and the Arab World: Religion, Royalty, and the New Rome

1. Figes, *Natasha's Dance*, 300.
2. MacCulloch, *A History of Christianity*, 522–3.
3. Sebag Montefiore, op. cit., 311.
4. Finkel, op. cit., 377–9; McMillan, op. cit., 79–80.
5. Said Makdisi, op. cit., 163.
6. Elon, *Israelis*, 50–1. As Barnet Litvinoff points out in *The Burning Bush*, the Jewish community was obliged to put forward a number of men as a percentage of the population for military service (ten out of every 1,000). This was a much higher quota than that for what he calls "true" Russians who had to provide four men per 7,000. The results of recruitment of the Jews were also unfair: rich people were able to buy their sons out of it, while the poor were left to make up the numbers: *The Burning Bush*, 154–5.
7. Lewis, *Jews of Islam*, 6–9.

5   The German Empire and the Arab World: Family Feuds and Eastern Ambitions

1. Hobsbawn, *Age of Empire*, 46–7, 174, 175, 178, 342, 345.
2. Ibid., 351.
3. Finkel, op. cit., 528.

6   The Ottoman Empire: How the Arab World
Was Won and Lost

1. Finkel, op. cit., 2. Similar stories were told of the Prophet Muhammad. Osman in Arabic is Uthman, which became Ottoman in English.
2. McMillan, op. cit., 71–5.
3. Ibid., 21–6.
4. Aburish, *House of Saud*, 31.
5. Imber, *Ottoman Empire*, 125.
6. Ibid., 249.
7. McMillan, op. cit., 76–9.
8. Quataert, *Ottoman Empire*, 78–9. See also Finkel, op. cit., 127–8.
9. I am grateful to Professor Alan Jones for drawing my attention to this.
10. Said Makdisi, op. cit., 150, 152, and 176.
11. These changes were also reflected in Ottoman law. See chapter 9, this volume.
12. Sebag Montefiore, op. cit., 342–3.
13. Owen, op. cit., 100–10.
14. Finkel, op. cit., 527–8.
15. Fromkin, *Peace to End All Peace*, 54–5.

7   London: Tuesday, December 21, 1915

1. For detailed and highly readable background studies of both men, see Barr, *A Line in the Sand*, 7–19 and 20–36.
2. Ibid., 8.
3. Fromkin, op. cit., 146.
4. Ibid., 146.
5. Ibid.
6. Barr, op. cit., 9.
7. Fromkin, op. cit., 147.
8. Ibid., 146.
9. Strachan, op. cit., 100.
10. The father was a founder of the Comité de l'Afrique Française. The son, Charles, was treasurer of the Comité de l'Asie Française. See Barr, op. cit., 20, and Fromkin, op. cit., 190.
11. Barr, op. cit., 20–1.
12. Fromkin, op. cit., 189.
13. Ibid., 191.
14. Ibid., 197.
15. Gilbert, op. cit., 244.
16. The Russian side fell out of the equation when they left the war on November 8, 1917.
17. Danahar, *The New Middle East*, 395.
18. Gilbert, op. cit., 123, 541.

19. Ibid., 541.
20. Fromkin, op. cit., 166; McMillan, op. cit., 93.
21. Ismael and Ismael, *Continuity and Change*, 1.

8 The Arab World before the War: The Facts on the Ground

1. Cesari, *Why the West Fears Islam*, 307.
2. Ibid., 309.
3. McMillan, *Fathers and Sons*, 141–5.
4. Quran 2:256. The translation is from Jones, 58.
5. See Lewis, op. cit., for a detailed study of the position of Jews in the Islamic world.
6. Hitti, op. cit., 620.
7. Lewis, op. cit., 42–3.
8. This is a brief overview of the diverse nature of Islam. For a more detailed account, see Hitti, op. cit., chapter 30 "Moslem Sects," 429–49.
9. Tribal identities remained important enough that there was a view among the early caliphs and their supporters that only someone from the Prophet's tribe of Quraysh was eligible to lead the community, a view that would appear to contradict the egalitarianism of Islam.
10. McMillan, *Mecca*, 102–13, 116–25, 144–58.
11. For details of the many dynasties that have ruled the Middle East, see Hitti, op. cit., 450–60, 461–83, 505–11, 520–5, 537–56, 617–24, 671–682, 709–18.
12. For studies on the Umayyad era, see Blankinship, *The End of the Jihad State*; Hawting, *First Dynasty of Islam*; McMillan, *The Meaning of Mecca*; Wellhausen, *Arab Kingdom*.
13. Hitti, op. cit., 154.
14. Leverett, *Inheriting Syria*, 2.
15. Hitti, op. cit., 155–9.
16. Al-Tabari, *Tarikh* II, 272–389.
17. In Kufa, a movement arose called the *Tawwabun*, or Penitents, because of this guilt. It did not last long in the face of the Umayyad armies, but it showed the strength of feeling about leaving al-Husayn to his fate. See al-Tabari, op. cit., II 497–513, 538–71.
18. Lapidus, op. cit., 234.
19. Al-Tabari, op. cit., III 84–6, 99–119, 330.
20. Al-Yaqubi, *Tarikh*, II 289–90. See also Hitti, op. cit., 285–6. One member of the family did survive to fight another day—a grandson of the caliph Hisham named Abd al-Rahman. He escaped from Palestine through North Africa (where he had tribal connections) to Spain where his descendants founded a new Umayyad caliphate in the tenth century.
21. Al-Tabari, op. cit., III 319–26.

22. The Cordoba caliphate belonged to the Umayyad family (929–1031), see note 20; the Cairo caliphate to the Fatimid family (969–1171).
23. Fromkin, op. cit., 450.

9   The Remaking of the Middle East: Enter the Nation-State

1. Reynolds, *The Long Shadow*, 5.
2. Lewis, op. cit., 156–8, 168.
3. Ibid., 158. The incident drew the attention—and intervention—of Britain and France. Britain saw itself as the protector of the Jewish community and intervened to help. France's intervention was more of a hindrance to the local Jewish community. The French Consul in Damascus used the situation to condemn local Jews.
4. Ismael and Ismael, op. cit., 80–1. See also chapter 6, this volume.
5. Lapidus, op. cit., 498–9.
6. Quataert, op. cit., 190.

10   From Sykes-Picot to the Treaty of Sèvres: Betrayals, Backstabbing, and Broken Promises

1. Fromkin, op. cit., 400.
2. For a more detailed account of the full range of diplomatic double-crossing that went on between Britain and France over the future of the Middle East right up until the 1940s, see Barr, op. cit.
3. Fromkin, op. cit., 336–8.
4. Barr, op. cit., 124–5.
5. Trotsky published details of the Sykes-Picot-Sazanov correspondence on November 27, 1917, in a bid to embarrass Russia's former rulers and the Allies.
6. Litvinoff, op. cit., 260–2.
7. Fromkin, op. cit., 298.
8. The Treaty of Brest-Litovsk was signed with Germany on March 3, 1918.
9. Fromkin, op. cit., 271, 285.
10. Ibid., 297.

11   The Poisoned Legacy and the War's Unanswered Questions

1. Ismael and Ismael, op. cit., 190 (emphasis added).
2. Fromkin, op. cit., 411.

12　Where to Begin?

1. Hitti, op. cit., 391.
2. Al-Tabari, op. cit., II 201 and II 1464–6.

13　Jerusalem: The Temple Mount

1. Sebag Montefiore, op. cit., 130.
2. MacCulloch, op. cit., 107; Sebag Montefiore, op. cit., 134.
3. Ibid., 137.
4. Litvinoff, op. cit., 21.
5. Ibid., 30.
6. Cook and Herzman, *Medieval World View*, 68–9.
7. Litvinoff, op. cit., 30.
8. MacCulloch, op. cit., 92.
9. Ibid., 93, citing John 18: 31.
10. Ibid., 93, citing Matthew 27: 24–5.
11. Sebag Montefiore, op. cit., 148.
12. Litvinoff, op. cit., 79.
13. Ibid., 60.
14. Ibid., 61.
15. Ibid., 130.
16. Ibid., 210.
17. Chaney, *Chanel*, 311.
18. Appelfeld, *The Age of Wonders*, 132.
19. Ibid., 135.
20. Ibid., 133.
21. Gellately, *Backing Hitler*, 12.
22. Ibid., 257.
23. Ibid., 27–8.
24. Gilbert, op. cit., 447. This was on August 4, 1918. Hitler had previously been awarded the Iron Cross, Second Class, back in 1914.
25. This story of Edwin Landau and his experiences is taken from Gellately, op. cit., 28.
26. Chaney, op. cit., 335–6.
27. Némirovsky, *Suite Française*, 246.
28. Elon, op. cit., 96–7.
29. Achcar, *Arabs and the Holocaust*, 18.
30. Ibid., 18.
31. Elon, op. cit., 22.
32. Litvinoff, op. cit., 388.
33. Danahar, op. cit., 145.
34. Sebag Montefiore, op. cit., 492–3.

14   Jerusalem: The Noble Sanctuary

1. From 661 to 750.
2. Al-Tabari, op. cit., II 1172–3.
3. Ibid., II 577. Other sources suggest the assassin was a slave girl acting on the orders of Marwan's disgruntled wife.
4. See McMillan, *Mecca*, 79–81.
5. Al-Yaqubi, op. cit., II 177–8. See also Ibn Kathir, *Bidayah*, VIII 280–1.
6. The source is al-Yaqubi. See McMillan, *Mecca*, 80, note 26, for the debate on this subject.
7. Guillaume, *Muhammad*, 289. It happened 18 months after Muhammad's hijra from Mecca in 622.
8. Quran 3: 67. See also 5: 15, 19, and 48.
9. See Quran 2: 92.
10. See Quran 2: 40, 41, 83–4, 87, 92, 93, 122; 4: 155, 160; 5: 13; 20: 80, 82.
11. See Quran 4: 171; 19: 88–92.
12. See Quran 4: 163–4; 19: 58.
13. See Quran 2: 40, 47, 122; 5: 69; 45: 16.
14. See also Quran 5: 51, 64, and 69. See also Quran 2: 88–96, 122, and 211.
15. These English translations come from the translation by Alan Jones, 113. Many translations of the Quran are difficult to read. This one is not; it does not read like a translation. In addition, it comes with equally easy-to-read explanatory notes.
16. Armstrong, *Muhammad*, 183.
17. Ibid., 207.
18. Ibid., 207–8.
19. Lewis, op. cit., 33.
20. Ibid., 19; see also 53 and 62.
21. Al-Tabari, op. cit., II 4.
22. Ibid., III 129.
23. Ibid., III 500.
24. Hitti, op. cit., 220–1.
25. McMillan, *Fathers and Sons*, 64–6.
26. Maalouf, *The Crusades through Arab Eyes*, ii.
27. Ibid., 53.
28. Ibid., 198.
29. Hitti, op. cit., 654.
30. Bloom and Blair, *Art and Architecture of Islam*, 92–3.
31. Ibid., 224.
32. Fromkin, op. cit., 297.
33. These figures come from Achcar, op. cit., 18.
34. Ibid., 19.
35. This sense of uncertainty is very well captured in Deborah Rohan's *The Olive Grove*.

15 Cairo: Wednesday, July 23, 1952

1. Mansfield, *Nasser's Egypt*, 42.
2. See, for example, Serageldin, *The Cairo House*, 41–2.
3. Mansfield, op. cit., 30.
4. Hopwood, *Egypt*, 30.
5. Mansfield, op. cit., 43.
6. Ibid., 43.
7. Hopwood, op. cit., 34.
8. Ibid., 35.
9. Calvert, *Sayyid Qutb*, 53–101.
10. Mansfield, op. cit., 35.
11. Hopwood, op. cit., 36.
12. Mansfield, op. cit., 45.

16 The Kings, the Colonels, and the Political Time Warp: The Return of the Middle Ages

1. For a more detailed discussion of the issues raised here, see McMillan, *Fathers and Sons*.
2. See, for example, 5: 18, 17: 111, and 25: 2. I am grateful to Professor Alan Jones for drawing my attention to these references. See McMillan, op. cit., 5–7.
3. Ibid., 5.
4. Ibid., 56.
5. Al-Tabari, op. cit., III 1368–70. See also 1372–3.
6. Ibid., III 1370, 1372–3, 1377–9, 1384–7, 1455–65, 1471–2. See also McMillan, op. cit., 59–60; and Miah, *Al-Mutawakkil*, 19–21.
7. Al-Tabari, op. cit., III 1697.
8. Hitti, op. cit., 461–83.
9. Holt, *Age of the Crusades*, 99, 142–3; McMillan, op. cit., 67.
10. Hitti, op. cit., 673.
11. Reynolds, op. cit., 47.
12. For a detailed study of Britain's relations with the elite of their empire, see David Cannadine's fascinating book *Ornamentalism*.
13. Halliday, *Arabia without Sultans*, 272, 279.
14. Lapidus, op. cit., 597. See also 595–6.
15. McMillan, op. cit., 114.
16. Lapidus, op. cit., 614.
17. McMillan, op. cit., 104–5.
18. Lapidus, op. cit., 604.
19. See, for example, van Dam, *Struggle for Power in Syria*, 29–74.
20. Lapidus, op. cit., 546.

17   I Am the State: Power, Politics, and the Cult of Personality

1. McMillan, op. cit., 117.
2. Ibid., 116.
3. Halliday, op. cit., 274–80, in particular 275.
4. Serageldin, op. cit., 90.
5. Hopwood, op. cit., 42.
6. Mansfield, op. cit., 51–2.
7. Ismael and Ismael, op. cit., 351.
8. Aburish, *Brutal Friendship*, 72.
9. Rasheed, *History of Saudi Arabia*, 131.
10. See Oufkir, *La Prisonnière: Twenty Years in a Desert Gaol.*
11. Mansfield, op. cit., 57.
12. Lapidus, op. cit., 567.
13. Ibid.
14. Ibid., 570.
15. Halliday, op. cit., 105–8, 109–18.
16. Ibid., 227–59; Lapidus, op. cit., 571; McMillan, op. cit., 113.
17. Shlaim, *Israel, Palestine and the Arab Uprisings*, 391, in Gerges, ed. *The New Middle East.*
18. Elon, op. cit., 298. Elon, op. cit., 296, also points out a number of factors why Israel might have ended up as an authoritarian state, the first of which is the security situation, and shows how this did not end up being the case.
19. Ibid., 294.
20. Al-Aswany, *On the State of Egypt*, 45.

18   The Problem of Absolute Power: From Stability to Stagnation

1. Dwight D. Eisenhower, John F. Kennedy, Lyndon Johnson, Richard Nixon, Gerald Ford, Jimmy Carter, Ronald Reagan, George H. Bush, and Bill Clinton.
2. McMillan, op. cit., 5.
3. Ibid., 128.
4. Ismael and Ismael, op. cit., 255. See also Leverett, op. cit., 83–4.
5. Owen, *Arab Presidents for Life*, 161–71.
6. Ibid., 163.
7. Ismael and Ismael, op. cit., 357.

19   Mecca: Tuesday, November 20, 1979

1. Al-Rasheed, op. cit., 18.
2. Ibid., 66.

3. Hiro, *Islamic Fundamentalism*, 128.
4. Ibid.
5. Calvert, op. cit., 261.
6. Ibid.
7. Keppel, *Jihad*, 50–2; Atwan, *Secret History*, 42.
8. Hiro, op. cit., 129.
9. Ibid.
10. Trofimov, *Siege of Mecca*, 23.
11. Al-Baladhuri, *Futuh*, 28; al-Yaqubi, op. cit., II 47. The caliph Umar (r. 634–44) expelled some of the Jewish and Christian communities from the peninsula, but Arabia remained home to many Jews (especially in Yemen) until the twentieth century.
12. Aburish's book, *The House of Saud*, explains this in detail.
13. The translation is from Jones, op. cit., 47.
14. This quotation is taken from Hiro, op. cit., 133.
15. Trofimov, op. cit., 226.
16. Ruthven, *Islam in the World*, 32.
17. Trofimov, op. cit., 239.

20   1979: The View from Tehran

1. Ismael and Ismael, op. cit., 138.
2. Lapidus, op. cit., 471.
3. Ibid.; Ismael and Ismael, 121.
4. Hiro, op. cit., 147–8.
5. Sharon, *Black Banners*, 33. See also McMillan, *Mecca*, 33.
6. McMillan, *Fathers and Sons*, 55, 149–50.
7. Ibid., 150.
8. Lapidus, op. cit., 475.
9. Kedourie, op. cit., 337, 339.
10. Lapidus, op. cit., 475.
11. Hiro, op. cit., 150.
12. Ismael and Ismael, op. cit., 123.
13. Ibid., 124.
14. Hiro, op. cit., 165, 167–8.
15. Ibid., 164, 167, 168.
16. Ibid., 169.
17. Ibid., 172.
18. Ibid., 177.
19. Rasheed, op. cit., 147.
20. Ibid.

21   1979: Holy War and Unholy Alliances

1. Trofimov, op. cit., 234–5.
2. Morris, *Heaven's Command*, 105–12.
3. Ibid., 112.
4. Vadney, *The World Since 1945*, 415.
5. For a detailed study of the US–Saudi relationship, see Bronson, *Thicker than Oil*.
6. Ismael and Ismael, op. cit., 201.
7. Atwan, *Country of Words*, 218.
8. Ibid. For the interview with Bin Laden, see Atwan's *Secret History*, 15–37.

22   The Arab Spring and the Democratic Alternative

1. Gerges, op. cit., 14, note 28.
2. The issue of Gulf money invested in the West is dealt with in greater detail in Christopher Davidson's *After the Sheikhs* and in Kristian Coates Ulrichsen's excellent *The Gulf States in International Political Economy*.
3. Filiu, *The Arab Revolution*, 5–16; Danahar, op. cit., 20–1; Gerges, op. cit., 21–4.
4. Calvert, *Sayyid Qutb*, 81.
5. Tamimi, *Hamas: Unwritten Chapters*, 4.
6. Calvert, op. cit., 119–20.
7. Ibid., 120.
8. Lapidus, op. cit., 606; McMillan, op. cit., 2.

Select Bibliography

Aarts, Paul, and Gerd Nonneman, eds. *Saudi Arabia in the Balance: Political Economy, Society, Foreign Affairs*. 2nd edition. London: C. Hurst & Co., 2006.

Abbott, Nabia. *Two Queens of Baghdad*. London: Saqi, 1986.

Abukhalil, As'ad. *The Battle for Saudi Arabia: Royalty, Fundamentalism, and Global Power*. New York: Seven Stories Press, 2004.

Aburish, Said. *The Rise, Corruption and Coming Fall of the House of Saud*. Updated edition. London: Bloomsbury, 1995.

———. *A Brutal Friendship: The West and the Arab Elite*. Updated edition. London: Indigo, 1998.

Achcar, Gilbert. *The Arabs and the Holocaust*. London: Saqi, 2010.

Afsaruddin, Asma. *Excellence & Precedence: Medieval Islamic Discourse on Legitimate Leadership*. Leiden: E. J. Brill, 2002.

———. *The First Muslims: History & Memory*. Oxford: Oneworld, 2009.

Ajami, Fuad. *The Arab Predicament: Arab Political Thought and Practice since 1967*. Updated edition. Cambridge: Cambridge University Press, 1992.

Alsharekh, Alanoud, ed. *The Gulf Family: Kinship Policies and Modernity*. London: Saqi, 2007.

Amabe, Fukuzo. *The Emergence of the 'Abbasid Autocracy: The 'Abbasid Army, Khurasan and Adharbayjan*. Kyoto: Kyoto University Press, 1995.

Appelfeld, Aharon. *The Age of Wonders*. London: Quartet Books, 1993.

Armstrong, Karen. *Islam: A Short History*. London: Phoenix, 2001.

———. *Muhammad: A Biography of the Prophet*. London: Phoenix, 2001.

Asad, Muhammad. *The Road to Mecca*. New York: Simon & Schuster, 1954.

Aslan, Reza. *No god but God: The Origins, Evolution and Future of Islam*. London: Arrow Books, 2006.

Al-Aswany, Alaa. *The Yacoubian Building*. Cairo and New York: The American University in Cairo Press, 2004.

———. *Friendly Fire*. London: Fourth Estate, 2010.

———. *On the State of Egypt: What Caused the Revolution*. Edinburgh: Canongate, 2011.

Atwan, Abdel Bari. *The Secret History of al-Qa'ida*. London: Saqi, 2006.

———. *A Country of Words: A Palestinian Journey from the Refugee Camp to the Front Page*. London: Saqi, 2008.

Al-Azmeh, Aziz. *Muslim Kingship: Power and the Sacred in Muslim, Christian and Pagan Polities*. London and New York: I. B. Tauris, 1997.

Barr, James. *A Line in the Sand: Britain, France and the Struggle for Mastery of the Middle East*. London: Simon & Schuster, 2011.

Bennison, Amira K. *The Great Caliphs: The Golden Age of the 'Abbasid Empire*. London: I. B. Tauris, 2011.

Berkey, Jonathan P. *The Formation of Islam: Religion and Society in the Near East 600–1800*. Cambridge and New York: Cambridge University Press, 2003.

Berlin, Isaiah. *Against the Current: Essays in the History of Ideas*. London: Pimlico, 1997.

Bianchi, Robert R. *Guests of God: Pilgrimage and Politics in the Islamic World*. New York: Oxford University Press, 2004.

Biddle, David White. *The Development of the Bureaucracy of the Islamic Empire during the Late Umayyad and Early 'Abbasid Period*. Ann Arbor and London: University Microfilms International, 1985.

Black, Antony. *A History of Islamic Political Thought: From the Prophet to the Present*. Edinburgh: Edinburgh University Press, 2001.

Blair, Shelia S., and Jonathan M. Bloom. *The Art and Architecture of Islam 1250–1800*. 2nd edition. Yale: Yale University Press, 1995.

Blankinship, Khalid Y. *The End of the Jihad State: The Reign of Hisham Ibn 'Abd al-Malik and the Collapse of the Umayyads*. Albany: State University of New York Press, 1994.

Blay-Abramski, Irit Irene. *From Damascus to Baghdad: The 'Abbasid Administrative System as a Product of the Umayyad Heritage (41/661 – 320/932)*. Ann Arbor and London: University Microfilms International, 1985.

Bonner, Michael D. *Aristocratic Violence and Holy War: Studies in the Jihad and the Arab-Byzantine Border*. New Haven: American Oriental Society, 1986.

Botton, Alain de. *Status Anxiety*. London: Penguin Books, 2005.

Bradley, John R. *After the Arab Spring: How Islamists Hijacked the Middle East Revolts*. New York: Palgrave Macmillan, 2012.

———. *Inside Egypt: The Road to Revolution in the Land of the Pharaohs*. Updated edition. New York: Palgrave Macmillan, 2012.

Bronson, Rachel. *Thicker than Oil: America's Uneasy Partnership with Saudi Arabia*. New York; Oxford: Oxford University Press, 2006.

Bulliet, Richard W. *The Camel and the Wheel*. New York: Columbia University Press, 1990.

———. *Islam: The View from the Edge*. New York: Columbia University Press, 1994.

———. *The Case for Islamo-Christian Civilization*. New York: Columbia University Press, 2004.

Bullock, Alan. *Hitler: A Study in Tyranny*. London: Penguin Books, 1990.

Calvert, John. *Sayyid Qutb and the Origins of Radical Islam*. London: C. Hurst & Co., 2010.

Cannadine, David. *Ornamentalism: How the British Saw Their Empire*. London: Penguin Books, 2002.

Cesari, Jocelyne. *Why the West Fears Islam: An Exploration of Muslims in Liberal Democracies*. New York: Palgrave Macmillan, 2013.

Chaney, Lisa. *Chanel: An Intimate Life*. London: Penguin Books, 2012.

Chejne, Anwar Georges. *Succession to the Rule in Islam: With Special Reference to the Early 'Abbasid Period*. Ann Arbor: University Microfilms International, 1985.

Coates Ulrichsen, Kristian. *The First World War in the Middle East*. London: C. Hurst & Co., 2014.

———. *The Gulf States in International Political Economy*. New York: Palgrave Macmillan, 2015.

Cobb, Paul M. *White Banners: Contention in 'Abbasid Syria 750–880*. Albany: State University of New York Press, 2001.

Cook, Michael A. *Muhammad*. Oxford: Oxford University Press, 1983.

———. *Forbidding Wrong in Islam*. Cambridge: Cambridge University Press, 2003.

Cook, William R., and Ronald B. Herzman. *The Medieval World View: An Introduction*. New York and Oxford: Oxford University Press, 1983.

Cooperson, Michael. *Al-Ma'mun*. Oxford: Oneworld, 2005.

Crone, Patricia. *Slaves on Horses: The Evolution of the Islamic Polity*. Cambridge: Cambridge University Press, 1980.

———. *Medieval Islamic Political Thought*. Edinburgh: Edinburgh University Press, 2004.

Crone, Patricia, and Martin Hinds. *God's Caliph: Religious Authority in the First Centuries of Islam*. Cambridge: Cambridge University Press, 1986.

Dabashi, Hamid. *The Arab Spring: The End of Postcolonialism*. London and New York: Zed Books, 2012.

———. *Being a Muslim in the World*. New York: Palgrave Macmillan, 2013.

Danahar, Paul. *The New Middle East: The World after the Arab Spring*. London: Bloomsbury, 2013.

Davidson, Christopher M. *After the Sheikhs: The Coming Collapse of the Gulf Monarchies*. London: C. Hurst & Co., 2012.

Al-Dhahabi, Shams al-Din Muhammad. *Ta'rikh al-Islam wa Tabaqat al-Mashahir wa'l-A'lam*. 6 volumes. Cairo: Maktabat al-Qudsi, 1947.

Dixon, 'Abd al-Ameer 'Abd. *The Umayyad Caliphate 65–86/684–705: A Political Study*. London: Luzac, 1971.

Eickelman, Dale F., and James Piscatori, eds. *Muslim Travellers: Pilgrimage, Migration and the Religious Imagination*. London and New York: Routledge, 1990.

Elad, Amikam. *Medieval Jerusalem and Islamic Worship: Holy Places, Ceremonies, Pilgrimage*. Leiden and New York: E. J. Brill, 1995.

Elon, Amos. *The Israelis: Founders and Sons*. London: Pelican Books, 1983.

Esposito, John L. *The Islamic Threat: Myth or Reality?* New York: Oxford University Press, 1992.

Fernández-Armesto, Felipe, ed. *The Times Guide to the Peoples of Europe*. Revised edition. London: Times Books, 1997

Filiu, Jean-Pierre. *The Arab Revolution: Ten Lessons from the Democratic Uprising*. London: C. Hurst & Co., 2011.

Figes, Orlando. *Natasha's Dance: A Cultural History of Russia*. London: Penguin Books, 2003.

Finkel, Caroline. *Osman's Dream: The Story of the Ottoman Empire 1300–1923*. London: John Murray, 2006.

Firestone, Reuven. *Jihad: The Origins of Holy War in Islam*. New York: Oxford University Press, 1999.

Flanders, Judith. *Consuming Passions: Leisure and Pleasure in Victorian Britain*. London: Harper Press, 2011.

Flood, Finbar B. *The Great Mosque of Damascus: Studies on the Makings of an Umayyad Visual Culture*. Leiden: E. J. Brill, 2001.

Fromkin, David. *A Peace to End All Peace: The Fall of the Ottoman Empire and the Creation of the Modern Middle East*. New York: Holt, 1989.

Gellately, Robert. *Backing Hitler: Consent and Coercion in Nazi Germany*. New York: Oxford University Press, 2001

Gerges, Fawaz A., ed. *The New Middle East: Protest and Revolution in the Arab World*. New York: Cambridge University Press, 2014.

Ghosh, Amitav. *In an Antique Land*. London: Granta Books, 1998.

Gilbert, Martin. *The First World War: A Complete History*. London: Phoenix, 2008.

Goitein, S. D. *Studies in Islamic History and Institutions*. Leiden: E. J. Brill, 1966.

Gordon, Matthew S. *The Breaking of a Thousand Swords: A History of the Turkish Military at Samarra (AH 200–275/815–889 CE)*. Albany: State University of New York Press, 2001.

Grass, Günter. *Dog Years*. London: Picador, 1989.

Grunebaum, G. E. von. *Medieval Islam*. Chicago: University of Chicago Press, 1953.

———. *Muhammadan Festivals*. London and New York: Abelard-Schuman, 1958.

Guillaume, Alfred. *The Life of Muhammad: A Translation of Ibn Ishaq's Sirat Rasul Allah*. Oxford: Oxford University Press, 2003.

Halliday, Fred. *Nation and Religion in the Middle East*. London: Saqi, 2000.

———. *Arabia Without Sultans*. 2nd edition. London: Saqi, 2002.

Hammoudi, Abdellah. *A Season in Mecca: Narrative of a Pilgrimage*. New York: Hill and Wang, 2006.

Hawting, Gerald R. *The First Dynasty of Islam*. London: Croon Helm, 1986.

———, ed. *The Development of Islamic Ritual*. Aldershot and Burlington: Ashgate/Varorium 2006.

Hinds, Martin. "The Siffin Arbitration Agreement." *Journal of Semitic Studies* 17 (1972): 93–129.

———. "The Murder of the Caliph 'Uthman.'" *International Journal of Middle East Studies* 3 (1972): 450–469.

Hiro, Dilip. *Islamic Fundamentalism*. 2nd edition. London: Paladin, 1989.

Hitti, Philip K. *A History of the Arabs*. 10th edition. Basingstoke: Palgrave Macmillan, 2002.

Hobsbawn, Eric. *The Age of Revolution 1789–1848*. London: Abacus, 2010.

———. *The Age of Empire 1875–1914*. London: Abacus, 2010.

Hodgson, Marshall G. S. *The Venture of Islam: Conscience and History in a World Civilization*. 3 volumes. 2nd edition. Chicago: University of Chicago Press, 1977.

Holt, P. M. *The Age of the Crusades: The Near East from the Eleventh Century to 1517*. London and New York: Longman, 1986.

Hopwood, Derek. *Egypt: Politics and Society 1945–90*. 3rd edition. London and New York: Routledge, 1993.

Hourani, Albert H. *A History of the Arab Peoples*. London: Faber and Faber, 1991.

Ibn 'Asakir, 'Ali al-Hasan. *Ta'rikh Madinat Dimashq*. 70 volumes. Edited by Muhibb al-Din Abi Sa'id 'Umar G. al-'Amrawi. Beirut: Dar al-Fikr, 1995–8.

Ibn A'tham, Abu Muhammad Ahmad al-Kufi. *Kitab al-Futuh*. 8 volumes. Edited by M. A. Khan. Hyderabad: Osmania Oriental Publications Bureau, 1968–75.

Ibn al-Athir, 'Izz al-Din, *al-Kamil fi'l-Ta'rikh*. 13 volumes. Edited by Carolus J. Tornberg. Beirut: Dar Beirut, 1982.

Ibn Hisham, 'Abd al-Malik. *Al-Sira al-Nabawiya*. 2 volumes. Edited by I. al-Abyari, M. al-Saqqa, and 'A. Shibbi. Cairo: Dar Sa'd Misr, 1955.

Ibn Kathir, Isma'il ibn 'Umar. *Bidaya wa'l-Nihaya*. 14 volumes. Beirut: Maktabat al-Ma'arif; Riyad: Maktabat al-Nasr, 1966.

Ibn Khayyat, Khalifah. *Ta'rikh*. 2 volumes. Edited by Akram Diya al-'Umari. Najaf: Imprimerie al-Adabe, 1967.

Imber, Colin. *The Ottoman Empire, 1300–1650: The Structure of Power*. 2nd edition. New York: Palgrave Macmillan, 2009.

Ismael, Tareq Y., and Jacqueline S. Ismael. *Government and Politics of the Contemporary Middle East: Continuity and Change*. Abingdon and New York: Routledge, 2011.

Ismail, O. S. A. "Mu'tasim and the Turks." *Bulletin of the School of Oriental and African Studies* 29 (1966): 12–24.

———. "The Founding of a New Capital: Samarra." *Bulletin of the School of Oriental and African Studies* 31 (1968): 1–13.

Johnston, Douglas, and Cynthia Sampson, eds. *Religion: The Missing Dimension of Statecraft*. New York and Oxford: Oxford University Press, 1994.

Joll, James. *Europe since 1870: An International History*. 3rd edition. London: Pelican, 1984.

Jones, Alan, trans. *The Qur'an*. E. J. W. Gibb Memorial Trust, 2007.

Kedourie, Elie. *Politics and the Middle East*. Oxford: Oxford University Press, 1992.

Kennedy, Hugh N. *The Early 'Abbasid Caliphate: A Political History*. London: Croon Helm, 1981.

———. *The Prophet and the Age of the Caliphates: The Islamic Near East from the Sixth to the Eleventh Century*. London and New York: Longman, 1986.

———. *The Armies of the Caliphs: Military & Society in the Early Islamic State*. London and New York: Routledge, 2001.

———. *The Court of the Caliphs: The Rise and Fall of Islam's Greatest Dynasty*. London: Weidenfield and Nicholson, 2004.

Kepel, Gilles. *The Prophet and Pharaoh: Muslim Extremism in Egypt*. London: Saqi, 1985.

——. *Jihad: The Trail of Political Islam*. London; New York: I. B. Tauris, 2002.

Kertész, Imre. *Fateless*. London: Vintage, 2006.

Kertzer, David I. *Ritual, Politics, and Power*. New Haven and London: Yale University Press, 1988.

Khalidi, Tarif. *Arabic Historical Thought in the Classical Period*. New York and Cambridge: Cambridge University Press, 1994.

Kienle, Eberhard, ed. *Politics from Above, Politics from Below: The Middle East in the Age of Economic Reform*. London: Saqi, 2003.

Kimber, Richard A. "Harun al-Rashid and the 'Abbasid Succession." PhD diss., University of Cambridge, 1989.

Kurzman, Charles. *The Missing Martyrs: Why There Are So Few Muslim Terrorists*. New York and Oxford: Oxford University Press, 2011.

Lapidus, Ira M. *A History of Islamic Societies*. 2nd edition. New York and Cambridge: Cambridge University Press, 2002.

Larson, Jayne Amelia. *Driving the Saudis: A Chauffeur's Tale of Life, Liberty, and the Pursuit of Happiness on Rodeo Drive*. New York: Simon & Schuster, 2012.

Lassner, Jacob. *The Shaping of 'Abbasid Rule*. Princeton: Princeton University Press, 1980.

Leverett, Flynt. *Inheriting Syria: Bashar's Trial by Fire*. Washington: Brookings Institution Press, 2005.

Lewis, Bernard. *The Jews of Islam*. Princeton: Princeton Paperbacks, 1987.

——. *The Political Language of Islam*. Chicago: University of Chicago Press, 1988.

——. *What Went Wrong? Western Impact and Middle Eastern Response*. New York: Oxford University Press, 2002.

Litvinoff, Barnet. *The Burning Bush: Antisemitism and World History*. Glasgow: Fontana Paperbacks, 1989.

Lustig, Arnošt. *Lovely Green Eyes*. London: Vintage, 2003.

——. *Waiting for Leah*. London: Vintage, 2005.

Maalouf, Amin. *The Crusades through Arab Eyes*. London: Saqi, 1984.

——. *On Identity*. London: The Harvill Press, 2000.

MacCulloch, Dairmaid. *A History of Christianity*. London: Penguin Books, 2010.

MacDonogh, Giles. *The Last Kaiser: William the Impetuous*. London: Phoenix, 2001.

Madelung, Wilfred. *The Succession to Muhammad: A Study of the Early Caliphate*. Cambridge: Cambridge University Press, 1997.

Makdisi, Jean Said. *Teta, Mother and Me*. London: Saqi, 2005.

Mansfield, Peter. *Nasser's Egypt*. London: Penguin Books, 1965.

Al-Mas'udi, Abu al-Hasan 'Ali. *Muruj al-Dhahab*. 7 volumes. Edited by Barbier de Maynard and P. de Courteille. Revised by Charles Pellat. Beirut: Université de Liban, 1965–79.

Maupaussant, Guy de. *Bel-Ami*. London: Penguin Books, 1975.

McMillan, M. E. *The Meaning of Mecca: The Politics of Pilgrimage in Early Islam*. London: Saqi, 2011.

———. *Fathers and Sons: The Rise and Fall of Political Dynasty in the Middle East*. New York: Palgrave Macmillan, 2013.

Menocal, María Rosa. *Ornament of the World: How Muslims, Jews, and Christians Created a Culture of Tolerance in Medieval Spain*. New York: Back Bay Books, 2002.

Miah, M. Shamsuddin. *The Reign of al-Mutawakkil*. Dacca: Asiatic Society of Pakistan, 1969.

Montague, James. *When Friday Comes: Football, War and Revolution in the Middle East*. London: deCoubertin Books, 2013.

Morris, Jan. *Heaven's Command: An Imperial Progress. Volume 1 of the Pax Britannica Trilogy*. London: Faber and Faber, 2012.

———. *Pax Britannica: The Climax of an Empire. Volume 2 of the Pax Britannica Trilogy*. London: Faber and Faber, 2012.

———. *Farewell the Trumpets: An Imperial Retreat. Volume 3 of the Pax Britannica Trilogy*. London: Faber and Faber, 2012.

Mottahedeh, Roy. *Loyalty and Leadership in an Early Islamic Society*. London and New York: I. B. Tauris, 2001.

Northedge, A. "Archaeology and New Urban Settlement in Early Islamic Syria and Iraq." In *The Byzantine and Early Islamic Near East*, edited by G. R. D. King and Averil Cameron, 231–65. Princeton: Darwin, 1994.

Norwich, John Julius. *The Middle Sea: A History of the Mediterranean*. London: Vintage, 2007.

Omar, Farouk. *The 'Abbasid Caliphate 132/750 – 170/786*. Baghdad: National Print and Publishing Co., 1969.

Oufkir, Malika. *La Prisonnière: Twenty Years in a Desert Gaol*. London: Random House, 2000.

Owen, Roger. *The Middle East in the World Economy 1800–1914*. London and New York: I. B. Tauris, 2011.

———. *The Rise and Fall of Arab Presidents for Life*. Cambridge and London: Harvard University Press, 2012.

Pappé, Ilan. *The Rise and Fall of a Palestinian Dynasty: The Husaynis 1700–1948*. London: Saqi, 2010.

Pargeter, Alison. *The Muslim Brotherhood: The Burden of Tradition*. London: Saqi, 2010.

Phares, Walid. *The Lost Spring: U.S. Policy in the Middle East and Catastrophes to Avoid*. New York: Palgrave Macmillan, 2014.

Quataert, Donald. *The Ottoman Empire 1700–1922*. 2nd edition. Cambridge and New York: Cambridge University Press, 2011.

Qutb, Sayyid. *A Child from the Village*. Translated by John Calvert and William Shepard. New York: Syracuse University Press, 2004.

Rabbat, Nasser. "The Meaning of the Umayyad Dome of the Rock." *Muqarnas* 6 (1989): 12–21.

Ramadan, Tariq. *The Messenger: The Meanings of the Life of Muhammad*. London: Penguin Books, 2008.

Al-Rasheed, Madawi. *A History of Saudi Arabia*. Cambridge: Cambridge University Press, 2002.

—— *Contesting the Saudi State: Islamic Voices from a New Generation*. Cambridge: Cambridge University Press, 2007.

Reynolds, David. *The Long Shadow: The Great War and the Twentieth Century*. London: Simon & Schuster, 2013.

Robinson, Chase F. *Islamic Historiography*. Cambridge and New York: Cambridge University Press, 2003.

——. *Makers of the Muslim World: 'Abd al-Malik*. Oxford: Oneworld, 2005.

Rodinson, Maxime. *Mohammed*. London: Pelican, 1973.

——. *Cult, Ghetto, and State: The Persistence of the Jewish Question*. London: Saqi, 1983.

Rogan, Eugene. *The Arabs: A History*. London: Penguin Books, 2010.

——. *The Fall of the Ottomans: The Great War in the Middle East 1914–20*. London: Penguin Books, 2015.

Rohan, Deborah. *The Olive Grove: A Palestinian Story*. London: Saqi, 2008.

Rounding, Virginia. *Catherine the Great: Love, Sex and Power*. London: Arrow Books, 2007.

Ruthven, Malise. *Islam in the World*. London: Penguin Books, 1991.

Said, Edward. *Orientalism: Western Concepts of the Orient*. London: Penguin Books, 1991.

——. *The Politics of Dispossession: The Struggle for Palestinian Self-Determination 1969–1994*. London: Chatto and Windus, 1994.

——. *Culture and Imperialism*. London: Vintage, 1994.

——. *Out of Place: A Memoir*. London: Granta Books, 2000.

Schacht, Joseph. *An Introduction to Islamic Law*. Oxford: Oxford University Press, 1982.

Sciolino, Elaine. *Persian Mirrors: The Elusive Face of Iran*. New York: Touchstone, 2000.

Sebag Montefiore, Simon. *Jerusalem: The Biography*. London: Phoenix, 2011.

Serageldin Samia. *The Cairo House*. London: Fourth Estate, 2004.

Sharon, Moshe. *Black Banners from the East*. Leiden: E. J. Brill, 1983.

——. *Revolt: The Social and Military Aspects of the 'Abbasid Revolution*. Jerusalem: The Max Schloessinger Memorial Fund at the Hebrew University, 1990.

Al-Sharqawi, Abdel Rahman. *Egyptian Earth*. London: Saqi, 1990.

Stetkevych, Suzanne P. *The Poetics of Islamic Legitimacy*. Bloomington: Indiana University Press, 2002.

Strachan, Hew. *The First World War*. London: Pocket Books, 2006.

Sweet, Matthew. *Inventing the Victorians*. London: Faber and Faber, 2002.

Al-Tabari, Abu Ja'far Muhammad b. Jarir. *Ta'rikh al-Rusul wa'l-Muluk*. 3 volumes. Edited by M. J. de Goeje and others. Leiden: E. J. Brill, 1879–1901.

Tamimi, Azzam. *Hamas: Unwritten Chapters*. London: C. Hurst & Co., 2007.

The Times Atlas of World History. London: Harper Collins, 1995.

Trofimov, Yaroslav. *The Siege of Mecca: The Forgotten Uprising in Islam's Holiest Shrine.* London: Penguin Books, 2008.

Turner, Victor, and Edith Turner. *Image and Pilgrimage in Christian Culture: Anthropological Perspectives.* Oxford: Blackwell, 1978.

Vadney, T. E. *The World since 1945.* New edition. London: Penguin Books, 1998.

Van Dam, Nikolaos. *The Struggle for Power in Syria: Politics and Society under Asad and the Ba'th Party.* 4th edition. London and New York: I. B. Tauris, 2011.

Vassiliev, Alexei. *The History of Saudi Arabia.* 2nd edition. London: Saqi, 2000.

Watt, W. Montgomery. *Muhammad: Prophet and Statesman.* Oxford: Oxford University Press, 1964.

Webster, Jason. *Andalus: Unlocking the Secrets of Moorish Spain.* London: Black Swan Books, 2005.

Wellhausen, Julius. *The Arab Kingdom and Its Fall.* Translated by Margaret G. Weir. London and New York: Routledge, 2002.

Whitaker, Brian. *What's Really Wrong with the Middle East.* Updated edition. London: Saqi, 2011.

Wiet, Gaston. *Baghdad: Metropolis of the 'Abbasid Caliphate.* Translated by Seymour Feiler. Ann Arbor: University Microfilms International, 1985.

Al-Ya'qubi, Ahmad. *Ta'rikh.* 2 volumes. Beirut: Mua'ssasat al-a'lami li'l-matbu'at, 1993.

Zaman, Muhammad Q. *Religion and Politics under the Early 'Abbasids: The Emergence of the Proto-Sunni Elite.* Leiden: E. J. Brill, 1997.

Index

Lightning Source UK Ltd.
Milton Keynes UK
UKOW06f1434311015

261830UK00006B/62/P